BOEING
707/720

BOEING 707/720

Jim Winchester

Airlife

Copyright © 2002 Airlife Publishing Ltd

First published in the UK in 2002
by Airlife Publishing Ltd

British Library Cataloguing-in-Publication Data
A catalogue record for this book
is available from the British Library

ISBN 1 84037 311 3

Typeset by Celtic, Wrexham
Printed in Hong Kong

*Contact us for a free catalogue that describes the complete range of
Airlife books for pilots and aviation enthusiasts.*

Airlife Publishing Ltd

101 Longden Road, Shrewsbury, SY3 9EB, England
E-mail: sales@airlife books.com
Website: www.airlifebooks.com

PREVIOUS PAGE: OO-SJA was the pride of Belgian airline Sabena's fleet. During
the Congo evacuation in July 1960, the aircraft carried 303 passengers on one flight
between Leopoldville and Brussels. After over twenty years of service it was
donated to the Brussels military museum. Currently only the nose section is on
display due to lack of space. *John Stroud Collection/The Aviation Picture Library*

BELOW: The 707-700 was a one-off aircraft built by Boeing in 1979 as a private
venture with CFM56 turbofans. It was later converted back to JT3D power. Other
707 projects included the double-deck 707-520, stretched 707-620 and 707-820 with
up to 279 passengers, designed to compete with the DC-8-61. Although it shared
few features, Boeing's Supersonic Transport (SST) project was designated the 2707.
The Aviation Picture Library

CONTENTS

1 Design and Development 6

2 In Detail 21

3 Customers 39

4 Military 707s 53

5 In Service 64

6 Production 79

7 The 707 Today 102

8 Accidents and Incidents 111

9 Chronology 126

Bibliography 127

Index 128

1 DESIGN AND DEVELOPMENT

By the end of the Second World War, the Boeing Aircraft Company had established itself as the United States' premier manufacturer of bomber aircraft. Before the war, the company had been known for its fighters, flying boats and airliners, but the demands of wartime had forced the company to concentrate on its heavy bomber designs, the B-17 Flying Fortress and B-29 Superfortress, of which over 12,700 and 2,750 were built respectively by 1945, many of them under a 'pool' arrangement with Douglas, Lockheed-Vega and Martin.

Boeing had certainly developed the skills, technology and expertise to build large, multi-engined aircraft, but had lost touch with the airlines and needs of the civilian market. Competitors Lockheed and Douglas had designs in production at the end of the war that had been designed as airliners or with easy conversion to civil use in mind. The airlines had bought many hundreds of Douglas DC-2s, DC-3s and Lockheed Models 10 through 14 before the war. To get a slice of the expected post-war air travel boom, Boeing would have to sell itself as a company to the airlines as much as it sold any new designs – and with a much less experienced sales force.

Thankfully, Boeing had able leadership. William M. Allen (1900–85) was a lawyer who had been appointed to the Boeing board of directors in 1931 and rose to become its Chairman and Chief Executive Officer in September 1945. He took the post reluctantly, not least because the Government cancelled all of Boeing's bomber contracts immediately and his first task was to lay off 87 per cent of the workforce, or 38,000 people. A much reduced contract for sixty B-50 Superfortresses, improved variants of the B-29, was soon reinstated however, and was followed by repeat orders that kept the line open until 1953.

The main hope for the future was the first jet in the company's history – the Model 450 or XB-47 Stratojet bomber. The Stratojet owed much to German research into swept-wing aerodynamics and the design changed from a straight-wing to a swept-wing configuration shortly after the war ended and German knowledge (and personnel) arrived in the USA. The B-47 story is outside the scope of this narrative, but suffice it to

BELOW: The 707 might have wound up looking something like this, one of the Model 473 designs, which was something of a hybrid between the 367 Stratocruiser and the B-47 bomber. In the end, the twin engine pods were abandoned in favour of spaced single pods. *Boeing via Aeroplane*

ABOVE: Before the Dash 80 could be built, the fit of parts, fuel and hydraulic pipes, control runs and control surfaces were tested on a full-scale wooden mock-up built in some secrecy at Renton in 1952. Note the trial of different structures and access panels on the two port engine cowls and pylons. *Aeroplane*

ABOVE: The thin wing of the 707 was designed to flex like that of the B-47, something that airline passengers took a long time to get used to. Structural testing of the Dash 80 saw the wing flexed up to 33 per cent of its design load (failure point) with a deflection of 49 in (124 cm). *Aeroplane*

say that the development problems experienced and overcome in developing this high-speed bomber with its thin, swept wing and engines in underslung pods proved hugely influential on the design of Boeing's first jet airliner.

The Model 377 Stratocruiser was the only commercial product on the drawing board in 1945 and Bill Allen went ahead with production of fifty airframes. There were no orders, but it was the only way to save the company's civil aircraft business. Although often described as a gamble, much of the development cost of the 377 had already been borne by the Model 367 Stratofreighter, which was essentially a transport version of the B-29 with a new pressurised 'double bubble' fuselage. The 367 became the C-97 transport and later the KC-97 tanker, which was ensured large orders by the need to refuel the growing fleet of Strategic Air Command (SAC) B-50 bombers. The B-50 and the Stratocruiser were built at and fully occupied Seattle Plant 2, so a part of the wartime plant at Renton was reopened for C-97 production. This plant would later see the production of over a thousand 707s and 800 C-135s. Bomber development was based at Wichita, Kansas, with the company's hopes for future SAC orders riding on the XB-47 Stratojet. If the XB-47 represented the future, with its swept wings and podded jet engines, the 377 was an extremely conservative basis for an airliner, being based to a large degree on technology a decade or more old.

Boeing only built fifty-six Model 377s, of which Pan Am bought twenty-five, and the company made a loss of $7 million on the much-loved but uneconomic 'Strat'. The Californian companies Douglas, with its long line of successful airliners from the DC-3 onwards and a reputation for listening to what airlines wanted, and Lockheed, which had developed its Constellation on the back of government contracts, were the undisputed leaders in commercial aircraft in the immediate post-war years.

By the time the 367-80 came along, total Boeing airliner production amounted to under 150 'modern' (multi-engined and all-metal) aircraft of which over half had been Model 247s of 1933 vintage.

With the feasibility of the large jet proved by the B-47, and turboprops tested on a version of the C-97, Boeing's thoughts

BELOW: As well as static rig tests as seen here, a full water tank test was made of a 707 fuselage. Boeing's engineers were avoiding the mistakes of the Comet, which was not as rigorously tested, with disastrous consequences. *Sabena via Aeroplane*

ABOVE: The 367-80 was rolled out on 15 May 1954 in front of thousands of invited guests and the world's media. Rarely has so much fanfare been accorded the debut of an aircraft which was little more than an engineering testbed. The first orders (for KC-135s) were still three months in the future. *Boeing*

turned towards a new transport for civil and military use. By 1950 the piston engine had reached the peak of its development, but Boeing and other manufacturers were at first reluctant to embrace jet propulsion.

Over 150 configurations were studied before the 707 layout as we know it emerged. Studies included designs based on the Model 367 Stratofreighter/377 Stratoliner and the Model 473, which owed much to the B-47, featuring a high-mounted swept wing. Versions of the latter included the twin-engined 473-11 and the six-engined 473-25 and 473-60, which had similarities to the B-52 design such as twin-podded engines and bicycle main landing-gear. The twin-engined 473-47 was very different, resembling the later 737 but with an 18-degree swept wing and Stratocruiser-like cockpit glazing.

The more conservative Model 367 line of development included the 367-60 design of 1950, which was a T-34

turboprop-powered version of the Stratocruiser/freighter. It had 'gull' wings to keep the large propellers clear of the ground and the undercarriage legs short.

Other studies based on the 'Strat' included the 367-64 (1951) and the 367-71 (1952) which were basically jet Stratocruisers with engines in twin pods like those on the B-47 and wings and tail surfaces with 25 degrees of sweepback. This was more conservative than the 35-degree sweep on the B-47 wing but was seen as a safer choice for a transport.

Much wind-tunnel time was expended on six wing designs until a version of the 25-degree configuration was chosen with an area of 2,500 sq ft (232 sq m). The wing structure was much more rigid, with upsweep or dihedral when at rest rather than the pronounced anhedral of the B-47. Married to a modified Model 367 fuselage with a new nose and a low-mounted wing, this configuration emerged in late 1951 under the designation 367-80.

DRAWING BOARD

The -80 wing was thicker than the -64 wing, which had been pared to the bone to meet the Mach requirement with the bulbous Stratocruiser fuselage, restricting the fuel capacity and

ABOVE: Guest of honour at the roll-out was 72-year-old William Boeing, who watched his wife Bertha break the traditional bottle of champagne over the nose and pronounce the 367-80 'the airplane of tomorrow, the Boeing Jet Stratoliner and Jet Stratotanker'. The Dash 80 itself was far from being either an airliner or a tanker. *Boeing via Aeroplane*

adding to manufacturing difficulties, but it had the same basic planform. The most critical difference was the new sweepback of 35 degrees, the same as the B-47. This reduced the wingspan by 10 ft (3 m), but retained the same 2,500 sq ft (232 sq m) area.

On 18 May 1952, Bill Allen gave the go-ahead for the construction of a jet prototype to demonstrate the feasibility of a jet airliner to the sceptical US airlines, a jet tanker to SAC and a jet freighter/troop transport for the Military Air Transport Service (MATS).

While it was not a secret that Boeing was working on a jet transport, the company felt no need to broadcast that this was an entirely new design and kept up the pretence that it was no more than a development of the Model 367 Stratofreighter. Thus the prototype was referred to as the 367-80 in documents and as the Dash 80 by the engineers and pilots. Boeing drawings and documents of the 1952–4 period also refer to the design as the Model 707 (the 500 and 600 series of numbers being allocated to products other than aircraft).

Detailed design of the 707 was of course a team effort, conducted by hundreds and thousands of people and would be worthy of a book in itself. The overall project leader was Ed

Wells, who led every large Boeing design effort from the B-17 to the 747. The aerodynamic design was the responsibility of a team led by the brilliant but demanding German engineer George Schairer, guru of the swept wing. He was the mentor and taskmaster of engineer and brilliant draftsman Jack Steiner, who turned theories into plans for the structural engineers, led by Maynard Pennell, an ex-Douglas man who became the main proponent within Boeing of a jet airliner, to turn into blueprints, and then into metal. The all-important cabin design (including the doors and seating arrangement) was the responsibility of former systems engineer Milt Heinemann. He wisely hired consultant designer Frank Del Giudice of the firm Walter Dorwin Teague to design the look of the interior and thus invent the modern airliner as most of us experience it today.

The Dash 80's engines were 10,000 lb static thrust (st) (44.4kN) Pratt & Whitney JT3 twin-spool turbojets, the civil version of the J57 as used on the B-52. Although airlines were

ABOVE: The flight test personnel for the early tests were (left to right) pilots Richards 'Dix' Loesch, Alvin 'Tex' Johnston and engineer L.A. 'Bert' Binegar. They are seen here at Boeing Field on their way to a post-flight conference. Note how the Dash 80's forward freight door doubled as a crew door. *Boeing via Aeroplane*

sceptical of jet engine reliability, Boeing knew that the J57 would be thoroughly proven (at government expense) on the B-52 by the time any civil airliner took off under their power.

Pylon-mounted engines were chosen for the 707 for several reasons. They are less susceptible to damage caused by failure of their neighbour than are engines buried in the wings, and they do not have unwanted shock-wave effects as do engines attached directly to the wing underside. If spaced carefully on the wing, the engines distribute the load evenly, reduce wing bending and allow a lighter structure. Wing flexibility was a critical issue – in certain conditions, the ailerons on a swept-back and upwards-flexing wing will move the wing rather than the airflow, and reverse their effect, rolling the aircraft in the opposite direction to that commanded. Aileron reversal was a major problem with the thin high-speed wing of the B-47.

WIDTH

Cabin width was the last major question to be resolved in the 707 design. Boeing hoped to utilise as much tooling as possible from the KC-135, but the US Air Force (USAF) insisted that the company recompense the Government for all costs that could be considered a subsidy for a commercial product. The USAF insisted that the KC-135 fuselage take standard pallets, which required it to be made 8 in (20 cm) wider than the Dash 80, which at 132 in (3.35 m) was the same as the Stratocruiser. The depth of the fuselage was also increased 2 in (5 cm) to 164 in (4.17 m) on the KC-135. Production plans went ahead on this basis until more details of the DC-8 emerged. The major airlines knew the plusses and minuses of the Douglas and Boeing cabins, and United even built partial mock-ups that showed graphically how much more volume the extra 3-in (7.5 cm) width and the lower floor gave to the DC-8. Douglas won United's first jet order, largely on this basis.

Pan American made the launch order for twenty 707-120s on 13 October 1956. Juan Trippe of Pan Am would never let another US airline be the first to operate a jet fleet, but at the same time he ordered twenty-five DC-8s that would not be

ABOVE: The Dash 80 made several record flights, notably Seattle–Washington in three hours, forty-eight minutes on 16 October 1955 at an average speed of 595 mph (957 kph). Tex Johnston was the pilot that day and is seen here on a later (11 March 1957) record flight from Baltimore to Seattle autographing a brochure for Pan Am stewardess Olga Podkrivacky. *Boeing via Aeroplane*

available for at least another six months. Trippe made it clear to Boeing that he ordered the 707s mainly for their earlier delivery date and regarded them as interim equipment that he would replace as soon as he had his DC-8s. Pan Am's preference was influenced by the DC-8's bigger wing (and thus longer range), higher gross weight and, most importantly, bigger cabin.

When Bill Allen saw how the DC-8's 147-in (3.73 m) cabin made the 707 look claustrophobic by comparison, and faced a meeting with C.R. Smith of American Airlines, he made a difficult but fateful decision – to widen the fuselage another 4 in (10 cm) and lower the floor. This did the trick, and American ordered thirty 707s on 8 November 1955. Pan Am accepted the change, which brought the width to 148 in (3.76 m), for their ordered jets. These were the final dimensions, which were to remain unchanged through 1,010 707s to follow, as well as 1,831 727s and over 4,100 737s to date, all of which have the same cross-section. In contrast, Douglas sold a total of 556 DC-8s. It could be argued that they lost the American Airlines order and eventually the lead in airliner development by an inch.

Programmes to refine the characteristics of the civil and military versions began at Boeing in April 1952. Construction of the actual prototype began in October. The previous month Bill Allen had publicly announced that a jet transport programme was underway and began to release information to the airlines. To have done so earlier would have given too much away to Boeing's competitors.

A wooden mock-up of the 707 cabin was secretly constructed in a warehouse in New York and a stream of airline executives and such luminaries as Charles Lindbergh (an adviser to TWA) were led through it. Not at all typical for Boeing, a few Hollywood-style gimmicks were added, such as recordings of engine noise and cabin announcements, to give an impression of jet flight. In Seattle a mostly wooden engineering mock-up was constructed to test the routeing of fuel, electrical and hydraulic systems, and control surface function.

The pilot chosen to lead the most important test programme in Boeing's history was Alvin M. Johnston. Known universally as 'Tex', more for his cowboy boots and manner than his origin (he was born in Kansas), Johnston began his test flying career in 1942 with Bell in New York on the P-39 Airacobra fighter. Moving on to the XP-63 King Cobra and the swept-wing L-39 testbed variant and then to America's first jet, the XP-59 Airacomet, Johnston also worked on the XS-1 research aircraft and on Bell's helicopter projects before joining Boeing in 1949. Soon he was senior experimental test pilot on the troubled XB-47 Stratojet bomber at Wichita and in no small measure helped save that project, which was eventually to result in production of over 2,000 aircraft. In mid-1950 Johnston gave Bill Allen his first jet flight, in a B-47. At this time Allen was at the centre of the argument as to whether the next Boeing would be a jet, a turboprop or piston-engined. Although it is not known how much Allen's flight influenced him, it was not long before the marketing men were sent out to discreetly test the waters among the big airlines for a jet transport, and propellers were never seriously considered again.

Johnston soon became project pilot on the YB-52 Stratofortress. On 15 April 1952 he piloted the first prototype of that intercontinental bomber on its three-hour maiden flight and led it through the test programme, which ensured the adoption into service of one of the most famous and longest-lived military aircraft of all time.

Despite the fanfare of the Dash 80 rollout on 15 May 1954, Boeing did not have any orders for the 707 or anything like it.

ABOVE: The Dash 80 test programme was not without its incidents, including two partial undercarriage collapses in the first months. The scene here is a later one, during testing for the very large aircraft programme. Here the fixed eighteen-wheel undercarriage has stuck in the surface of Harper Dry Lake, California. *Aeroplane*

The company's future was riding on its success. The insurance policy on the prototype was the largest aviation policy taken out to that time, with a value of $15 million. Unusually, it stipulated that, at least for the initial flights, only one pilot – Tex Johnston – was allowed to fly it.

Outwardly similar to the 707s that were to follow, the Dash 80 was in fact very different. It was shorter, lower and lighter and had a narrower cross-section and smaller wingspan than any 707. Most notable was its striking yellow and chocolate brown colour scheme.

Even a casual observer would have noted the lack of cabin

BELOW: By August 1954, the Dash 80 was being used for refuelling trials with a 'flying boom', part of which is just visible here above the tailplane. The Dash 80 was actually in tanker configuration when Tex Johnson rolled it over Lake Washington. *Aeroplane*

windows (only eight oval and two rectangular windows on the starboard side and four ovals on the port side), and the large freight doors fore and aft of the wing. Despite its civil colour scheme, the Dash 80 was much more of a military transport than an airliner.

By this time the pretence that this was a development of the 367 had been dropped, and Boeing was referring to the '707 Jet Prototype' in all publicity. Registered N70700, the Dash 80 soon gained 'Boeing 707' titles on the vertical fin. To bring it to this point had required 432,000 direct design-engineering man-hours. The 707-120 was to require a further 772,000, demonstrating how far from being a commercial airliner the 367-80 actually was.

Bill Allen was asked by a reporter shortly before the 367-80's first flight why a company in Boeing's position should 'take such a gamble with 15 million of its own dollars'. His reply mixed patriotism with a sense of adventure that did not really suit the conservative-minded lawyer; 'We felt strongly that it was high time *some* American manufacturer took the plunge, got a jet transport off of paper and into the air. We felt our national welfare demanded it, both from the military and the commercial standpoint.'

The Dash 80 was, however, less of a risk than is often suggested. Douglas had already launched the DC-8 by the time the go-ahead for the Dash 80 was given (although they waited for orders before building a prototype) and Britain, France and the Soviet Union were developing jet transports. Even Canada had built a jet prototype, although it was not put into production. Boeing also knew that the B-52 bombers it was beginning to

build in great numbers would need jet tankers and that orders for a military Dash 80, if not a civil airliner, were all but a certainty. In fact, as it turned out, the decision to build a prototype *made* military orders a certainty. The USAF announced its jet tanker competition one month before the Dash 80 rolled out, and selected Lockheed's L-193 design (with aft-mounted engines) as the winner of the 'paper' contest in March 1955. Meanwhile SAC Commander General Curtis LeMay had flown the Dash 80 and been sold on it by Boeing's Vice President Wellwood Beall. He knew that a tanker from Lockheed, the likely competition winner, would be years away and effectively said, 'Meanwhile, build me some of these.' The USAF ordered twenty-nine 'interim' KC-135s on 3 August 1954, soon followed by another eighty-eight. Lockheed's design was never built, mainly because the logistics of having two tanker platforms in service was deemed too costly.

The first flight of the 367-80 was delayed by a weakness in the main landing gear. During a braking test on 21 May, the port main-gear attachment failed and the Dash 80's No. 1 engine nacelle and left wingtip struck the ground. Damage was relatively slight, but the test programme was delayed while repairs were carried out. Although the failure was caused by a metallurgical failure, modifications were made to the landing gear to counter excessive structural loads under braking.

ABOVE: As part of 1963 tests into supersonic and very large transports, the Dash 80 mounted a long instrumented nose probe. At this time the wings were modified with a full set of blown leading-edge flaps and a tailplane with an inverted leading edge. *Boeing via the Aviation Picture Library*

Finally, at 2:14 p.m. on 15 July 1954, the 367-80 made its first flight from Renton. In the left seat was Tex Johnston and the co-pilot was Richards L. 'Dix' Loesch. Because there were no escape hatches, the crew was kept to a minimum and there was no flight engineer. The first flight, watched by thousands of workers and locals and escorted by an F-86 chase plane, was notable only for its lack of drama. After two hours, twenty-four minutes of high- and low-speed handling tests, the Dash 80 landed at Boeing Field to a hearty welcome from Bill Allen, Ed Wells, George Schairer and others who had brought Boeing's gamble to life.

The test programme soon settled into a familiar routine, but on 5 August 1954, disaster nearly struck. Johnston carried out some high-speed taxi runs with hard braking before conducting a short flight. On landing, the brakes failed completely. The only way to stop the stampeding jet was to cut the engines and steer it onto the grass – and it nearly worked. Unfortunately a hidden pile of concrete pieces brought the Dash 80 to an abrupt halt just as it was slowing to a safe speed and the nose gear collapsed. There was little other damage, but the event, attributed to foaming of overheated hydraulic fluid, was an embarrassment to Boeing, and the Dash 80 was out of the air until 20 September.

If the Dash 80 is known for one thing, it is that Tex Johnston rolled it in public. The annual Seattle Sea Fair is a celebration of the city's maritime heritage and has for many years featured hydroplane or powerboat racing on Lake Washington. Between the races there are usually air show acts and flybys of Boeing's latest models. At the 1955 event, Johnston had received permission for a low-level, high-speed flypast, but to the amazement of the crowd and the chagrin of Bill Allen and other Boeing executives who were watching from the VIP enclosure alongside representatives of the major US airlines, the Dash 80 approached at 400 ft (120 m), pulled up its nose and completed a gentle barrel roll overhead. The engineer took a photo of the starboard wing with its engines pointing upwards over the Seattle suburbs, but no photos or film from the ground seem to have survived. Then Johnston made a pass in the opposite direction and rolled the Dash 80 again. Of course, there was little risk to Boeing's precious prototype – the airframe never exceeded 1 *g* and Johnston had tested the manoeuvre twice at high altitude. Nevertheless, Allen was furious that his potential customers might think the new Boeing was being tested and developed by 'cowboys' and never really forgave Johnston, although the pilot was not punished in any way for his spectacular display.

It is often said that nobody has since rolled a jet airliner (or at least not deliberately or under full control). It is possible, however that the loss of a Lufthansa 720 (D-ABOP) on a training flight in July 1964 was the result of the pilot in command 'proving it could be done' to his companions. One roll was accomplished successfully, but on a second attempt, the aircraft lost control when inverted, broke up and crashed near Nuremberg, killing the three crew on board.

ABOVE: One of the many tests performed by the Dash 80 was to evaluate the rear mounting of the JT8D engine for the 727. The exhaust of the fifth engine was directed over the tailplane by a duct pipe. N70700's colour scheme, particularly the wings, took a battering from the test airfoils, experimental control surfaces and engineers' boots. *The Aviation Picture Library*

Publicly, Tex Johnston praised the performance of the Dash 80. Without going into specifics, he said that 'this airplane [was] not likely to be outperformed by anything this side of the supersonic era'. In his official flight test report to Boeing, however, he criticised the stability as 'marginal' in some flight regimes. Unfortunately, this finding was somewhat forgotten in the aftermath of the undercarriage collapse incident, and no corrective modifications were made until after several early 707 accidents.

Flight testing showed that the Dash 80 could take off too soon at too high an angle of attack, resulting in an over-rotation and a much-increased take-off run. A small leading-edge flap cured this problem and was introduced into the early 707 production line. Fixed and moveable flaps were tested on the Dash 80 and a sudden application of the latter was found to convert a take-off roll to a climb of 700–800 ft (213–244 m) per minute without application of elevator or trailing edge flaps.

Another incident in which the skill and experience of Tex Johnston saved the day occurred on a flight in July 1955 when overheated brakes caused a fire in the main wheel wells of the 367-80. The F-86 chase aircraft pilot reported flames coming from the wheel doors and Johnson lowered the landing gear and dived the aircraft, blowing out the fire.

The model number 707 came about in a roundabout fashion. The 367-80 designation was, of course, a front to disguise the new jet as a version of an older design, and the 400, 500 and 600 model numbers had already been used for missiles and other products, leaving the 700s as the next available sequence. The number seven had been associated with earlier important Boeings such as the 247, 377 and even B-17, and 'seven-oh-seven' had a certain ring to it. From hereafter, Boeing was to use the same basic formula for all subsequent transport – 717 (thrice), 727, 737, 747, 757, 767 and 777. Unbuilt projects include the 7J7 (a collaboration with Japan) and the 2707 SST. The future 'Sonic Cruiser' may or may not become the 787 when it appears in the late 2000s. Boeing's 'seven' series jetliners are among the most recognised brands in the world.

Most of the Dash 80's flights were less than two hours long and the aircraft never travelled out of North American airspace. In 1955 a total of 222 flights were made for a total of 268.5

ABOVE: A rare image of the Dash 80 and a 707 together. In this case it is the first production 707 and the two aircraft were engaged at the time on sound-suppressor trials. Four years and many thousands of hours of engineering development separated the two, which had few common parts. *Boeing via the Aviation Picture Library*

flight hours, and the following year there were 237 flights and 284 hours in the air. The final tally when it was retired from test duties in 1970 was 1,691 sorties and 2,349.75 hours. By way of comparison, over 70,000 hours was not uncommon for a 1968 707 still in service in 1998, 2,500–3,500 hours per year being the norm, with the highest usage coming in the early years of service.

The first production 707 was rolled out at Renton on 28 October 1957 and assigned the registration N708PA on 17 December. Three days later it made its first flight, with Tex Johnston at the controls. The flight was only seven minutes long and concluded at Boeing Field, where the first US domestic jet airmail letter was handed to Bill Allen. Later in the day the test programme began in earnest with a seventy-minute flight.

The test programme for the 707 included many tests, one of which was applying the thrust-reversers and airbrakes in flight. The results were not as drastic as expected but nevertheless had to be used with caution; application of airbrakes in approach configuration gave a rate of descent of 12,000 ft (3,650 m) per minute and reverse thrust gave a rate two to three times that figure.

707-300

Although the 707-120 could operate transatlantic sectors, this usually required stops at Gander eastbound and Keflavik on the return. The DC-8, with its bigger wing, was not so hampered and threatened to take the sales lead. The only solution, decided on before the 707-100 had even flown, was to develop a longer wing with greater area. The changes in the wing as redesigned by W.T. Hamilton were much greater than that

ABOVE: The first JT3D-engined 707 was destined for Qantas as VH-EBH, but first tested in promotional 707 turbofan colours with the registration N93134. It was later converted to VIP configuration and is currently owned by Omni International. Although usually parked in Arizona, it is said still to be used for the occasional VIP charter. *Boeing via the Aviation Picture Library*

BELOW AND RIGHT: As part of tests for the very large aircraft (later C-5) programme, a double-wheel undercarriage was installed on the Dash 80 and many take-offs and landings were made on the Harper Dry Lake, California in 1959. The temporary landing gear was not retractable. *Boeing via the Aviation Picture Library*

ABOVE: Another modification to the Dash 80 saw the addition of a large radome for the Bendix AN/AMQ-15 weather reconnaissance radar. Extra equipment collected high-altitude atmospheric data and monitored drop and rocket sonde weather probes. This nose appears to have come and gone within 1959. *Boeing via Aeroplane*

suggests, and the design was subtly refined in almost every way. The only changes obvious even to an alert eye, however, were a revised wing/fuselage junction at the trailing edge, altered wingtips and greater forward protrusion of the engines. The result, however was that the 707 outperformed the DC-8 by a small but economically important margin and Boeing never looked back. More 707-300s were sold than all DC-8 models combined. The 'Intercontinental' 707 was longer, with a tourist-class capacity of 189 passengers, and could 'cross the pond' with ease. The first -300 flew only nine months after the first -100, and again Pan Am was the launch customer.

BOEING 720

What became the Boeing 720 began as a design for a short-range derivative of the 707 designated the 707-020. By 1957, this had evolved into the 717, a designation shared with the military K/C-135 family. The two types had little in common, however, with different fuselage diameters, different wings and very different structural design. Understandably, the Model 717 designation was quickly dispensed with in favour of the 'rounder' number 720, but of course was revived after

the merger with McDonnell Douglas in 1997 and applied to the MD95 (née the Douglas DC-9). Some airlines called their 720s 707-020s if they preferred to for marketing reasons.

The main change to the 720 over the 707 was again the wing, which was fitted with a 'glove' or leading-edge extension between the fuselage and the inboard engines. This reduced the wing's thickness-to-chord ratio, which increased the cruising speed by Mach 0.02. The inboard leading-edge slats were moved to the outboard wings. Passenger capacity was 165 in all-tourist configuration. The 720 first flew and entered service in 1960 and although produced until 1967, it was competing with Boeing's own Model 727 by 1964 and sales were relatively modest, with 154 sold.

The foreign certification process for any airliner required Federal Aviation Authority (FAA) certification plus compliance with any special conditions laid down by the importing country. For example, the UK's Air Registration Board (ARB) had twenty-three conditions for the Conway-engined 707-400 over and above the FAA's requirements, each of which could mean complying with a wide range of performance points. One particular concern was over-rotation on take-off and a 707-436 for BOAC was put through some deliberately mishandled take-offs at Edwards Air Force Base (AFB) before the ARB decided that an underfin would both cure this tendency and aid in-flight stability.

BOAC's own acceptance procedure involved a team of

ABOVE: Final assembly of most 707s was carried out outdoors at Renton and these are some of the very first. N710PA (line number 4) heads a line-up of PAA and American Airlines jets, some of which have yet to be fitted with tailfins. *Boeing via the Aviation Picture Library*

company pilots based in Seattle. After three to ten hours of initial test flying by Boeing, and a two-hour acceptance flight by the FAA, the aircraft would be handed over to the airline for its own acceptance tests. This would see autopilot checks, flight to maximum speed, emergency descent and let-down, depressurisation and fuel dumping. One flight was enough for acceptance of ten out of the first thirteen 707-436s, delivered by November 1960. After this and the completion of other paperwork, the balance of the aircraft cost, about $3.85 million, was handed over by BOAC's representative in Seattle.

Most of the first -436s were delivered direct to London with empty cabins, but two were fitted with seats shipped from the UK and picked up passengers in Montreal *en route*. Other nations had different requirements but usually went along with FAA or other major certification authority decisions when it came to large complex aircraft like the 707.

But what of the original Dash 80? Although it was very different from the 707s that were to follow and by no means a jet airliner, it was involved in a great number of test programmes designed to improve the efficiency, safety and comfort of commercial aircraft. Most of these began after 707s began to roll off the Seattle production line and included noise reduction, cabin interior linings, boundary layer control (BLC) and slotted flap studies. Several test projects involved major changes to the Dash 80's appearance. A fifth engine was fitted at the rear of the fuselage to validate this location for the 727's engines, a

long nose probe was installed as part of studies for the anticipated Boeing SST (or 2707) and a spray rig was fitted ahead of the starboard inner engine to create ice in the intake for ice resistance tests.

In late 1960, JT3D-1 turbofans were installed, making N70700 the 367-80B, although it was rarely referred to as such. Two years later these were replaced with JT8Ds as part of the 727 development programme. During studies for the proposed 707-820, the tail fin height was increased and leading-edge slots were added to the wing, allowing extremely low landing speeds and reduced landing runs. These slots were formed with simple sheet metal structures and their use necessitated hiring a Beech 18 as a chase plane as the usual F-86 Sabre was unable to match such low speeds. For tests associated with the very heavy transport aircraft programme that was to lead to the C-5 Galaxy (and in a roundabout way, to the 747), a fixed undercarriage was fitted having four nosewheels, and sixteen mainwheels fitted, with very low-pressure 'balloon' tyres. Landings were made on dry lakebeds in California in September 1964 to evaluate these multi-wheel units on unprepared runways. A tour of military bases then followed during which the Dash 80 made several take-offs and landings on grass surfaces to demonstrate the rough-field abilities of these tyres to Military Airlift Command officers and others.

Military equipment tested on the Dash 80 included a dummy rig of the Boeing 'flying boom' refuelling system and an AN/AMQ-15 weather reconnaissance radar in a large 'thimble' radome as later adopted on the WC-135B.

Civil tests included the Automatic Landing System (ALS), installed in 1969. In 1970 the Dash 80's last test tasks were in conjunction with the development of a similar system for the Space Shuttle, and the final flight of the 367-80 in Boeing test service was made on 22 January 1970 at Paine Field, Everett, Washington.

Each of these programmes left its scars on the Dash 80, which then became a ground-test airframe. Stored in the Arizona desert at Davis-Monthan AFB, the historical importance of N70700 was recognised by the agreement in 1972 to donate it to the Smithsonian Institution's National Air and Space Museum (NASM). In that year, a massive international aviation trade fair (later encompassing transport in general) was planned for Washington's Dulles Airport under the title Transpo '72. A star attraction was to be the Dash 80 and this was ferried to Seattle where Boeing employees refurbished the airframe and repainted it in its original house colour scheme

and fitted a 707 nose radome. In a ceremony at Transpo, the Smithsonian formally named the Dash 80 as one of the 'twelve most significant aircraft of all time'. At that time NASM had not even opened its new building in the Mall in Washington and the Dulles exhibition and restoration centre was only a distant dream, so the Dash 80 returned to Arizona for storage. In 1990 it returned to Seattle where it was repainted once again and appeared at a number of events in conjunction with the seventy-fifth anniversary of the Boeing Company the following year.

At the time of writing the Dash 80, ancestor of over 10,000 Boeing jetliners, was in storage in Seattle, awaiting the time to make one final flight, again to Dulles, for display in NASM's Udvar-Hazy Restoration and Display Centre which will open on 17 December 2003, the centenary of powered flight.

BELOW: This view of the underside of N70700 shows various details of the brown, yellow and aluminium colour scheme as first flown on the 367-80. These house colours were used in modified form on the 727 and 737 prototypes, but subsequent designs have first appeared in a less garish white scheme with red and blue trim. *Author's collection*

2 IN DETAIL

Boeing 707-385C N68657 first flew on 13 September 1965, and it was bought by LAN Chile, as CC-CEB, on 20 December 1969. In 1981 the aircraft was named *Lago Ranco*. Ten years later *Lago Ranco* was bought by the Chilean Air Force. *(Jerry C. Scutts)*

This chapter gives a 'nose-to-tail' description of the main features of the 707 and 720. The past tense is used throughout, but most of the information remains true for the many examples still in service today. Likewise, flight crew are referred to in the masculine, although women have increasingly occupied these positions in recent years. This is done because most of what follows refers to the 707 as built and the heyday of operations in the late 1950s and the 1960s.

The Boeing designation system for its civil airlines that we know today began with the 707. Major model changes were usually, but not always, marked by the basic series number, for example: 707-100 (original model), 707-200 (JT-4 engines), 707-300 (intercontinental version), 707-400 (Conway engines). Within each series, further gradations of ten marked changes of configuration such as engine model and weight class, although this was not always consistently applied. Suffix letters identified

other important changes. A 'B' suffix identified turbofan engines and 'C' stood for 'convertible' or 'combi' as in combined freighter-passenger layout. The initial model was the 707-120, and re-engined versions were -120Bs. The remaining element was the customer number. As the first 707 customer, Pan Am's aircraft became 707-121s. The sequence proceeded through the next customers, United (22), American (23), and so on, eventually reaching 99 (Caledonian) before filling in from 01 (Piedmont) to 19 (Air New Zealand). Boeing reserved 20 for its prototypes and test aircraft. Of course there have been well over a hundred customers for Boeing jetliners and alphanumeric combinations such as D3 for Alia Royal Jordanian Airlines and X9 for the Indonesian Air Force have since been used.

Occasionally, usually later in the sales life of a Boeing airliner, the title 'Advanced' is bestowed on models that have been

ABOVE: During testing associated with Boeing's proposed Supersonic Transport (SST) in 1975, this 'Pinocchio' nose probe was fitted to the Dash 80. Sensors in the probe fed to a computer in the cockpit that allowed the aircraft's control responses to simulate those of a supersonic airliner or a very heavy transport aircraft. *Boeing via Author*

ABOVE: Cockpits changed relatively little through the life of the 707, but the keen-eyed will note differences between the Boeing factory pictures and this photo of a ZAS Airline of Egypt 707-328C at Bristol, England, in July 1984. The flyswatter was not standard Boeing equipment. *Austin J. Brown/The Aviation Picture Library*
BELOW: The overhead and flight engineer's panels are shown in this view of ZAS 707-328C SU-DAA. This ex-Air France aircraft (once F-BLCK *Chateau de Langeais*) last served with Air Memphis. In November 1997 it made a landing at Ostend, Belgium, with its nosegear retracted and was stored for some time but is now back in service. *Austin J. Brown/The Aviation Picture Library*

BELOW: Boeing 720 cockpits were basically the same as those on 707s, and airlines with both types in their fleets cross-qualified their crews to fly either as required. Seen at Luton in March 1981, this was the cockpit of Monarch Airlines' G-AZNX, a former TWA and Northwest Orient aircraft. It served with Monarch from 1972 to 1983 when it was sold to the Boeing Military Airplane Company and stripped for parts at Davis-Monthan AFB, Arizona. *Austin J. Brown/The Aviation Picture Library*

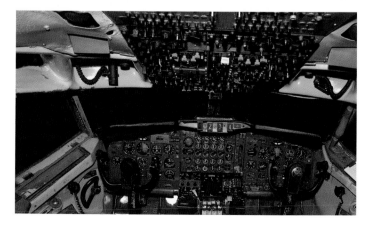

refined in some way, such as the 'Advanced 707-300B' which had wing modifications, namely additional leading-edge flaps and revisions to the trailing-edge flaps. This is more of a marketing term and is not reflected in the model designation.

NOSE

The nose of the 707 was an elegant design, certainly compared to the blunt snout of the Stratocruiser and Stratofreighter, mainly due to the integration of weather radar from the outset of the design. The nose cone or radome of the production 707 was longer and more pointed than that on the 367-80, and was not pressurised.

COCKPIT

Although the cockpit equipment of the 707 appears incredibly complex to the uninitiated, it was greatly simplified and more standardised than that found in the previous generation of transports. The photographs show the major features of the main instrument panel of a typical 707. As the 707 evolved, the design was further simplified and made easier to read. The panel itself was modular in design, with quick disconnect fittings to ease maintenance.

The pedestal or control stand between the pilots housed the throttles, engine start levers, trim wheels, flap controls, speed brake and parking brake handles and two electronics control panels. The controls were basically mounted symmetrically for use by either pilot, although the speed brake lever was on the left and the flap handle on the right.

The greater importance of longitudinal trim is reflected in the relative size and position of the stabiliser trim compared with those affecting roll and yaw. The stabiliser trim control wheels were mounted on either side of the pedestal adjacent to the throttles and were turned with an integral handle. The rear of the horizontal portion of the pedestal mounted the smaller rudder trim control, operated by a crank handle, the position of which marked the degree of trim set. Aileron trim was adjusted by a rotating knob on the rear vertical surface of the pedestal. To the left of this was a hand-held microphone for making cabin announcements.

The overhead panel controlled various functions such as cockpit and exterior lighting, de-icing, rudder damping and the windscreen wipers. Most importantly, engine start switches were located at the rear of the panel.

The flight engineer sat behind the co-pilot with the traditional wall-mounted instrument and control panel. This was divided into four parts. At top left was the electrical panel with its generator instruments and selectors and circuit breakers. Top right was the pressurisation and air-conditioning panel, based around a schematic of the aircraft and its engine-driven pumps. Two large switches at the bottom allowed cockpit and cabin temperature to be independently adjusted in the range

between 65 and 85° F (18–29° C). The lower left panel and instruments controlled the fuel system. Gauges and boost switches for the five main tanks were the main feature of this panel, with indicators for the gravity-fed reserve tanks below the main panel. The bottom right corner of the flight engineer's panel contained repeaters of the altimeter and climb-rate indicator, as well as cabin pressure gauges. Below these were oil quantity, pressure and temperature instruments, hydraulic level indicators and shutoffs and an airborne vibration monitor unit.

The flight engineer had a duplicate set of throttles which allowed him to 'trim' the engines for maximum efficiency for a given cruise speed as requested by the captain. The engineer's seat could rotate to face forwards so that he could view the main instrument panel and handle the main throttles if necessary. To the right of his panel was a locker for stowing the crew's coats.

Where a navigator was carried, his position was at the left rear of the cockpit, with his seat back-to-back but slightly aft of

ABOVE: The cockpit window arrangement, nose profile and cabin diameter of the 707 were left basically unchanged throughout production and were adopted for the many 727s and 737s to follow, right up to the New Generation 737s in service today. *Author*

BELOW: A Boeing general arrangement drawing of the 707-220. This version was bought only by Braniff, but apart from its JT4 engines, it was externally identical to the widely used 707-120 series. *John Stroud Collection/ The Aviation Picture Library*

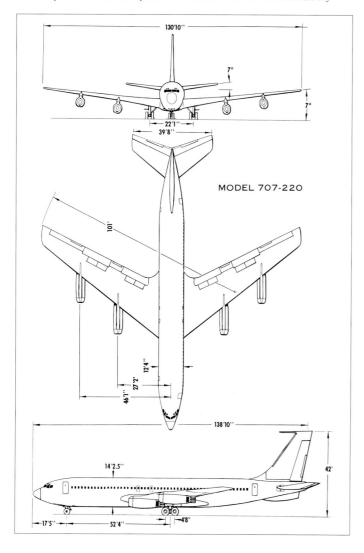

MODEL 707-220

the engineer's. There was a mount for a periscopic sextant in the cockpit ceiling although modern navigation equipment was fitted.

A hatch to the lower deck and its electronics compartment (known as the 'hell hole') was situated under the navigator's table. Occasionally burned out components needed replacing in flight.

Finally, there was a seat for a 'supernumerary' behind the captain's seat. This could be an instructor, a check pilot or a visitor to the cockpit. If the captain was tall and had his seat adjusted to the rear, the leg-room in this seat was minimal. With the sharp tapering of the nose section ahead of the cabin door, the 707's cockpit was cosy to say the least, particularly with up to five seated occupants.

Avionics included LORAN, dual ADFs, weather radar, DME and VOR equipment. Customer options included dual Doppler and inertial navigation systems. The 707-300 was one of the first airliners to be fitted with an automatic bad weather landing equipment. The Precision Approach and Landing System (PALS) could guide the aircraft automatically to within 50 ft (15 m) either side of the runway centreline and within 12 ft (3.5 m) of glidescope in conditions of up to Category II weather minima (100 ft (30 m) ceiling and 1,200 ft (365 m) runway visual range) and with lateral or longitudinal windshear of up to 4 knots and crosswind of 20 knots. On 7 July 1967, Pan Am's N419PA was the first jetliner to make a fully automatic approach and landing with passengers aboard.

FUSELAGE

Despite its smooth-contoured oval shape, the 707 fuselage was actually a 'double-bubble' under the skin. Where the two circles of the cross-section intersected, a 'crease beam' ran the length of the fuselage and disguised the join. The fuselage was constructed in four sections – the nose to a point behind the

BELOW: Converting the interior of a 707 for freight duty involved removing the carpeting and laying roller tracks on the floor. Numbered panels replaced the regular interior mouldings and protected the windows from damage. Here Boeing engineers demonstrate loading freight pallets on a -321C. Later purpose-built freighters often had blanked-off windows. *Boeing via the Aviation Picture Library*

ABOVE: The forward fuselage and engines of an American Airlines 720B are seen at the end of one of Edwards AFB's long runways during testing of the JT3D engine installation. Notice the test equipment visible in the cabin and the centre of gravity marking on the fuselage top. *Boeing via the Aviation Picture Library*

ABOVE: The 707's seat tracks could accommodate two- or three-seat units, allowing for four, five or six abreast seating arrangements. This is the first class seating in a BOAC 707-400. Moveable divider panels allowed easy reconfiguration between classes. The overhead passenger service units or 'pods' were also moveable to suit different seat arrangements. *BOAC via the Aviation Picture Library*

BELOW: This is the conference room of one of the USAF's first three VC-137As, located at the centre section of the aircraft. The projection screen was for in-flight briefings and the sofas on each side converted into bunks. *Boeing via Aeroplane*

starboard entry door, the forward fuselage to the trailing edge of the wing, the rear fuselage to the aft pressure bulkhead, which was in line with the tailfin forward spar, and the extreme tail. At the centre section the floor was attached to the top of the wing structure.

The plug-type doors on the 707 were an innovation that was quickly adopted by all airliner manufacturers. On earlier airliners, passenger doors either opened outwards, and thus provided poor structural integrity, or inwards, taking up a row of seats. Boeing's door design was slightly larger than the opening and thus was pushed to a tighter seal by the higher internal pressure, but in operation rotated just enough about its vertical axis to fit through the aperture and swing outside to lie alongside the fuselage. The forward starboard door was mounted aft of that on the port side and the starboard aft door was forward of its opposite number. The starboard doors were smaller and sometimes called 'buffet' or service doors. The short-fuselage 707s and 720 had two emergency exits per side. Many, but not all -300s had an exit just aft of the port trailing edge, and some also on the starboard side.

Most previous airliners had featured a window alongside each row of seats. On the 707 the windows were somewhat smaller than previously and were mounted between each fuselage frame rather than aligned with the seats, which of course could be repositioned. This meant that each passenger had two windows, or at least part of two. Structural engineers of course would prefer to have no windows at all in a pressurised airframe, as every penetration of the pressure hull is a potential point of failure. American Airlines specified a larger window size (10 × 14 in (25 × 36 cm) versus 9 × 12.5 in (23 × 32 cm)) for its new-build aircraft. Each window was fitted with a tinted Plexiglas shade on early 707s, but this later gave way to the more familiar opaque shade.

Closeable overhead stowage-bins were an innovation on the

707 and offered much more room for cabin baggage than did the open racks and closets of earlier airliners. Some airlines preferred open racks, one advantage of which was that they could be folded down against the fuselage sides on the C versions to allow the insertion of cargo containers.

American's 707 'Flagships' were operated in a two-class configuration with first class in the forward cabin named 'Mercury' and tourist class aft dubbed 'Royal Coachman'. The order of these classes was reversed compared to the DC-7 because the noise levels were higher towards the front of the jet rather than to the rear as with the propliner. Each class on the 707 had fifty-six seats, arranged in pairs with a card table between each. The Royal Coachman seats were in threes with

ABOVE: Many airlines revamped their 707s in the early 1970s. New lighting, overhead bins and service unit panels, and such things as in-flight movies, were an attempt to compete with airlines with new equipment such as 747s. Demonstrating the 'wide-body look' here is a 1971 American Airlines 707-300 'LuxuryJet' cabin. *American Airlines via Author*

ABOVE: Although lounge areas are a rarity today, they were a feature of early 747s and DC-10s such as American's 'LuxuryLiners'. American rebranded its 707s along the same lines as 'LuxuryJets' in 1971, with the lounge seen here and even a stand-up bar, resplendent with brown, red, beige and orange carpets and red seats. *Author's Collection*

BELOW: Passengers in a 'jetliner of the future' enjoy the delights of the new style of airline catering. Actually, this is the interior mock-up built in a coffee warehouse in Manhattan to demonstrate design features to the airlines. One innovation was the 'snap in' sections of hard wall covering, a departure from the cloth coverings of the previous generation of airliners. The panels could be printed with the airline's choice of pattern. *Aeroplane*

BELOW: A stewardess serves cocktails with a smile at 30,000 ft (9,000 m) in the forward lounge of a Pan Am 707-121. Actually, this is probably a view of the mock-up but it gives an idea of the glamorous world of the 'jet set' (a word actually coined in 1960) that the airlines were keen to promote. Publicity stressed the 'over the weather' and vibration-free flying of the new jetliners. *Pan Am/John Stroud Collection/The Aviation Picture Library*

the familiar swing-down tray tables in the backs of the seats. At least initially American offered a buffet food service rather than a trolley service. There were two buffets at the forward left Mercury cabin and one at the rear left side of the Royal Coachman cabin, where there was also a six-place lounge. BOAC called this area an observation salon as the two seating units faced outwards and five of the windows.

Seat pitch on 707s of the era was in the order of 42 in (107 cm) for first-class areas and 34 in (86 cm) in tourist class. By comparison, 30–31 in (76–79 cm) is typical in today's economy-class cabins. With four-abreast 'luxury' seating, the aisle was 30 in (76 cm) wide, reducing to 18 in (46 cm) in six-abreast tourist seating. The latter dimension shows why a buffet service was preferred to trolleys by some airlines.

The air-conditioning system on the first (Pan Am and AA) 707-120s used freon gas, but this proved somewhat

troublesome and later aircraft used an air-cycle system. This, however, required a separate source of conditioned air for ground use rather than just electrical power as with the freon system. Both systems took pressurised, heated air from engine-driven superchargers and passed it through air-conditioning packs in the lower centre fuselage. The air-conditioning and pressurisation systems were driven by three engine-mounted turbocompressors and four engine bleeds. The turbocompressor inlets were mounted on extensions of the pylon fairings with their intakes just above the lip of the main engine intakes, excluding the port outer unit.

In the days before airbridges and piers at airports, cabins were often arranged for entrance from the right side, with the doors on the left used for food and cleaning service. This was the case on early American Airlines 707s at least. Standardisation on the opposite arrangement came as terminals

ABOVE: The lavatories of the 707-100 were designed to 'duplicate the effect of a small powder room in a family home'. Note the curve of the wall – the aft lavatories were in the tapering part of the rear fuselage. This is actually a view of the $500,000 cabin mock-up constructed in a New York warehouse by Walter Dorwin Teague and Associates. *Boeing via Aeroplane*

ABOVE: The aft cabin of the VC-137A contained fourteen sets of double seats and four tables. The forward cabin contained a communications centre with a high-frequency communications set and radio teletype machine as well as the usual galley and toilets and an eight-person seating area. *Boeing via Aeroplane*

BELOW: In order to reduce the ear-splitting noise of the early 707's JT3C engines, noise-reducer nozzles were developed. A dozen models were flight-tested after 200 different paper designs were studied, but the one seen here with test pilot Jim Gannet (left) and flight test engineer Bruce Mengel was not adopted. *Boeing via author*

were upgraded to provide covered walkways of various sorts between the building and the aircraft. Because the captain, in the left seat, was 'driving' on the ground, it was easiest for him to line up the aircraft with the pier or bridge for disembarking from the left.

Convertible passenger/freight 707s could take 108-in (274 cm) wide cargo containers which allowed space to the port side for an accessway between the cockpit and the passenger cabin. A typical mixed load was four pallets and 119 passengers seated six abreast. The pure freighter versions could take larger (125 in/317 cm) containers with no racks or bins and a protective lining panel attached to the interior. The standard 707 container was just over 86 in (218 cm) high at the top. In freighter configuration, the 707-300C could take fourteen full-width pallets for a total cargo volume of 9,785 cu ft (277 cu m). The Combi had a capacity for 7,415 cu ft (210 cu m) in all-freight configuration. The upward-hinging freight door was not of the plug type like the passenger doors, but there are no known incidents of one coming adrift in flight.

ENGINES

Four different types of engine were supplied with production 707s: the Pratt & Whitney JT3 turbojet, JT3D and JT4 turbofans, and the Rolls-Royce Conway turbofan. Additionally there was a CFM-56 testbed, which led to the CFM-powered

ABOVE: By 1960 707-100s were returning to the factory for conversion to turbofan power. At the same time the opportunity was taken to fit the wing and tail modifications and the whole process took three to five weeks. The JT3C itself was convertible to a JT3D by adding a front fan and a fourth-stage turbine. Accessories were repositioned below the engine for better accessibility. *Author's Collection*

AWACS variants and the E-6. The production engines were all of similar diameter, leading to few obvious visual differences between 707 models apart from fuselage length.

The original JT3 two-shaft turbojet was designed in the late 1940s and first flew in 1951. It was a version of the military J57 as used in Boeing's own B-52 and KC-135. It had many other military uses, including on the F-100, F-101 and F-102 fighters and the U-2 spyplane, and over 21,100 JT3s and J57s were built. The length of the JT3C-6 variant without cowlings was 167.5 in (4.25 m) and the diameter was 38.9 in (98.7 cm). Without fuel the weight was 4,234 lb (1,921 kg). Take-off thrust was 11,000 lb (48.9 kN) dry or 13,000 lb (57.8 kN) with water injection.

The JT3D was the turbofan version of the JT3. It was developed in 1959 by replacing the first three stages of the low-pressure compressor with a two-stage fan, and a third stage was added to an enlarged low-pressure turbine. This allowed it to handle two and a half times the air mass flow at take-off, giving 50 per cent more thrust and much better fuel consumption and reduced noise. In military service, the JT3D was called the TF33 and was used on the C-141 and the B-52H. Most C-135s were re-engined with TF33s and about 8,600 JT3Ds and TF33s were made in twenty-four years of production. The JT3D-3B was 135 in (3.43 m) long and 53 in (1.35 m) in diameter. Dry weight was 4,260 lb (1,932 kg). At take-off it was rated at 18,000 lb st (80 kN) dry. Thrust reversers were fitted in the fan and core sections, the former using hinged blocker doors and the latter involving a sliding reverser sleeve, cascade vanes and a clamshell reverser.

The JT4A of the 707-220 and -320 was the military's J75, used in the F-105 and F-106 fighters. In civil use it also powered the DC-8-20 and -30 series airliners.

A JT4-9 was 144 in (3.66 m) long with a diameter of 43 in (1.09 m) and weighed 5,050 lb (2,290 kg). Take-off thrust was 16,800 lb st (74.7 kN).

The Rolls-Royce Conway was the first large turbofan to be developed and was of two-spool, axial-flow configuration. The first production version was the Mk 508 for the 707-420.

ABOVE: The noise-reducer nozzle design eventually chosen for production was this deceptively simple device consisting of two rings of eight pipes. Seen here with the Dash 80, the nozzles were fitted to most 707s with JT3C turbojets. *Boeing via author*

LEFT: This view of the starboard JT3D-3B engines of a 707-320B shows the auxiliary air intake doors in action just after take-off. These doors were a distinguishing feature of the JT3D turbofans. *Author*

The Mk 509 was the equivalent DC-8-40 engine. When operated, a rear-mounted clamshell thrust reverser directed the thrust forward through cascade vanes in the jetpipe walls. The reverse thrust was equal to 50 per cent of the forward thrust. The 707's Conways were fitted with the multiple-exhaust silencing nozzle.

Other applications for the Conway were the VC10 and Super VC10 airliner and the Victor bomber, for a total production of 907. The length was 154 in (3.91 m), the diameter was 50 in (1.27 m) and the no-fuel weight was 5,148 lb (2,335 kg), making it the heaviest 707 engine. Take-off power was 22,500lb st (100kN).

The CFM-56-2 (military F108) as tested on the 707-700 and used on the E-6 and some E-3s has a fan diameter (excluding cowls) of 68.3 in (1.735 m), a length (excluding

spinner) of 95.7 in (2.43 m) a dry weight of 4,820 lb (2187 kg). It is rated at 24,000 lb st (106.8 kN)s.

ABOVE: This view of the Dash 80 shows the starboard JT3L engines and an experimental leading-edge flap section, bolted rather crudely in a fixed mounting. *Boeing via the Aviation Picture Library*

WATER INJECTION

One memorable feature of the early 707s for pilots and spectators on the ground alike was the use of water injection to boost take-off performance. Otherwise used mainly on large military aircraft, some smaller jets like the BAC-111 and a few civil turboprops, water injection on the 707 involved the addition of demineralised water into the combustion chamber of each engine during take-off.

The principle of water injection is that the air inside the compressor is extremely hot, up to 250° C, and the injection of vaporised water cools it, which makes it denser and thus gives more mass flow from the exhaust for a given volume at the intake. This allows more fuel (energy) to be burnt without a meltdown, although it pushes materials and components towards their limits.

The performance increase was dependent on temperature; the airfield altitude and aircraft weight and had to be calculated using tables before take-off. In approximate terms, the injection of a total of 400 gall (1,818 l) of water gave an extra 2,000 pounds (8.9 kN) of thrust per engine. The tanks (between the wheel wells) ran dry after two and a half minutes at take-off power with injection operating, thus preventing freezing problems at altitude.

Water injection was only used on 707-120s with the JT3C-6 engine, notably those of Pan Am and Qantas, who operated from many short runways in the tropics. One problem with its use was the need to ensure supplies of demineralised (or 'demin' water) along the route and this was an expensive commodity.

Water injection was mainly used when the aircraft was weight-limited and thus gave some exciting moments to 707 crews when it failed on one engine, as everything else was giving its maximum. Even when working as designed, the reduction in thrust as the water ran out took some getting used to. Viewed from the ground, the use of water injection was spectacular, producing clouds of black smoke and a large increase in noise. The development of more powerful turbofans and the extension of many runways to cope with jet operations in time obviated the need for water injection on the 707, to the relief of aircrews and those living near airports. 'Wet' engines did make a comeback on some versions of the JT-9 used on the 747, albeit with reduced pollution levels.

failure of one hydraulic drive motor, the opposite pumps could be crossed over to operate the flaps and there were standby electrical motors for use in an emergency. Hydraulic fluid was the new non-flammable Skydrol 500, a break from the mineral oil-based fluids used before.

The electrical system was 115 volts, three-phase, 400 cycles and was driven by a 30 kVA alternator on each engine. In the event of a malfunction, individual alternators could be directed to fill specific loads such as the flap motors, standby hydraulics and fuel booster pumps. One alternator could handle the 'essential' loads needed for a safe emergency landing.

PYLONS

The engine pylons were attached to strengthened wing ribs, which were parallel to the line of flight but diagonal to the main ribs. They were largely made of magnesium. This allowed them to burn through in the event of an uncontained engine fire, letting the engine fall free. This happened on a number of occasions, notably to BOAC's Conway-powered 707-465 G-ARWE at Heathrow, when the aircraft suffered an explosion and fire in the port inner (No. 2) engine and was able to make a successful landing after the unit fell away, fortunately falling into a gravel pit near the airport. The fire spread after landing, however, owing to non-activation of the fire extinguishers in the confusion, and the aircraft was burnt-out on the ground.

ABOVE: A close look at the underside of Omega's 707AR tanker/transport reveals its special features, namely the twin refuelling baskets in the retracted position, refuelling readiness lights and, further forward, the twin-lens video camera that monitors the refuelling process. *Author*

FUEL

Fuel was carried in seven tanks positioned between the wing spars, and in the centre section. Total capacity for the 707-120 was 17,406 US gall or 113,139 lbs (51,319 kg) of JP-1 or JP-4 fuel. Capacity for the 707-320B was 23,855 gall (155,058 lb/70,334 kg). The six wing tanks were integral between the wing spars whereas the centre tank was made up of bladder cells. The outboard pair of tanks were reserve tanks which fed by gravity to the adjacent main tanks. The main wing tanks were used for take-off with these and the main tanks used in the cruise. The outboard tanks then fed into these as fuel was used. The engines were supplied by boost pumps in each tank or by a central manifold which could supply any engine. Fuelling was through underwing pressure openings, with gravity hatches for each tank above the wing provided as an alternative where pressure refuelling was not available.

HYDRAULICS

The dual 3,000 psi (211 kg/cm²) hydraulic system was run by pumps on all engines and powered the flaps, undercarriage, spoilers, wheel brakes and nosewheel steering. In the case of

BELOW: On JT3Cs and JT4s, all four engines had an intake in the 'knuckle' of the pylon for the cabin air turbo compressor. JT3Ds as seen here usually had this only on engines 2, 3 and 4. There was a compressor outlet port on the outboard side of the pylon, midway along its length. *Boeing via the Aviation Picture Library*

FIRE EXTINGUISHERS

The engine fire extinguishing system was controlled through the fire shut-off handles situated above the centre of the instrument panel. Pulling out the knobs for each engine cut off the fuel supply to the engine and the hydraulic oil supply to the engine-driven pumps. It also armed the fire-extinguishing circuit. Activation of the extinguishers fired the contents of two inert gas bottles into the engine. If this failed to work, the contents of the bottle on the adjoining engine could be fired into the burning engine by selecting 'transfer' on the extinguisher switch for the adjacent engine.

CONTROL SYSTEM

The 707 used control cables for some applications where British designers preferred to use mechanical push-pull rods, such as for the elevator trim. On the 707 this was activated by a control cable run from the cockpit trim wheel to an electrical actuator at the tail. The reason was the development of more effective cable-tensioners in the USA that could better handle temperature and altitude variations, preventing cable stretch and sag.

ABOVE: An anonymous Pakistan International Airlines (PIA) 720B (one of three ordered new) undergoes control surface checks at Renton. Here the slotted flaps and fillet flaps are at full down position and the spoilers are full up. The inboard left aileron is also deflected up. *Boeing via the Aviation Picture Library*

RIGHT: A view of the underside of the wing of a 707-320B shows details of the outboard leading-edge flap, position light and exhausts of the JT3D engines. *Author*

CONTROL SURFACES

Hinged spoilers were fitted ahead of the slotted flaps in the area of greatest lift and operated completely independently of the flaps. They worked together with the ailerons for roll control. In flight, 30 degrees deflection gave maximum roll rate. Maximum deflection for landing was 60 degrees. In the retracted position the flaps and spoiler fitted together to form the trailing edge of the wing with an unbroken upper and lower surface.

The ailerons were unconventional compared to earlier airliners in that there were two pairs, one in the usual outboard wing positions and the second at roughly mid-span. These operated throughout the speed range whereas those at the

wingtips were locked in neutral position most of the time and only used at low speeds when the flaps were lowered. The ailerons were activated by a cable moving a trim tab and it was the air load on this tab that moved the aileron. Pressure changes on the aileron surface were partly balanced by air entering a balance bay cavity forward of the hinge line, thus reducing the control forces needed by the pilot as speed increased.

There were two sets of double-slotted flaps on either side of the inboard ailerons and fillet flaps at the fuselage junction. In the event of hydraulic failure they could be wound down electrically or manually. Split flaps were fitted under the centre section. Normal take-off setting was either 20 or 30 degrees. Landing settings were 40 or 50 degrees.

Small inboard leading-edge flaps on the 707-100 operated when the trailing-edge flaps were lowered to 9.5 degrees for take-off and greatly increased lift, converting acceleration into climb at a critical point when over-rotation into a semi-stalled state was otherwise possible. They retracted again when the trailing flaps retracted above 6 degrees.

The 707-300s had full leading-edge flaps, which greatly improved landing performance, reducing approach speeds by 12 per cent over the 707-100. Aided by better brakes, the required landing length was reduced by up to 16 per cent, to

ABOVE: Some of the complexity of the 707's control surfaces can be seen here, including the triple-slotted flaps and the inboard aileron. Vortex generators placed ahead of the inboard aileron cured a tendency for the wing to shake in high-speed cruise. *Boeing via the Aviation Picture Library*

BELOW: The 707-320B (as seen here) featured several improvements over the standard -320, mainly to the wing. These included curved, low-drag wingtips, full-span leading-edge flaps and larger trailing-edge flaps. *Author*

about 5,500 ft (1,676 m) at 200,000 lb (90,720 kg). At maximum landing weight of about 190,000 lb (86,184 kg) the requirement for a 707-120B was for over 6,500 ft (1,981 m) of runway.

The 720's 'glove' extension added only 77 sq ft (7.2 sq m) to the wing area but helped increase the maximum Mach to 0.906 by reducing the thickness/chord ratio. This also gave better fuel consumption figures.

UNDERCARRIAGE

The undercarriage consisted of twin nosewheels and eight mainwheels on four-wheel trucks mounted on single oleos. On a 707–300 the nosewheels were 59 ft (18 m) ahead of the main wheels. Ground handling was conducted by differential thrust and hydraulic nosewheel steering, controlled by a half wheel on the cockpit wall on the first pilot's (left) side. The nosewheels had a steering arc of 55 degrees each way.

The main gear units retracted inwards to lie in wells aft of the rear wing spar powered by the left-side hydraulics. The main gear doors closed after the undercarriage extension. The retraction sequence took 10 seconds. The nose gear retracted forwards and the main doors closed after them, leaving the trailing door open.

ABOVE: A view from the factory roof at Renton shows the wing details of Sabena's first 707-329, rolled out in December 1959. The wingtip HF aerial was only specified by some airlines. OO-SJA had an eventful career, including airlifting over 300 evacuees from the Congo. The nose section is preserved in the Brussels military museum. *Boeing via the Aviation Picture Library*

BELOW: The nose undercarriage of the 707 was a sturdy twin-wheeled unit, mostly hidden within the fuselage. Jet engines did not require the ground clearance for propellers that piston engines did, allowing much shorter gear legs. *Author*

ABOVE: The starboard main landing gear unit of a 707-321B. The -300C had a stronger undercarriage to allow for greater landing weights and different brakes, Goodyear as opposed to Goodrich multiple-disc units. *Author*

BELOW: The mainwheel well bays of the 707-300 were usually enclosed by doors except when retracting or extending, but could be opened on the ground for access to the hydraulic panel and other equipment. *Author*

Brakes were hydraulically operated with anti-skid, but even under normal braking they were said to have an effectiveness equivalent to stopping 432 automobiles from 50 mph (80 kph). An emergency pneumatic system was good for seven applications of 50 per cent capacity.

TAILPLANE

The all-moving tailplane or 'flying tail' was of two-spar construction and attached to a tilting box structure mounted in a rectangular cutout in the rear fuselage. The tailplane incidence was controlled electrically by a jackscrew (with manual back-up) and ranged only a few degrees nose up and nose down. Above Mach 0.81 and with autopilot off, a Mach trim system automatically adjusted the incidence. This was involved in the February 1959 incident in which a Pan Am aircraft dived from cruise altitude to 6,000 ft (1,829 m) before it was recovered, albeit with some damage. The Mach trimmer had disengaged when the autopilot was off and Captain Waldo Wright was in the cabin. Slowly, the 707 nosed into a dive while the co-pilot was distracted by paperwork. Fighting the g-forces from the worsening spiral dive, Captain Wright crawled back to the cockpit and helped the co-pilot pull out. The aircraft

landed safely at Gander, but with a permanent set to the wings. A modification was made to the control system to prevent deactivation of the trimmer in the cruise when the autopilot was disengaged.

The tailfin was of two-spar construction with a 'false spar' carrying the rudder hinges and had electric leading-edge de-icing. On all 707s and most 720s, the fin tip mounted the high-frequency (HF) probe antenna so characteristic of the type. This combined the HF communications No.1 antenna and the No.2 transmitter. The No.2 receiver was inside the fairing on top of the fin. The fin was hinged so that it could be folded down to fit the aircraft into a standard hangar, although this feature appears to have been rarely used.

The original rudder system was operated three different ways according its deflection. For the first 10 degrees deflection, the powered trim tab moved the rudder aerodynamically. Between 10 and 15 degrees the power booster began to take over and above 15 degrees it was fully effective. However, this meant that there was no trim relief at higher angles and for structural safety reasons, the boost 'gave way' at air loads greater than 180 ft lb. To use this effectively required training and practice as a heavy application of rudder gave a noticeable

BELOW: The so-called ARB fin on 737-436 G-APFB. When the marginal stability characteristics of the 707 in some modes was realised, Tex Johnston, backed up by the aerodynamicists, recommended a taller fin, a boosted rudder and the ventral fin seen here. Bill Allen and Boeing's board accepted his findings, as did the British. Johnston answered BOAC's question, 'Who pays for it?' with 'Boeing' – an answer that reassured the customers and ensured the success of the 707, but which delayed profitability even further. *Boeing via the Aviation Picture Library*

BELOW: The tail surfaces of this Northwest Orient 720B shows the distinctive high frequency (HF) antenna on the fin which was not specified by all 720 operators, but was later refitted to many aircraft. The shallow ventral fin used on the 720s is also well shown. *Boeing via the Aviation Picture Library*

'lag' as the booster became effective and then a rapid deflection to the booster's limit. The tendency was to add aileron and spoiler inputs, leading to an overcorrection and Dutch roll. A new booster that worked throughout the full range of deflection was designed to meet UK ARB certification requirements and was later fitted to all 707s.

Dutch roll was a problem inherent in swept-wing jets and was kept in check by the yaw damper function of the autopilot. The yaw damper could not be used at take-off or on the landing approach. Unlike piston transports, the 707 had to be 'flown' positively onto the runway rather than aimed at the threshold and 'floated' on. Pilots who tried to land the 707 like a piston risked undershooting the runway.

The solution was greater fin area and Boeing increased the tail-fin height by 40 in (102 cm) for greater stability. BOAC 707-400s and later aircraft were delivered with the larger fin, but the programme to refit earlier aircraft took several years. Most 707-100s were fitted with the tail modifications when they were returned re-engined with JT3Ds in the 1960–4 period.

Another improvement required for British certification was increased keel area. The so-called 'ARB fin' not only increased stability but also acted as a tail bumper to prevent over-rotation on take-off. The ventral fins were of at least three different shapes, with straight or curved leading edges and different areas.

3 CUSTOMERS

Fifty airlines bought 707s and 720s as 'first-tier' customers and numerous others picked up second-hand examples over the years. Space precludes coverage of them all in this chapter, so what follows is a look at some of the more important and more interesting customers for Boeing's first jet airliner.

PAN AMERICAN

Pan American World Airways (Pan Am) had shown its confidence in Boeing by making the first order for 707s in October 1955 (but hedged its bets by ordering a slightly larger number of DC-8s). In all, the airline was to buy 126 new 707s and other second-hand 720s, but no more DC-8s or any other Douglas jets. After a period of crew training at Seattle, the first Pan Am 707, N710PA was handed over on 16 October 1958. First Lady Mamie Eisenhower christened the aircraft *Clipper America* in a ceremony in a hangar at Washington National Airport attended by several hundred invited guests. The aircraft then set off for London on a 'jet preview flight' with a passenger list that included Pan Am's famous president, Juan T. Trippe.

Actually four of Pan Am's first 707 deliveries were named *(Jet) Clipper America*, including N707PA (so named from January to December 1958), N709PA (August–November 1958), N710PA (1958–1970) and N711PA (October–November 1958). The reason for this may have been uncertainty at Boeing over which aircraft would be ready for the scheduled naming ceremony and the transatlantic flight to follow directly afterwards, and so the manufacturer was hedging its bets.

BELOW: Pan Am was the first 707 customer, taking something of a gamble with the 707 (and DC-8) as much for Juan Trippe's desire not to be second in anything as for any other reason. One reason airlines were initially reluctant to embrace jets was their high purchase cost. In 1953 it was thought a four-engine jetliner might cost $4 million, compared to the $1.5 million price of a new DC-7. The final cost of a 707-100 was well over $5 million. *The Aviation Picture Library*

The historic *Clipper* names dated from the days of the Sikorsky flying boats of the 1930s. Most of the 707s reused historic *Clipper* (or *Jet Clipper*) names such as *Bald Eagle*, *Friendship* and *Constitution*. At least one was renamed for a new destination; *Clipper Beograd* (Belgrade), and for the Beatles' US tour in February 1964 one aircraft was temporarily redubbed *Clipper Beatles*.

Delivery price of the first 707-100s was said to be about $6 million, although the declared value for insurance purposes of Pan Am's first aircraft was $4.5 million and BOAC's -436s cost about $5.1 million The actual price paid depended on the number ordered, the amount of training and support purchased from Boeing and other factors.

The first commercial 707 service was flown from Idlewild Airport, New York, to Paris Le Bourget and Rome ten days later with N711PA *Clipper Mayflower* amid much fanfare, including a send-off from an army band. Just as the 707 was not the first jet airliner to fly, having been beaten to that honour by the Comet I, Avro C.102 and Tupolev Tu-104, the Boeing was not the first to offer a transatlantic service, being pipped to the post by the Comet 4 which BOAC put into service between New York and London on 4 October 1958. Officials in Paris only reluctantly approved 707 revenue operations into that city after making noise measurements during proving flights in late 1958.

A year later, Pan Am inaugurated the first round-the-world jet service with its 707-321s. The route was San Francisco to Manila via Hawaii, then Manila–Karachi–Rome and over the

ABOVE: The first production 707 was N708PA, *Jet Clipper Constitution*. Line number 1 was to be N707PA, but for some reason, this identity was swapped with the second aircraft before roll-out. In February 1959 an engine was torn off during a 'Dutch roll' incident in France and this encouraged Boeing to modify the tails of all existing and future 707s. N708PA was lost in September 1965 when it crashed into Chance Mountain on Montserrat. *Mike Hooks*

BELOW: American Airlines went through a change of image in 1968 and this 720B (N7528A) was the first of the airline's aircraft to receive the new colour scheme, which is basically the same as that worn today. *Mike Hooks*

Pole via Anchorage back to San Francisco. The first round-the-world jet airliner flight was flown on 10 October by N717PA *Clipper Fleetwing*, taking fifty-five hours and sixteen stops over three days, but this was more of a publicity flight than a route-proving exercise.

The Douglas DC-7C was the pride of the Pan Am fleet until the 707-120's arrival, but the jet soon showed its superiority in every respect. The 707 could fly nearly twice as fast with nearly twice the passenger load, and at a lower cost per seat-mile. Soon Pan Am was achieving 100 per cent load factors on the transatlantic routes and was paying off, or amortising the cost of one 707 with the profits of each month's operations.

The 707-321 Intercontinental version, delivered from July 1959, extended Pan Am's non-stop destinations from New York as far as Frankfurt, Rome and Rio de Janeiro. By buying large numbers of -321C convertible cargo versions when they became available from 1963, Pan Am stole a march on its competitors with its 'cargo Clippers' and captured a large part of the civil long-haul freight market. During the Vietnam War, the airline received lucrative contracts to shift military equipment to the war zone as US involvement increased. On the other hand, the military tasks impeded the growth of Pan Am's civil freight business until this was reorganised in 1966.

Only nine 720s, all ex-Lufthansa and American Airlines aircraft, were to see Pan Am service from 1963 to 1974. They were used mainly on Caribbean and South American services until 1965 when they were replaced by 727s, but also supplemented 707s on short-range US services.

As the 727, and later the 747 were established in service, the 707s were sold off. The last Pan Am 707, N492PA *Clipper Eagle Wing* was sold on to a parts company in November 1984. The previous October a special commemorative flight was made on the twenty-fifth anniversary of the first New York–Paris service. Unlike the original flight (in a -121), the 1983 re-enactment (in -321 N880PA) did not require a refuelling stop in Gander, Newfoundland, to enable it to make it across the Atlantic.

AMERICAN AIRLINES

Pan Am's great rival was the first customer to put the 707 into scheduled domestic services. The first commercial coast-to-coast jet service was flown by N7502 *Flagship Oklahoma* from Los Angeles to Idlewild, New York, on 25 January, 1959, returning the same day. The limited range of the 707-120 often led to weather diversions and occasionally to embarrassment. In October 1959 a New York–Los Angeles flight diverted to Phoenix due to bad weather at the destination and was impounded by local authorities, as Phoenix had no insurance cover for jets. It took five days to arrange the necessary documents so that the jet could continue to LA.

After two months of 707 operations, American Airlines

BELOW: A classic view of one of American Airlines' 707-123Bs over the plains of the central USA. Although markings have changed over the years, American still retains the classic polished metal surface on its fleet of Boeing, McDonnell Douglas and Airbus jets today. *The Aviation Picture Library*

ABOVE: N7501A was American Airlines' first jet and the first of twenty-three 707-123s. It was followed by twenty-nine -123Bs, ten -323Bs, forty-seven -323Cs, ten 720-023s, twenty-five 720-023Bs and one -385C. Later named *Flagship Michigan*, N7501A was sold on in 1978 and served briefly with Cyprus Airways before a minor accident grounded it at Bahrain, where it was broken up. *Boeing via author*

produced an internal report on operations with the four aircraft by then in full service. There were several problems that came about indirectly as a result of the new jets. These included the difficulty of setting up a schedule based on predicted winds at the higher altitudes (which the airline's IBM punchcard computer was initially unable to deal with), and the military occasionally blocking off 10,000 ft (3,048 m) of airspace at a time when the jet routeings and altitudes available were already restricted. There were in fact only three transcontinental jet routes between New York and Los Angeles in 1959. Because of these and other factors, up to 66 per cent of flights were late by 10 minutes or more and a further ten per cent were early.

Air traffic control procedures required some adjustment for jets. The regular reporting points were the same as for slower aircraft, so that the 707 crew could barely make one location report before passing the next checkpoint. American introduced a third pilot or second officer to handle navigation and communications duties. He would also take over the left or right seats or flight engineer's station if that pilot vacated it. This four-crew arrangement was also designed to ensure a constant visual scan in the increasingly crowded airways. American

was the only US airline to adopt this crew arrangement and it was fairly short-lived.

In Italy, the arrival of jets seemed to catch the authorities by surprise, even though they had experience of Comet operations in 1952–4. In 1958 the Italian Undersecretary for Civil Aviation refused to allow scheduled jet services as Rome's Ciampino Airport was overcrowded, the new Fiumicino Airport was not finished, and Milan's Malpensa Airport needed extending. Air traffic control was also considered inadequate and overall the 707 was thought to risk 'an undue strain on safety regulations'. The situation did not completely resolve itself until Fiumicino was opened in 1960.

Problems with the aircraft itself included damage to skin, flaps and cargo doors by snow and slush thrown up by higher taxi speeds and trouble with the complex electrical wiring. Spare parts availability was an early teething problem, made worse by minor changes on the Boeing line that came about as part of a pre-delivery design improvement programme which saw changes made between the specification given to the airlines and delivery itself, including everything from new doormats to leading-edge flaps. American found that if a part was to be changed on the production line, subcontractors would often stop making it immediately, leaving Seattle's stocks as the only source. A change in air-conditioning manufacturer after Pan Am and American's first aircraft were delivered was one such case.

These were minor issues, however, and no more than was to be expected. The further introduction of 707s by the main US airlines saw better ATC procedures, high-altitude forecasting and spares distribution. Most importantly, the travelling public took to the 707 with enthusiasm. 'Passenger acceptance of the 707 has exceeded our fondest hope,' the American report concluded proudly. 'We are satisfied that the 707 will have a long and useful history in airline operation.'

After a year of service, a world-wide fleet of fifty-three 707s had flown over 51,000 hours and accumulated over 2.5 billion passenger miles, mostly on US domestic services. The basic soundness of the design had been proved, but a few troubles, mainly with hydraulics, air conditioning and water injection had shown up within the fleet, as had several incidents of 'inadvertent flight manoeuvres'. These included a number of incidents of engine pods scraping on the runway (something that could happen with only 7–8 degrees of roll on landing), two major 'Dutch roll' incidents in training, one of which resulted in the loss of an engine and pylon (see chapter 8) and an unintended dive from altitude on a scheduled transatlantic flight that was only recovered with a 5–6-*g* pullout. Certain weaknesses in the main landing gear truck beams and outboard foreflaps resulted in damage on landing on a number of occasions and led to a redesign of these components. One embarrassing incident involved a Pan Am jet arriving at New York with a damaged undercarriage. Publicity on local TV and radio brought thousands of New Yorkers to Idlewild for a 'Roman Holiday' in expectation of a crash. A safe landing was made with little damage to the aircraft, but there was traffic chaos around the airport.

The phenomenon of 'sonic fatigue' or stress caused by engine noise was a problem in certain parts of the airframe, such as the tailcone. This was cured by replacing some magnesium components with aluminium ones and by lining the tailcone interior with fibreglass. The water injection system proved troublesome with many failures of the engine-driven and electrically driven pumps.

Notwithstanding these initial problems, American and TWA were soon achieving fleet utilisation of 4,000 hours per month. Despite, or perhaps because of, having the first deliveries, Pan Am was only getting 2,000 hours out of its fleet after seven months of service.

QANTAS

Boeing was prepared to make a lot of modifications in order to win orders, unlike Douglas, who offered the DC-8 in only one fuselage length until the later 60-Series aircraft. This was an expensive way to do business, but paved the way for repeat orders and proved to be a wise path in the long run. The prime example was Australia's Qantas, which had the particular problem of Nadi (pronounced 'Nandi') on Fiji. The runway at this important tourist destination and essential stopover on the route to the US West Coast was short and had a distinct hump, the so-called 'Nadi Bump'. To meet the take-off requirements at this airfield and some others on the Sydney–London route in the other direction, Boeing sold the airline the unique 707-138 with a fuselage shortened by 10 ft (3.05 m) behind the wing. This reduced the seating capacity to 154. The engines were an uprated version of the JT3C, but after only a short period of service, the aircraft were returned to Boeing for re-engining with the JT3D turbofan, which had since become available. The seven aircraft returned to service from late 1961 as -138Bs and now had the ventral fins, wing fillets and a fully boosted rudder and other improvements. The airline adopted the branding 'V-Jet' for its fan-engined 707s, the V, rather obscurely, arising from the Latin for fan, *vannus*.

In total, Qantas was to operate up to thirty-five different 707s, with a peak of twenty-seven in service in 1968, even though the -138s were on their way out by then. At the same time, six of the airline's -338s were modified to all-cargo configuration (all had cargo doors for 'combi' operations), thus ensuring another decade of service. On 25 March 1979, the last Qantas 707 service was flown, just three months short of the twentieth anniversary of the arrival of the first aircraft, and a period as 'the world's only all-747 airline' began.

BRANIFF

Another version only used by one airline was the 707-220 for Braniff (as 707-227s). Although the same size as the 707-120, the -220 had the JT4A-3 engine with 15,800 lb st (70.2 kN) thrust, which was useful for the 'hot and high' South American destinations. Only five of this model were built, with one lost on an acceptance flight, as related elsewhere. The others were exchanged with British West Indian Airlines (BWIA) for 727-100s and have now all been scrapped or dismantled. Braniff later ordered five 720s and nine -327Cs and also operated a number of second-hand 707s, including four ex-Qantas -138Bs.

Braniff became famous for the individual colour schemes on their 707s and 720s. Years before special colour schemes were taken up by other airlines, Braniff International's 'pastel fleet' appeared in a riot of colour schemes, from ochre to 'Panagra green' (Braniff had taken over the routes once operated by Pan American Grace, or Panagra). Braniff announced 'the end of the plain plane' and each aircraft had a bold one-colour fuselage with white wings, nacelles and tail surfaces with a large 'BI' logo on the fin.

The change of colours from an interesting, but more conventional red and white scheme was brought about in 1965 by designer Alexander Girard, who in fact came up with over 17,000 changes to logos, uniforms and interiors, completely 'rebranding' the airline. The interiors were as striking as the exteriors, with the use of fifty-two fabric patterns. Eight different exterior colours were used across the fleet, with some duplications when the existing aircraft were repainted at the time the airline changed its name from Braniff Airways in 1965. The new 707-327s were delivered from the factory in 1967 in a revised range of colours. Some of the more striking (or repulsive, depending on your point of view) hues such as the purplish blue, lemon yellow and beige were dropped in favour of dark blue, red and 'Panagra yellow'. Although the colours persisted on other types, such as the 747, the pastel 707

ABOVE: United Airlines was not one of Boeing's best customers in the late 1950s, buying only eleven 720s, which entered service in July 1960. One reason is that UAL had already bought DC-8s and ordered Caravelles, thus having the most mixed jet fleet in US service by 1961. The 720s were phased out in favour of 727s in 1972, as were the Caravelles. *The Aviation Picture Library*

OPPOSITE ABOVE: World Airways is a largely-forgotten carrier, having got out of the scheduled passenger business in the mid-1980s, but still going today as a freight and charter operator with DC-10s and MD-11s. The eighth of nine new 707-300s for the airline, N375WA (18707) served from 1963 to 1971 before sale to Britannia. *John Stroud Collection/The Aviation Picture Library*

OPPOSITE BELOW: N791TW was TWA's first 720B 'SuperJet', although it was originally built for Northwest Orient, which chose to delay delivery of the order. Before it wore TWA colours, N791TW (c/n 18381) spent some time as a company demonstrator, oddly enough, wearing 'Boeing 707' titles. TWA only operated four 720Bs and leased them back to Northwest after a year. *John Stroud Collection/The Aviation Picture Library*

ABOVE: The Aer Lingus Boeing 707/720 story is a complicated one but suffice to say that sixteen 707s and five 720s were bought, sold, leased in and leased out by the Irish national carrier between 1960 and 1986. EI-ALA served on and off from 1960 to 1971, which is when it was photographed at Dublin. *Austin J. Brown/The Aviation Picture Library*

ABOVE: EI-AMW was the first of Aer Lingus's 707-348Cs. Supplementing 720s, the Intercontinental jets allowed destinations beyond New York and Boston to be served by the airline. Last flown by Alyemda, the fuselage of -AMW was last reported giving service as a restaurant in Damascus, Syria. *The Aviation Picture Library*

era was a short one as the Braniff fleet was rationalised in 1971 and the 707s sold on. This was partly due to the winding down of the Vietnam War, which had seen heavy use of Braniff aircraft on military charter flights. Even though this flourish of brightness was brief, some aircraft wore up to three different schemes, changing after major overhauls. In 1982 the original Braniff went out of business, although there have been attempts to revive the name since.

SABENA

Beginning with the national airline Sabena, Belgian companies have been enthusiastic 707 users, with almost 40 airframes recorded on the Belgian civil register. National airline Sabena (Societe Anonyme Belge d'Exploitations de la Navigation Aerienne) ordered four 707-329s in December 1955 alongside Air France's order for 10 -328s.

Sabena's first passenger flight to New York was on 23 January 1960, beating Air France to the honour of having the first non-US transatlantic 707 service by a week. Within six months, however, Sabena's 707s and DC-7s were being used for a different kind of passenger service as the outbreak of civil war in the former Belgian Congo (later Zaire and today the Democratic Republic of Congo) called for the mass evacuation of Belgian citizens. Sabena suspended transatlantic services from 9 to 22 July 1960 in order that its five 707s could be used for the airlift. The 707s evacuated over 7,000 civilians in this period, with up to 303 people including crew carried on one flight (143 adults, 118 children, 32 babies and 10 crew aboard OO-SJA on 16 July). Regular seating capacity for these aircraft was 147, but space was found for children on the floor and babies in the luggage racks on the seven-hour flights to Brussels. Use of jet transports for this airlift helped influence the USAF to acquire transport C-135s for use by Military Airlift Command, which was to prove useful in 1964 when more trouble in the Congo led to American intervention. C-135s supplemented slower piston transports in delivering

aid, personnel and equipment for Belgian forces and the UN.

On the subject of huge passenger loads on 707s, it is believed that over 500 people were carried on some flights of a leased Uganda Airlines 707-300 (5X-UCM) that airlifted Serbian civilians and Yugoslav federal soldiers out of Bosnia and Croatia at the outbreak of the Yugoslav civil war in 1991. Other large passenger loads include 327 civilians evacuated from Darwin after Cyclone Tracy aboard Qantas' VH-EBU on 27 December 1974. In May 1967 El Al 707s helped evacuate over 11,000 tourists from Israel during the Six-Day War.

In May 1978, eight Sabena 707s were used to airlift paratroopers to quell further unrest in the Congo. Over 1,100 were transported on these and two Sabena 727s. The jets were used to spare the Belgian para-commandos a 22-hour C-130 Hercules flight before jumping. They were transferred to C-130s on arrival at secure airfields in the country.

Unlike many other airlines which replaced their 707 fleets completely with 747s on their long-haul services, Sabena only bought two 'Jumbos', partially for reasons of national prestige in 1971. Otherwise it retained 707s, latterly -329Cs bought in 1966, until the 1980s although a number were written off in Sabena service or while on lease to other companies operating in Africa. The 707s opened up jet routes to traditional Sabena destinations in North America and Africa, but also to new ones in the Far East and South America, and the airline grew to operate a large jet fleet. Boeing types gave way to various Airbus models and to the (then) McDonnell Douglas MD-11. Seldom making a profit, Sabena's 78-year history came to an end in 2001 when it was forced to close amidst the world-wide airline crisis and the failure of majority shareholders Swissair.

MIDDLE EAST AIRLINES

One of the major customers for the Intercontinental versions of the 707 was Middle East Airlines (MEA) of Lebanon. MEA eventually owned twenty-nine 707s and leased eight others, but

ABOVE: As one result of President Nixon's historic visit to China in 1972 and the improvement of relations with the West, the Chinese government ordered 707s as the first Western equipment for state airline CAAC (Civil Aviation Administration of China). Delivered in 1974, B-2420 is seen landing at Gatwick on 4 May 1981. It was sold to Royal Jordanian in 1985, where it carries freight today with Comtran hushkits as JY-ADO. *Graham Finch/ The Aviation Picture Library*

RIGHT: Sudan Airways has been a large user of the 707 over the years, although most of their aircraft have been leased, particularly for Haj flights. Two 707-3J8Cs were purchased new in 1974 and both have served with the airline ever since. ST-AFA is one of a dwindling number of passenger-carrying 707s (although operated in a mixed freight/passenger layout). Sistership ST-AFB is currently in freighter configuration. *Boeing via author*

it had not really wanted 707s at all, initially ordering DC-8s as its first long-range jet equipment. The collapse of Lebanon's Intra Bank (which held 65 per cent of MEA's shares) in 1966 caused Douglas to cancel the order, but when things had stabilised, MEA turned to Boeing with an order for four 707-320Cs in August 1968, leasing three 720s and two VC-10s in the interim. These were completed very quickly and the first was delivered in November of that year – but was to only survive another month, falling victim to the regional and internal strife that would blight Lebanon and MEA over the next thirty years. On 28 December 1968 Israeli commandos raided the airport by helicopter in retaliation for a PLO hijacking and blew up three MEA Comets, three Caravelles, a VC-10 leased from Ghana Airways – and the first 707. Six other airliners were destroyed in the attack. Showing the spirit that would often be needed in the future, MEA was back in business the next day using its remaining 707, a Caravelle and a Viscount. By leasing aircraft and investing the insurance money, MEA soon had an all-707 and 720 fleet, which cut costs and brought the airline into profit.

ABOVE: Cameroon Airlines has always had a very small international fleet. From 1972 to 1987 it consisted of 707-3H7C TJ-CAA supplemented by other leased 707s as needed. This aircraft was sold on to Israel and rebuilt to electronic warfare configuration for the air force. It has worn the IDF/AF serials 248, 929 and 255 in its time. *Boeing via author*

ABOVE: Malaysia-Singapore Airlines was the new name for Malaysian Airways after January 1967. The airline was equally owned by both countries and the new name reflected this. It was a short-lived title, however as Malaysia and Singapore set up their own airlines in 1972. The 707s were split between the two, 9V-BBA going to Singapore Airlines with whom it flew until 1979. *Boeing via author*

BELOW: Nigeria Airways bought three 707-359Cs over a period of eight years but leased over thirty others of all basic models except the -200 at different times. Two of Nigeria's own aircraft, including 5N-ABJ, were impounded for non-payment of maintenance bills at Shannon, Ireland, and were broken up in the late 1990s. *Boeing via author*

BELOW: Engine adjustments are made to the JT3Ds of a PIA 720-047B before its flight test programme begins. The weather in Seattle is notably different from California, where the other US jetliner builders were, but none the less, considerable finishing work was completed in the open, exposed to the elements. *John Stroud Collection/ The Aviation Picture Library*

By 1975 Lebanon was slipping into civil war (with much external involvement) and another 707 was lost on 27 June 1976 as it tried to taxi away from Israeli shelling. The passengers had disembarked but two of the crew were killed. For eight months MEA left Beirut and operated from Paris-Orly, mainly on charter flights with a few scheduled routes in Arabia and the Horn of Africa. More 707s were acquired and there was more political turmoil. In June 1982, during the Israeli invasion of Lebanon, six 707s were destroyed by shelling and by 1984, Beirut International Airport was untenable. In 1987 some operations were carried out from a widened stretch of the Beirut–Tripoli highway. MEA was banned from the US and lost much of its other trade. In 1989 MEA returned to Paris, now with some 'hushkitted' 707s and other aircraft, including a pair of 747s. The 707s were later all hushkitted and wore a prominent 'New Q' marking to indicate their 'quiet' status.

Although the airline had wanted to phase out the elderly Boeings for some years, a worsening financial position delayed the introduction of new equipment, in the form of Airbus A310s, until 1992. By 1995 the last of the Boeing 720s had been phased out, ending nearly twenty-seven years of passenger service with Boeing's first jetliners.

Other Lebanese airlines, primarily Trans Mediterranean Airways (TMA) have operated many 707s. After the 1968 disaster (in which TMA also lost several aircraft), the Lebanese government gave MEA exclusive passenger rights and TMA concentrated on freight, building up a fleet of 707s with a few DC-8s and 747s. In 2001 they still operate six 707-300 freighters, making them the largest civilian operator. Some of TMA's aircraft are notable mainly for their plainness, usually bearing no titles at all, just a Lebanese registration and a small national flag on otherwise all-white airframes, but others have

ABOVE: Zambia Airways was one of many operators to pick up surplus 707-300Cs in the 1970s, most of them leased from European airlines such as Aer Lingus and Alitalia. This ex-Northwest Orient -351C was with Zambia from 1975 to 1989 when it was sold to Florida West Gateway who fitted hushkits and used it on cargo flights out of Miami where it was eventually scrapped. *Austin J. Brown/ The Aviation Picture Library*

BELOW: The first 707 for Air France, F-BHSA *Chateau de Versailles* is greeted on its arrival at Orly on 6 November 1959. This was the first 707 delivered to an overseas airline and was used to inaugurate transatlantic services in February 1960. F-BHSA's career was short as it was written off in an aborted take-off at Hamburg July 1961, fortunately without loss of life. *John Stroud Collection/ The Aviation Picture Library*

worn striking green and yellow schemes reminiscent of the heyday of Braniff.

ASIA

Asian airlines were quick to take up the 707. Although the first jet services in the region were flown by Comets, the 707 was the first to fly services with local operators. Air-India International ordered three Conway-powered 707-437s in September 1956 and the first arrived on a record-breaking flight via London on 21 February 1960. Pakistan International Airlines (PIA) had just pipped them to the post by operating a leased Pan Am 707 from 7 March 1960. After a series of proving flights, regular Air-India International services to London began on 19 April and on 14 May, to New York. Tokyo services began in January 1961. The 707s, now numbering six, replaced Air-India International's Super Constellations by June 1962, and served alongside leased BOAC Comets, making it the world's only all-jet passenger airline for a time. At the same time the airline shortened its name to Air-India.

One of the 707-437s was lost in January 1966 with all on board when it struck the Swiss side of Mont Blanc in 'white-out' conditions *en route* to Geneva, a tragic replica of an accident fifteen years before when a Super Connie struck the French side in similar conditions.

New 707-337s arrived from 1964 and a number of these became freighters as the airline introduced 747s in 1971. In 1984, Air-India announced a purchase of a further nine Airbus A310s to replace the half-dozen 707s still in service. The last Air-India 707 service, from Harare to Delhi, was operated on 29 October 1986.

As mentioned before, Pakistan International Airlines (PIA) was the first far eastern 707 operator, beginning services from Karachi to London with a leased aircraft in 1960, but it was two more years before the next Boeings – three 720Bs – arrived. These were followed by many others, nine of which were new-build 720Bs, and another nine 707-300s (two -351Cs and seven -340Cs). Another fifteen or so 707s were leased in at different times, often to operate Haj services to Mecca. Some of PIA's aircraft were passed on to the Pakistan Air Force as 747s,

BELOW: Avianca of Colombia was one of seventeen airlines to purchase Boeing 720s from new. The others were Aer Lingus, American, Braniff, Continental, Eastern Air Lines, El Al, Ethiopian, the Federal Aviation Administration, Lufthansa, Northwest Airlines, PIA, Pacific Northern, Saudi Arabian, TWA, United, and Western. HK-724 was a 720-059B which flew nearly 50,000 hours in Avianca service. It was broken up at Miami in 1989. *Boeing via author*

ABOVE: Ecuatoriana, the state airline of Ecuador, became famous for its flamboyant colour schemes in the 1970s. Its three 720s were painted in different wild schemes based on Indian art motifs. The 720-023B HC-BDP seen here landing at Miami in February 1978 also carried the Ecuador Air Force serial FAE 8037, making it one of the most unusually coloured military aircraft ever. *Austin J. Brown/The Aviation Picture Library*

BELOW: A BOAC 707-436 lifts off from Renton under the power of four Rolls-Royce Conways. The certification programme for BOAC's jets was long and complex. First flown in May 1959, FAA certification took until February 1960 and the British nod was another two months in coming. A taller tail and a new underfin would be needed before the -436s were ready for delivery. *John Stroud Collection/The Aviation Picture Library*

DC-10s, Airbus A300s and A310s were introduced. One or two aircraft served on past 2000 in a freight role making PIA the longest continuous operator of the 707.

Flying Tiger Line was one of the customers for the freighter version of the 707-300, receiving four -349Cs in 1965, although the airline is better known as a DC-8 operator and only operated the Boeings (plus three leased examples) for about four years. One event in this short period is of note, however. Two months after delivery, on 14 November 1965, N322F, specially named *Pole Cat*, took off from Honolulu on the first round-the-world flight by the polar route. The flight was organised by the Explorer's Club of New York and routed Honolulu–London–Lisbon–Buenos Aires–Christchurch-Honolulu for a total distance of 27,000 miles (43,200 km) and flight time of sixty-two hours and twenty-eight minutes. This is thought to be the only 707 to fly over the South Pole, although examples from World Airways and Northwest Orient operated between the USA and Christchurch, New Zealand in the mid 1970s in support of Naval Support Force Antarctica.

BOAC

The British Overseas Airways Corporation (BOAC) was the launch customer for an Intercontinental version with Rolls-Royce power. The Conway-engined 707-400 came about because of the Comet 1 disasters and the resulting delay to the development of the 'definitive' Comet 4. The state-owned but independent BOAC rejected the proposed Vickers VC7 which was cancelled in November 1955 and demanded access to the foreign exchange reserves to buy Boeings for the North

Atlantic routes. As a compromise, the UK government demanded a high local content if BOAC were going to buy an American jetliner and Rolls-Royce Conway turbofans were specified, along with British-made furnishings and other components, married to the 707-300 Intercontinental airframe.

Fifteen 707-436s were ordered by BOAC in October 1956 and the first was rolled out on 12 December 1958. First flight was on 19 May 1959, but the UK ARB demanded a number of changes before certification, mostly relating to stability, as described in chapter 1, but this was eventually awarded on 24 April 1960. BOAC also operated Conway 707s on behalf of Cunard Eagle and later under the BOAC Cunard banner. From 1972, the -400s were traded back to Boeing or passed to BEA Airtours, which later merged with BOAC to form British Airways. The last was retired in October 1977.

The 'Rolls-Royce 707s' used slightly more fuel and were less popular with passengers and crews than the VC10s that were their intended replacements, and less profitable. Nevertheless, BOAC ordered more 707s, this time -300s, and even suggested that they be built in the UK. British airliner manufacturing never quite recovered from BOAC's indifference

to its products since the 1960s.

The first Conway 707 user was actually Lufthansa, who began services in March 1960 while the BOAC aircraft were still undergoing certification. Their aircraft were returned to Boeing for modification with the enlarged fin and ventral fin in 1961.

The only other purchasers of new Conway 707s were Air-India, Varig and El Al, but airlines as varied as Syrian Air, Air Mauritius and Wolf Air of Zaire leased or purchased second-hand examples. None of the thirty-seven built remain in service and only three have been preserved.

Although Boeing was prepared to delay profitability by buying market share with customised versions for different airlines, each new development of the basic airframe pushed the break-even point further and further back. Boeing estimated in 1958 that the hundredth 707 would make a profit, but this goal slipped away until it was closer to the 400th example, delivered in 1965, before it was achieved . Of course, there were another 600 airframes to go, and the profit they began to make allowed the go-ahead for the 747 to be given later that year. Now *there* was a gamble...

4 MILITARY 707s

The original Boeing 367-80 was built primarily to meet a military requirement for a tanker able to refuel the new B-47 and B-52 jet bombers. The success of the subsequent Model 717 or KC-135 did much to secure the future of the 707 as a commercial airliner and make jet passenger travel available to the ordinary person. A total of 820 aircraft were built on the 717 airframe design, which as noted earlier was shorter and narrower than the 707 with only 20 per cent shared components. The bulk of these were KC-135 tankers, along with C-135 transports, although numerous specialised EC- and RC-135 models were built for reconnaissance, missile tracking, command post and other specialised duties. The Model 717/C-135 story is outside the scope of this book, but the use of 707 airframes for military purposes is a fascinating story in itself.

Over a hundred 707s were built by Boeing for military customers, and many other second-hand commercial models were later converted for various military and government roles. Military 707s can be broken down into those used for VIP or tanker use and those built in specialist military configurations for the USA and its allies. These latter aircraft include the E-3 Sentry AWACS (Airborne Warning and Control System), the E-6 Mercury TACAMO (take charge and move out), and the E-8 J-STARS (Joint Surveillance Target Attack Radar System) platforms.

BELOW: Seen in its original MATS (Military Air Transport Service) colour scheme, VC-137A 58-6970 undergoes final preparations before its first flight in April 1959 alongside American -123s and a TWA -131. In August it took President Eisenhower on a trip to Western Europe. The following year it was modified with hidden cameras in preparation for his first visit to the USSR, but the U-2 spyplane incident in May caused the trip's cancellation and the cameras were never used. This historic aircraft was retired to the Museum of Flight at Renton in 1996. *Boeing via the Aviation Picture Library*

ABOVE: Canada operated a fleet of five Boeing 707s or CC-137s in the tanker and transport role. They were replaced as transports by Airbus A310s (or CC-150 Polaris) twinjets in 1997, but it was not until late 2001 that a decision was made to equip two of the five Airbuses as aerial refuellers. *Austin J. Brown/ the Aviation Picture Library*

The AWACS programme began as long ago as 1963 when the USAF first sought to replace the EC-121 Warning Star version of the Lockheed Super Constellation. As with the EC-121s, the hardware solution chosen was a large dorsally mounted radome on an airliner airframe. The main difference was that the radar antenna itself was to be mounted horizontally in a rotating dome or 'rotodome', which would allow it to be much longer, and thus have longer range than with a vertical housing, as in the EC-121. Two new-build 707-320Bs were acquired from Boeing to test the Hughes and Westinghouse radar systems and were both flown in February 1972.

Westinghouse was chosen as the winning radar contractor in October 1972 and a production order for the first of thirty-four E-3A (originally VC-137D) Sentry aircraft with AN/APY-1 radar was made in April 1975.

The first of thirty-four production Sentries was delivered to the USAF in March 1977 and entered service in 1978 to the 552nd Airborne Warning and Control Wing at Tinker AFB, Oklahoma. A thirty-fifth airframe remained with Boeing as a JE-3 test aircraft until delivery in April 1994, after which it was immediately leased back to Boeing. These aircraft have all been converted to E-3Bs or E-3Cs, having AN/APY-2 radar, upgraded computers, maritime tracking capability, secure radios and jam-resistant systems. The E-3 programme was highly controversial in the 1970s, not only for its vast cost, but

also because of the decision to supply aircraft to Saudi Arabia, thus giving them a capability not fielded by any other country in the Middle East. Five CFM-56-powered E-3Bs were eventually supplied in 1986 and 1987 and serve with 18 Squadron Royal Saudi Air Force, as do eight KE-3A tankers, also based on the 707-320 with CFMs. Despite the designation, these aircraft have no AWACS equipment, but have a flying boom refuelling system as used on the KC-135. At least one of the Saudi aircraft KE-3s is believed actually to be an RC-707 or RE-3 intelligence-gathering aircraft.

Other users of the E-3 include NATO, using seventeen of eighteen E-3As delivered from 1982 and four 707s used as

BELOW: Seen landing at RAF Waddington in June 2000 is Israeli Air Force VC-707 transport IDF 264, also registered as 4X-JYH. This aircraft was built for CAAC of China and was sold to Israel in 1993. Its visit to 'Waddo' was in support of the visit of two F-15I Strike Eagles to the International Air Show held on the base. *Graham Robson*

ABOVE: The E-3 Sentry or AWACS has been a big success for Boeing with large numbers sold to the USAF and others to France, the United Kingdom, Saudi Arabia and NATO. This is a NATO E-3A, pictured over the North Sea. NATO E-3s were sent to the USA in late 2001 to supplement USAF E-3s monitoring flights and controlling fighters over potential terrorist targets. *Graham Robson*

RIGHT: The bulbous nose of an EC-18B (81-0891) contains a 7 ft (2.13 m) steerable radar antenna for tracking missiles and space vehicles. The code-name for this role is ARIA (advanced range instrumented aircraft) and this example was seen at the 1997 Point Mugu airshow in California. *Author*

'bounce bird' trainers for aircrews. These aircraft are to the highest (E-3C) modification standard, with side and undernose fairings for ESM (electronic support measures), although they retain the E-3A designation. France has four E-3Fs with CFM-56 engines and refuelling probes based with the 36e Escadre at Avord, and the Royal Air Force has seven similar E-3D Sentry AEW.1s at Waddington. The British aircraft replaced the venerable Avro Shackleton after the failure of the Nimrod AEW.3 programme in the 1980s. The seventh RAF aircraft, ZH107, has the distinction of being the very last 707 produced, making its first flight on 14 June1991 and ending thirty-four years of continuous production. This aircraft was the 1,013th 707/720 airframe produced and the ninety-fifth AWACS. Although Japan and Australia have ordered AWACS-type aircraft since 1992, they are based on the Boeing 767 and 737 respectively.

US and Saudi E-3s were heavily involved in the1991 Gulf War, and US and NATO aircraft monitored the skies over the former Yugoslavia from 1994 through the Allied force campaign in 1999, directing the fighters that enforced the no-fly

zones and scored a number of kills over Serbian and Yugoslav aircraft. A similar role has been performed in enforcing UN resolutions against Iraq. Following the attacks on the USA of 11 September 2001, USAF AWACS were despatched to the Middle East to control aircraft on missions over Afghanistan, and two NATO aircraft were sent to the USA to bolster forces engaged in providing combat air patrol (CAP) over major US cities and other potential targets.

One US and one NATO aircraft have been lost in accidents, both attributed to birdstrikes. In September 1995, a 961st Air Control Squadron (ACS) aircraft lost its left-hand engines when it struck a flock of Canada geese just after take-off from Elmendorf AFB in Alaska. While dumping fuel and attempting to return for a landing, the aircraft struck a hill and all twenty-four crew were killed. More fortunate were the crew of a NATO AEWF (Airborne Early Warning Force) aircraft which encountered birds on its take-off run from Preveza AFB, Iraklion, Crete, in July 1996. Take-off was aborted, but the aircraft overran the runway and collided with a sea wall, breaking in two. All fourteen aboard survived with few injuries. Neither of these E-3s was replaced.

Currently the US, Saudi and NATO AWACS, along with all other military 707s use 1960s-vintage design TF33 or JT3D-7 engines. French and British E-3s are CFM-56

ABOVE: The first two of almost 100 AWACS aircraft based on the 707 airframe were designated as EC-137Ds at first and flew within a day of each other in February 1972. They were later converted to E-3A Sentries and are in service today. The US military has reused the EC-137D designation for an ex-Caledonian Airways 707-355C (67-19417) operated as a communications aircraft for Special Operations Command. *Author's collection*

BELOW: One of the most extraordinary-looking of all 707s is Chile's Phalcon, known locally as the Condor. Using an electronic and radar system developed by Israel, the Phalcon/Condor combines the roles of AWACS with a sophisticated electronics and communications intelligence (ELINT/COMINT) system. Its nose houses an electronically steered surveillance radar. *Robert Hewson*

ABOVE: The Northrop Grumman Joint Surveillance Attack Radar System (Joint STARS or J-Stars) is the official name for an ex-airline Boeing 707-300 converted to a sophisticated airborne targeting and battle management platform. Officially in service from late 1997, the J-stars was trialled successfully in the 1991 Gulf War. *Northrop Grumman via the Aviation Picture Library*

BELOW: Originally intended to be a Navy E-6 Mercury, c/n 24503 was converted to the prototype YE-8B J-stars for the USAF. In the end the cheaper option was to convert existing airliner airframes supplied by Omega Air and it was exchanged for five of these and converted back to JT3D power. Omega lease it to Northrop Grumman as a company 'hack' as N707UM. It is seen here at RAF Waddington on return from the 1993 Dubai Air Show. *Graham Robson*

powered. A consortium involving Pratt & Whitney, the Seven Q Seven group (including Omega Air), Goodrich Aerospace and Nordam is bidding to replace the engines of NATO E-3s with the quieter, more fuel-efficient JT8D-219 as used in the McDonnell Douglas DC-9 series. The 707RE (re-engined) would require relatively few airframe changes and offer considerable cost savings. A demonstrator aircraft made a tour of European airfields and air bases in late 2001 prior to an expected NATO request for proposals in 2002. After the NATO E-3s, the consortium has its sights on a possible contract to re-engine the E-8 J-STARS, and there are numerous other potential civil and military customers for the new engines.

E-6 MERCURY

The problem of communicating with submerged ballistic-missile submarines in time of war was solved by the use of relay aircraft transmitting very low-frequency (VLF) signals by way of a long trailing wire aerial. For many years this was the role of the EC-130Q Hercules under the name TACAMO, but, following trials with borrowed USAF NKC-135As, the US Navy chose to adopt a platform based on the 707 airframe. The first of these, designated as the E-6A Hermes was delivered in 1989. Two squadrons of Sea Control Wing One (SCW-1), VQ-3 'Ironmen' and VQ-4 'Shadows' operate the E-6A. The original 'Hermes' name attracted too many jokes about social diseases and VQ-4 were successful in lobbying for the name to be changed to Mercury, the Roman name for the same legendary messenger of the gods.

The heart of the E-6 system is the AN/USC VLF transmitter/receiver and its two trailing antennae, the longer of which is an amazing 26,000 ft (7,925 m) or nearly five miles (8 km) in length. Naturally, this hangs a great distance below the aircraft when reeled out and as the E-6 flies an orbiting pattern, the antenna forms a spiral. This flight profile causes considerable stress to the airframe, which was strengthened after some initial problems with damage to the vertical tails of early aircraft. The transmitter/receiver system and communications suite was transferred from the EC-130Qs to the fourteen E-6s delivered. In 1997 the first E-6B conversion was handed over and the last will be delivered in 2003. This improved model includes a communication system able to relay orders from national command authorities to the B-2 bomber and other strategic platforms and as such makes the Mercury a joint-service asset, replacing the EC-135 'Looking Glass' command aircraft. E-6Bs can be identified by the large satellite antenna housing above the forward fuselage. The Airborne Launch Control System (ALCS) allows the E-6B to command the launch of land-based ballistic missiles. The base airframe was the 707-320, fitted with CFM-56 engines, like the British and French aircraft benefiting from Boeing's private-venture CFM-56 work in the early 1980s.

The newest and probably last 707 variant to join the US forces is the E-8 J-STARS, or Joint Surveillance Target Attack Radar System. 'Joint' in this case means US Air Force and US Army; the latter had a long-standing requirement for a platform able to survey an entire battlefield and supply real-time

information on vehicle movements to commanders on the ground. By the time the go-ahead for the programme was given, Boeing was winding down 707 production and it proved expedient to use second-hand ex-airline airframes on this as yet untried system rather than try and keep the line open. A number of the airframes were originally Qantas 707-338Cs, although they had passed through several other hands in the interim. Northrop Grumman at Melbourne, Florida, were given the job of converting the aircraft and integrating the Westinghouse-Norden AN/APY-3 side-looking phased array radar, which is fitted in a ventral canoe fitting under the forward fuselage. J-STARS are therefore usually listed in official documents as Northrop Grumman E-8s rather than Boeing aircraft.

The E-8 has not yet received an official name, but 'Sentinel', 'Excalibur' and 'Night Owl' have been considered.

The total requirement for J-STARS airframes has varied since the programme began. At one point up to thirty-five aircraft were seen as necessary in order to provide constant surveillance over the battlefield in a two-theatre war, the basis of US defence strategy through the 1990s, but funding has only been given for thirteen as of the end of 2001. A more likely final total is nineteen aircraft. The E-8s are operated by the 93rd ACW at Warner-Robbins AFB, Georgia.

VIP 707

The 707 is or has been used in the government and military transport role or in a dual tanker/transport role by two dozen countries around the world. These have included Argentina, Canada, Germany, Iran, Morocco, Portugal, Qatar, Romania and Saudi Arabia, as well as the USA, which all bought some

BELOW: The most famous military 707 must be 62-6000, popularly but wrongly thought of as 'Air Force One'. Unlike the earlier VC-137A, the VC-137C was officially designated as a presidential aircraft, the first jet to be so assigned. It is perhaps best known for returning the body of President John F. Kennedy to Washington and the on-board inauguration of Lyndon B. Johnson on 22 November 1963. Among its many important missions was President Nixon's 1972 visit to China, which helped reopen that country to the West. *The Aviation Picture Library*

new-build aircraft. Additionally Angola, Australia, Brazil, Chile, Colombia, India, Indonesia, Italy, NATO, Pakistan, Paraguay, Peru, South Africa, Spain, Togo, Venezuela and Yugoslavia have used ex-airline 707s, and Taiwan has used a 720. Countries using civil-registered 707s for government use include Democratic Republic of Congo, Egypt, Libya, Morocco, the United Arab Emirates (UAE) and Saudi Arabia.

The only Boeing 720 in military service belonged to the Republic of China (Taiwan) Air Force and was used as a presidential aircraft for over twenty years before it was retired to a museum in the mid 1990s. Togo, the UAE and Congo-Brazzaville have used 720s as government aircraft on the local civil registers.

RC-707

Several nations' aircraft with an ostensible transport role are believed to have more or less clandestine roles as RC-707s, although this is not any kind of official designation and covers a wide variety of configurations for electronic intelligence (ELINT) missions. ELINT covers communications intelligence (COMINT) or listening to messages transmitted by radio signal, and signals intelligence (SIGINT) or recording radar and other electronic emissions.

The South African Air Force (SAAF) has an ELINT 707 with large cheek radomes which can be removed to avoid undue attention when on overseas visits, although the mounting points can be seen on close inspection.

BELOW: Almost dwarfed by its bigger brethren at London's Heathrow Airport is A7-AAA, a 707-3P1C built as a VIP aircraft for the government of Qatar. This aircraft was sold in 1999 to Commodore Aviation in 1999 and then to Israel, where it was converted to tanker-transport configuration. It flies today as IDF 275 in a plain white and grey colour scheme. *Peter J. Cooper*

Many of the foreign listening or electronic aircraft are only identifiable as such by proliferations of small aerials on the fuselage. The Israeli Phalcon conversion on the other hand is nothing if not distinctive, and the aircraft has caused a great deal of interest since it first appeared in public in 1993.

With electronics by Elta and airframe modifications by IAI, the Phalcon system is a combination of ELINT and COMINT sensors and AEW&C (airborne early warning and control) radar. A sophisticated sensor fusion system cross-relates the data gathered by all the sensors and directs a complementary sensor to begin a search when a contact is detected. The most distinct features are the side-mounted phased-array radar antenna housings on the sides of the forward fuselage and the bulbous nose radar, which extends well below the line of the lower fuselage. The electronically (rather than mechanically) steered radar beam can survey a 360-degree arc around the aircraft with less weight and aerodynamic and mechanical complexity than a rotodome system. One ex-South African Airways 707-344C was converted to Phalcon configuration as a testbed, albeit without the nose radome and another (an ex-LAN Chile 707-385C) has been delivered to Chile and is known locally as the Condor. The Condor does not have the rear antenna array of the prototype, restricting radar coverage to 260 degrees.

After strong US objections and to great Chinese annoyance, Israel withdrew an offer to sell the Phalcon system to China in July 2000. The system is said to be suitable for many platforms other than the 707 and the Chinese would probably have fitted it to a version of the Ilyushin Il-76 transport. The Chinese government announced at the end of 2001 that they were to sue Israel for $2 billion over the Phalcon deal.

This technology is a generation ahead of that used on the E-3, and will likely be employed in many future surveillance aircraft.

Argentina may have received an RC-707 modified in Israel to go alongside its standard 707s (a variety of aircraft have served with the Fuerza Aerea Argentina over the years with a usual inventory of three aircraft). The Falklands War of 1982 showed up a need for a better intelligence platform and an airborne command and control post. During the war, the 707s were used as long-range patrol aircraft to shadow the British task force as it approached the Falkland Islands and were escorted away by Sea Harriers on a number of occasions. Less well known are the transport missions to the UK undertaken in the weeks before the Argentine invasion of the islands to pick up spare parts and ammunition which was soon to be turned on its suppliers.

Iran bought four 707-329Cs in tanker configuration with a Boeing flying boom and wingtip hose reels and may have converted others from its fleet of ten transports. The tankers were used to refuel Iran's F-4s (with the boom) and F-14s (with the hose-and-drogue) system and extended their effective range by about 2,500 miles (4,000 km), giving an important strategic advantage against Iraq until that nation acquired Iluyshin Il-78 tankers.

One of the Iranian aircraft is believed to have been modified for electronic reconnaissance duties, but since converted back to standard configuration.

The original aircraft have been joined by a number of other aircraft, including one ex-Iraqi Airways jet that had been stored in Jordan before the Islamic Republic of Iran Air Force (IIrAF) acquired it in 1995.

The Shah of Iran had ordered seven E-3s in late 1977, but these were cancelled after the 1979 Islamic revolution.

The Indian Air Force has two 707 aircraft that it prefers not to acknowledge. These belong to the Air Research Centre and Analysis Wing at Palam. These are a 337C (K-2899) and a -337B (K-2900), both ex-Air-India, and they are thought to have an ELINT role.

TANKER CONVERSIONS

Israel has had a hand in many tanker conversions as well as with electronic surveillance installations. The US turned down Israeli requests for surplus KC-135 tankers or for refuelling boom kits, so Israel Aircraft Industries (IAI) developed their own conversion package for 707 airliners, mostly ex-El Al. The first IAI tankers delivered to the Israeli Defence Force/Air Force (IDF/AF) had triple-point hose drum units (HDUs) and the service's F-4 Phantom and Kfir fighters were modified with refuelling probes to use the system. Later conversions included a flying boom for refuelling the F-15 and F-16 as well as having wingtip HDUs. Unlike KC-135s, the Israeli and other 707 tankers do not have a visual refuelling window or a boom operator's station, relying instead on a video camera system monitored by an operator in the cockpit or, in the case of boom-equipped 707s, in the rear fuselage. This reduces the number of fuselage penetrations and structural modifications needed to the aircraft, thus simplifying the conversion.

The large number of 707s passing through IAI's hands, and the frequent re-registering or re-serialling of IDF/AF aircraft makes it hard to get a full picture of Israeli military 707s. One is known to be used as an 'Air Force One' governmental transport and several have been seen with extra aerial fits, suggesting ELINT duties. These specialised aircraft may or may not be known within the IDF/AF by the Hebrew names Barboor ('swan') and/or Chasidah ('stork').

IAI supplied conversion kits using Flight Refuelling Ltd (FRL) pods to the Royal Australian Air Force (RAAF) which converted four of the service's five aircraft to refuel F/A-18 fighters. Two of these No. 33 Squadron aircraft were deployed to Diego Garcia in November 2001 together with four F/A-18s to support US and other forces operating in Afghanistan.

The Australian aircraft are mostly ex-Qantas 707-338Cs acquired in 1979 and 1983, although two more aircraft were obtained from Saudia in 1988. At one time it was planned that these aircraft would receive a boom system for refuelling the RAAF's F-111s. One of the ex-Saudia aircraft was lost in a training accident in New South Wales in 1991. All of the ex-Qantas aircraft have a dual tanker/transport role with the latter duty occupying about 85 per cent of the flying hours, and the surviving Saudia aircraft is in VIP configuration. Noise regulations around the world are reducing the utility of the JT3-engined aircraft and it was announced in December 2001

ABOVE: The Iranian (then Imperial, now Islamic Republic) Air Force has been a big 707 user. Their purpose-built -3J9Cs were equipped with both boom and hose refuelling systems. Despite revolution, war and sanctions, most are still believed to be in service at Tehran-Mehrabad Airport. *Beech via Aeroplane*

RIGHT: Boeing converted an ex-TWA 707-331C to tanker-transport (also called KC-707 or KC-137E) configuration in late 1982. Like the -3J9Cs built for Iran, the modification involved wingtip pods with a hinged guide chute that lowered the refuelling drogue out of the disturbed airflow. This proved more successful than some third-party conversions using Flight Refuelling Ltd pods, and it was not until 1989 that the aircraft was sold – to Spain as T.17-2. It is seen here conducting trials with an F-105G Thunderchief. *Author's Collection*

that the 707s would be replaced in the transport role with two new 737s and three Bombardier Challenger 604s on a 12-year lease deal.

Other nations with hose-and-drogue-equipped tankers include Brazil with four KC-137s (ex-Varig), Italy with four 707T/Ts (ex-TAP) and Spain with four T.17s (ex-TWA, Olympic and Saudia). All are based on 707-300 airframes. Canada has retired its CC-137s, which were bought new from Boeing in 1970. Morocco had its 707 transport (the former CFM-56 testbed) converted to a tanker, but this aircraft has subsequently joined the Israeli Air Force and has been converted to VIP configuration. Both Peru and Venezuela operate hose-equipped 707 tankers supplied via IAI and South Africa's No. 60 Squadron has four. The catchall designation of KC-137E is used in some US military documents to describe former 707-320 series airframes converted to tankers by foreign nations.

OTHER MILITARY CONVERSIONS

The most famous individual military 707s, and probably of the whole breed were those used as VIP transports for the US military under the VC-137 designation, often called collectively (and thus inaccurately) 'Air Force One'. The first VC-137A, serial 58-6970 was delivered in 1959 and was the first jet aircraft used by a US president when Dwight Eisenhower used it to visit Western Europe in December 1959. It was soon joined at the 89th Military Airlift Wing (MAW) by two others. In 1963 they were converted to turbofan power becoming VC-137Bs and repainted in the familiar blue and white colours. They were later stripped of some VIP fittings and downgraded to C-137B status and used as general passenger transports.

The first officially-designated presidential jet aircraft wasVC-137C 62-6000 (usually abbreviated to 26000), which entered service with Wing (MAW) in October 1962. It was the aircraft that took President John F. Kennedy to Dallas, Texas on 22 November 1962 and on board which Lyndon B. Johnson was sworn in as President following Kennedy's assassination that day. It later carried President Nixon on historic visits to China and the USSR. The second VC-137C, 72-7000 (27000) was delivered in 1972 and was mainly used as a backup aircraft. Like 62000 it was based on the 707-300 and Boeing designated it a 353B. In 1981 it carried former Presidents Nixon, Ford and Carter to Cairo for the funeral of Egypt's President Anwar Sadat. This aircraft was mainly used by President Ronald Reagan and was retired for display at the Reagan Presidential Library in Simi Valley, California on 16 August 2001. In May 1998 62000 was delivered to the USAF Museum at Dayton, Ohio.

The VC-137s, only known as 'Air Force One' when carrying the President, were appointed with a communications centre, a conference room with projection screens and convertible sofa-bunks, two galleys and other features not found on the three VC-137A (707-153) VIP aircraft.

In contrast to the well-known VC-137s, officially called Stratoliners by the USAF, the C-18 has mostly remained in obscurity through many years of service and has not been blessed with a popular name, let alone an official one. Like the VC-137C, the C-18A and derivatives are based on the 707-300, and all twelve that have served with the USAF and USN are in fact ex-airliners, mainly American 707-323Cs and TWA 707-331Cs. The primary version is the EC-18B which fulfilled the advanced range instrumentation aircraft (ARIA) role by

BELOW: The West German air force or *Luftwaffe* purchased four B707-307Cs in 1968. This, the first, was named *Otto Lilienthal*. The others were *Hans Grade*, *August Euler* and *Hermann Kohl* and all served with Transport Squadron 1 of the Special Air Missions Unit at Cologne–Bonn until replacement by Airbus A310s in 1999. 10+01 was sold to NATO in 1998 and serves today as LX-N19997 as an aircrew trainer or 'bounce bird' based at Geilenkirchen, Germany. *Boeing vis the Aviation Picture Library*

ABOVE: The Chilean Air Force (Fuerza Aérea de Chile, FAC) has operated four 707-300s, although it has swapped the identities of several of them over the years. For example aircraft 905 became 904 and 904 then became 901. This anonymous example is probably 903, the FAC's only known 707 tanker. *Robert Hewson*

tracking military and NASA missile launches with a large steerable radar antenna in a greatly extended nose radome. As such they replaced the similar but smaller EC-135N. The initial EC-18As (without the radome) were converted to EC-18Bs or EC-18D cruise missile mission control aircraft or TC-18E crew trainers with the cockpit layout of the E-3 but no mission avionics. Finally, two TC-18Fs are ex-TAP Air Portugal -382BAs used as flight crew trainers for the E-6.

The US forces have been known to operate other 707s from time to time. One such was N2138T, a former Pan Am aircraft (N404PA, *Clipper Seven Seas*). Used by E-Systems Inc., which developed the J-STARS radar, it passed to Air Force Systems Command (later Air Force Material Command) in the early 1990s and wore a very anonymous white colour scheme with a thin black cheat-line and a 'Boeing 707' title prominently displayed on the nose. The exact role or purpose of this aircraft is not known. It was last reported in storage and the registration has been used at least twice since by non-governmental aircraft.

The latest military conversion of a 707 is for Angola, which has acquired a former Pan Am, Lan Chile and Chilean Air Force -321B (c/n 19374) for electronic warfare (EW) uses. These are said to include the detection and jamming of air defence systems used by UNITA rebels in the country and the aircraft has received a sophisticated electronics suite installed by Elisra and IAI Taman of Israel.

5 IN SERVICE

This chapter takes a look at the early days of jet travel from an operational perspective and at some of the things that were new about the 707 from a passenger's point of view.

The introduction of the 707 cut travelling times almost in half – if only at first for a privileged few. The 707 reduced the average flight time from Los Angeles to New York from seven hours, twenty minutes to four hours, thirty minutes. The return journey was scheduled an hour longer due to prevailing winds, but there was no longer the requirement for an intermediate stop or the likelihood of a fuel diversion, as there was with the piston airliners. Other typical domestic sector times were one hour, twenty-eight minutes New York to Chicago and two hours, thirty minutes Boston to Miami. Important international sector times included six hours, thirteen minutes New York to London, seven hours, thirty minutes New York to Rome, and nine hours, thirty minutes Seattle to Tokyo. All of these were 'zero wind condition' figures, so are accurate in relative terms only. Headwinds affected transatlantic services too, and such destinations as Shannon, Ireland, Keflavik, Iceland, and Gander, Newfoundland, became almost as familiar to early 707 passengers as they had been to those aboard the slower, lower-flying Constellations, Stratocruisers and DC-7s.

The absence of vibration of the jet was a big selling point compared to piston engines that transmitted the throbbing of their pistons to the cabin. This vibration was claimed to be the main cause of travel fatigue and it was said that this would almost completely disappear with jets. The phenomenon of jet-lag had yet to be discovered, first being recorded in dictionaries in about 1969.

Pilots transitioning to the 707 were on average slightly over fifty years old, reflecting the experience needed and the prestige of flying the new jets. Each would be a senior pilot with many thousands of hours on Constellations, Stratocruisers or DC-7s. About twelve hours' flying time was needed for each pilot to transition to the 707. A *Flight* magazine review of the first year of service noted that the thrill of flying the 707 had 'brought

BELOW: F-BLCC *Le Pelican I* awaits loading with another 'cargon' at Orly. Air France's 707-328Cs 'Pelican' freighters were delivered from August 1965 and served into the early 1980s. F-BLCC (l/n 18881) was later bought by a leasing company and after several leases and sub-leases was operating for Angola Air Charter when it crashed into a river while attempting to land at Lagos, Nigeria, in July 1988. *Air France via the Aviation Picture Library*

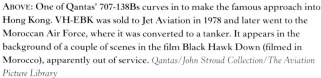

ABOVE: One of Qantas' 707-138Bs curves in to make the famous approach into Hong Kong. VH-EBK was sold to Jet Aviation in 1978 and later went to the Moroccan Air Force, where it was converted to a tanker. It appears in the background of a couple of scenes in the film Black Hawk Down (filmed in Morocco), apparently out of service. *Qantas/John Stroud Collection/The Aviation Picture Library*

ABOVE: Qantas stewardess Pat Willbrandt models the new Boeing uniform in front of one of the airline's new 707-138s. The aircraft's white tail with red trim only lasted for a couple of years before the new 'V-Jet' livery came in with the conversion to turbofan power. *Qantas/John Stroud Collection/The Aviation Picture Library*

back to senior pilots the gleam in their eyes'. On the other hand there were early problems with the US Airline Pilots Association (ALPA) over pay for jet crews and the status of the flight engineer, who the unions insisted should be a rated pilot. The dispute meant that Pan Am's and American's services began in the hands of supervisory staff such as check pilots not subject to ALPA's rulings.

Some aspects of the transition to jets took a bit of getting used to. Piston-engined transports decelerate quickly when power is reduced, owing to the drag of the propellers, but jets maintain speed for a long time and pilots had to be taught to reduce speed for the landing pattern earlier, using the speed-brakes when necessary. The cockpit instrumentation and controls were not much more complex, and in many cases simpler than on four-engined piston aircraft, but new methods of speed measurement had to be learned, namely Mach (percentage of the speed of sound), and new calculations for take-off and landing speeds for given weights calculated. The fuel burn of jets, particularly at the higher altitudes at which they flew, and the effect on performance and landing distance, took on a much greater importance. For reasons of flight economy, the need to reach cruising altitude quickly and stay there as long as possible was drilled into pilots in training.

The Dutch roll problem was later fixed by modifications to the tail surfaces, but initially was dealt with by emphasis on yaw prevention and recovery. Pilots were warned strictly against exceeding more than 10 degrees of yaw, as an irrecoverable condition could develop beyond 15 degrees in some circumstances. The yaw damper in the autopilot was one of the most important parts of the flight control system, but if it was not rigged correctly, a mild yet disturbing form of Dutch roll could develop, with passengers in the rear of the cabin suffering the most as the tail made a circular motion around the longitudinal axis of the aircraft.

Runway requirements were longer than those seen before on a commercial airliner. At the maximum take-off weight of 245,000 lb (111,132 kg) the 707-120 required 10,000 ft (3,048 m) of runway under standard day sea-level conditions. It should be noted that this was the required length, allowing for an aborted take-off rather than the actual take-off distance. The 707-220 with its greater weight but higher thrust required 9,400 ft (2,865 m) of concrete, and the -320 needed 'only' 8,800 ft (2,682 m) at a maximum weight of 295,000 lb (133, 812 kg) because of its bigger wings and even greater thrust engines.

The infrastructure requirements of the 707 and its contemporaries initially hampered the spread of jet services. The extra capacity of the 707, DC-8 and Convair 880 compared to the previous generation of airliners created parking difficulties on

OPPOSITE ABOVE: Qantas bought seven 707-138s which were later converted to JT3D-powered -138Bs, and six new-build -138Bs. These specialised versions were followed by twenty-two -338Cs, of which VH-EAJ *City of Geelong* (later *City of Broken Hill*) was one. In Uganda Airlines service it was one of the last passenger 707s to be lost in an accident, crashing at Rome in October 1988. *John Stroud Collection/The Aviation Picture Library*

OPPOSITE BELOW: A steward and stewardess serve drinks in the first class cabin of a BOAC 707. The joys of jet travel appear to have passed at least one passenger by. *BOAC via The Aviation Picture Library*

ABOVE: HK-724 was one of seven 720Bs purchased new or second hand by Colombian airline Avianca to replace Lockheed Constellations mainly on services to New York. It served from 1961 to 1983, after which it was stored at Miami and eventually broken up. *The Aviation Picture Library*

the airport ramp and congestion in the terminal buildings, leading to a frantic round of airport modernising and building by municipal authorities desperate to avoid missing the 'jet age'. New fuel-storage facilities and larger hangars were also needed. The 707 used kerosene fuel, new grades of oil and synthetic hydraulic fluid (which if mixed in the system with older mineral fluids congealed to an unpleasant jelly-like substance).

Once the infrastructure was in place, the arrival of jet services pleased the city fathers and chambers of commerce of municipalities across the USA and the world, but they were a mixed blessing to those living near airports who were subjected to the ear-splitting roar and clouds of smoke produced by the early turbojet airliners. Despite various technical measures such as the multi-nozzle exhaust, the 707 became a by-word for noisy operation. A JT3C-engined 707 landing at a distance of 1 mile (1.6 km) gave a noise reading of 106 dB(A) or eight

times as loud as a busy city street or a nearby television. The first limits on noise output set down by the International Civil Aviation Organisation (ICAO) in the early 1970s specified the 707 and DC-8 as 'Stage I' (or 'Chapter I') aircraft, meaning they were the baseline against which noise improvement and regulation would be measured. No new aircraft would be approved for service after 1973 if it did not meet Chapter II/Stage II standards. The harsher Chapter III was introduced in 1976 and specified a reduction of around 20 decibels as measured at take-off compared to Chapter I aircraft. Today all Chapter I and II aircraft are banned from the US, and since the beginning of 2002, Chapter II aircraft can be banned from operating in EU states at each state's discretion. The introduction of JT3D turbofans and the re-engining of many earlier aircraft greatly reduced the noise and smoke nuisance as did the development of 'hushkits'. After 1985, foreign-registered 707s were increasingly restricted in their operations to the USA, needing special permissions and being limited to coastal airports.

Even in 1959, airlines and regulators understood that there was a danger from portable electronic devices carried aboard by passengers and issued warning leaflets to passengers. The US

ABOVE: Inclusive tour operator Monarch Airlines of Luton, England, operated 720s and 707s from 1971 to 1983. G-BCBB, seen at Luton in 1981, was an ex-American 023B and the second jet purchased by the airline, who had previously operated Bristol Britannia turboprops. Today they operate a fleet of nearly thirty jets, a mix of Airbus types from the A320 to the A330, Boeing 757s and a DC-10. *Austin J. Brown/The Aviation Picture Library*

BELOW: Now known better for its Airbuses, Antonovs and remaining Shorts Belfast, HeavyLift Cargo Airlines operated five different 707s between 1990 and 1996. G-HEVY was an ex-Continental -324C and the only one actually owned by the airline as opposed to being leased in. It is seen lifting off from Shannon, Ireland in April 1991. *HeavyLift via the Aviation Picture Library*

ABOVE: Braniff's 'Jellybean Jets' certainly livened up the skies of the late 1960s and early 1970s. N7095 was a -327C operated from May 1966 to April 1971 and unlike many other Braniff aircraft, stayed in the same colour scheme (ochre) throughout. It is still in service with its subsequent owner, TMA of Lebanon as OD-AGX. *Boeing via the Aviation Picture Library*

RIGHT: Flying Tiger Line only bought four 707s and leased a couple more, but the first one, N322F seen here, achieved a measure of fame in November 1965 by flying around the world, pole to pole. This was the first civil aircraft to do this and it required additional fuel tanks in the cabin. The flight (with four intermediate stops) took sixty-two hours in total. The aircraft was given the name *Tigers Pole Cat* to mark the event. *Boeing via the Aviation Picture Library*

Radio Technical Commission for Aeronautics recommended that passengers not use electronic equipment such as televisions, radios, recorders or dictating machines until they could determine which devices would not interfere with the navigation instruments. Just as aircraft instruments and control systems have become so much more sophisticated, so have the gadgets passengers are inclined to travel with, from telephones to computers.

The new jets required more cabin service staff. Applicants for positions as stewardesses with American were trained at the 'unique' American Airlines Stewardess College near Fort Worth which featured a 'swimming pool, lighted tennis courts … even a built in beauty parlour!' according to 1959 recruiting material. Built in 1957, the American school was the first such institute in the world. Applicants had to be between nineteen and a half and twenty-six years old, single, attractive, 5 ft 3 in to 5 ft 8 in (1.6–1.7 m) tall and between 105 and 135 lb (47.6–61.2 kg) in weight, in proportion to height. A high-school diploma and 20/50 vision or better (contact lenses

OPPOSITE ABOVE : South African Airways' ZS-CKC was the first of three 707-344s ordered in February 1958, followed later by seven further new 707s. In 1961 it inaugurated non-stop Johannesburg–London services and in 1968 it was re-registered ZS-SAA. In 1984 it was bought by Columbia Pictures and burnt out in the making of a film. *Boeing via the Aviation Picture Library*

ABOVE: It is not very often that you see two jet airliners in formation, but in February 1961 both 707-430 D-ABOG *Bonn* and 720-030B D-ABOH *Köln* were undertaking test flights prior to delivery to Lufthansa and the opportunity for a family photo was taken. Apart from the obvious length and engine differences, note the smaller ventral fin on the 720. *John Stroud Collection/The Aviation Picture Library*

OPPOSITE BELOW: Air Manila International evolved from a domestic competitor to Philippine Airlines into a charter airline by 1973, when this photo was taken at London Heathrow. At the time this 707-331 (RP-C7073) was on a brief lease to Egyptair. *Austin J. Brown/The Aviation Picture Library*

considered) and a friendly, helpful personality were other requirements. Aside from such dated notions of the role of the cabin crew, Frank Del Giudice, who designed the look of the 707 cabin interior actively sought the opinions and ideas of stewardesses. After all, the 707 cabin is where they would spend their working day, looking after more passengers than on any previous aircraft, and if they couldn't do their job easily, the customers would not be satisfied and the costly jets would be a flop.

Personal oxygen masks were new to the 707 compared with earlier airliners, which had relied on portable bottles, obviously an impracticality in a cabin with over a hundred passengers. At the time of the 707's debut, the major aircraft manufacturers supplied different systems with different methods of operation. On some early 707s, the masks were not always automatically deployed from the overhead unit, but were passed out by cabin staff and then plugged in by the passengers, who were using walk-around air bottles. Soon the manufacturers standardised on the 'pull down to operate' masks with the elastic headband in use today. Not only was it simple to use, but passengers did not have to learn a new procedure for each type of airliner they flew on.

Air outlets, lights and stewardess call buttons were provided above each seat unit, but the seats were not yet wired up with controls for these and headphone outlets as they are now. In fact entertainment was anything but personal as it was piped in through speakers above alternating rows. American Airlines publicity spoke of 'scientifically programmed' background music 'that does not require active listening'. Among the music the AA passenger could expect were such tunes as 'You Do Something to Me', 'You and the Night and the Music', 'Goodnight My Someone' and 'What Is This Thing Called

ABOVE: One of these Qantas first class passengers seems more impressed by the cheese selection than the other, but there were seven other courses on offer, according to the airline's publicity, even if one of them was only a mint. *Qantas/The Aviation Picture Library*

BELOW: Dinner is served on white linen in the first class cabin of a Qantas 707. The excesses of the Stratocruiser and the great flying boats, with their lounges and bars, did not translate to the single-deck 707 with its comparatively short sector lengths. *Qantas/John Stroud Collection/The Aviation Picture Library*

BELOW: Breakfast over India. The crew of this BOAC 707-430 were the subject of a 1963 BBC documentary, *The Pilots* about the men who flew Britain's airliners. At left, Captain E.E Rodley, centre, Flight Engineer H.T.L Leedham and right, First Officer Brian Walpole. *John Stroud Collection/The Aviation Picture Library*

ABOVE: El Al's 707-358C 4X-ATX had an eventful career with the airline, suffering fires and a serious birdstrike while operating on freight services to New York. In 1994 it was largely rebuilt using components of 4X-ATU before being sold to a Zairean company, later serving with Congo Air Lines. By 2001 it was grounded at Kinshasa being stripped for components. *Mike Hooks*

RIGHT: PIA leased a new 707-321 (N723PA) from Pan Am in October 1959 for route proving. Initially American flight crew were used with PIA cabin staff, but local crews were soon trained and introduced. The airline later purchased and leased many 707-300s and 720s. The last 707 freighters left service in 2001. *John Stroud Collection/the Aviation Picture Library*

Love?' One early BOAC passenger grumbled that the 'Lord High Executioner's Song' from *The Mikado* was hardly appropriate as before-take-off entertainment.

Food service was revised for jet operations. The greater speed and higher capacity of the 707 meant not only less time to serve meals on any given route, but the rapid passage of time zones made the timing of meals to coincide with passengers' needs or expectations harder to meet. Airlines stressed that quality of food would not suffer but the number of courses would have to be reduced consistent with the passengers' ability to eat them. Already aware of the need to save weight and thus fuel, airlines quickly moved to plastic trays, dishes and condiment containers.

For the children such distractions as BOAC's Junior Jet Club were developed. Members were given a logbook endorsed by the captains on the flights they made and awarded certificates for every 25,000 miles (40,000 km) travelled. This can perhaps be seen as the precursor of the 'frequent flyer' and Air

OPPOSITE ABOVE: Most of the major US carriers were part of the Civil Reserve Air Fleet (CRAF) scheme which meant that they were bound to supply aircraft and crews for military airlift in time of conflict. Pan Am's scheduling was particularly disrupted by the demands of the Vietnam War and the diversion of aircraft such as N799PA, *Jet Clipper Racer*, which was actually written off on 26 December 1968 at Elmendorf, Alaska while carrying freight bound for Vietnam. *Author's collection*

ABOVE: The 707 will always be associated with New York. When this photo was taken on a June evening in 1959, New York International Airport was known as Idlewild. In December 1963 it was renamed John F. Kennedy International Airport. The international terminal was built in 1958 in time for the arrival of the big jets. *John Stroud Collection/The Aviation Picture Library*

OPPOSITE BELOW: Continental Airlines acquired 720Bs in 1962, using them alongside 707-120s for trunk domestic routes. In all, eight 720s were bought, the last serving until 1976. N57203 was sold to Ethiopian as AT-AFA in 1973 and to Boeing for spares recovery in 1985. *Author's collection*

Miles schemes popular today. American Airlines gave out order coupons for Revell model kits with their *Welcome Aboard* booklets. A 707 'Astrojet' kit – in AA livery, of course – was $1 in 1959 ($5 fully assembled).

For the less confident flyer, this was the era of coin-operated insurance machines at airports that would issue a policy of (for example) $62,500 for $2.50. Such schemes were revised after the 1962 Continental Airlines bomb disaster and other incidents where murder or suicide was committed for insurance money.

Not all passengers chose to make their journey. Many US airlines' 707s were part of the Civil Reserve Air Fleet which meant they were available in times of crisis for the airlift of military personnel and cargo. Supplemental carriers were smaller airlines granted licences only for charter services and to supplement Military Airlift Command (MAC) in time of war. During the Vietnam War, both types of carrier were heavily employed shifting men and materiel to Southeast Asia. With the 707's adjustable seating allowing for varied seat pitch, 161 soldiers could be carried at 38-inch pitch on a 707-100, meeting MAC's requirements.

Although it took about seven years of deliveries before Boeing made a profit on the 707, the airlines were raking in the money almost as soon as they could get their jets in service.

American Airlines were soon achieving 90 per cent load factors (seats filled) on domestic routes and Pan Am were claiming

OPPOSITE ABOVE: Cunard Eagle Airways was a short-lived concern which took delivery of two 707-465s in February 1962 to compete with BOAC across the Atlantic. Because of BOAC opposition, the aircraft were put on the Bermudan register to allow charters from London to Bermuda via New York, but Cunard withdrew from partnership with Eagle Airlines in June 1962 and formed BOAC-Cunard instead. G-ARWD/VR-BBW served under the BOAC-Cunard, BOAC, BEA Airtours and British Airtours names until 1981. *Boeing via the Aviation Picture Library*

OPPOSITE BELOW: The US Federal Aviation Administration (FAA) bought a 720-061 in 1961 for training of operations inspectors and other tasks. Standards for jet crews could not be regulated without inspectors who were also qualified in large jet transports. With under 11,000 hours on the clock by 1984, the 720 was deliberately crashed at Edwards AFB to investigate safer fuels and other safety improvements. *Boeing via the Aviation Picture Library*

ABOVE: Iraqi Airways had some of the most attractive 707s in service. On the port side of the fuselage 'Iraqi Airways' was written in Arabic and 'Iraqi' written in Roman script on the tail. When a UN embargo on Iraqi Airways flights was imposed in 1991, several 707s were stored in Jordan. YI-AGE is believed still to be there, while sister 707-320C YI-AGF somehow joined the Iranian Air Force. *The Aviation Picture Library*

100 per cent on the North Atlantic run. In the first six weeks Pan Am's two aircraft, which replaced six piston aircraft on the route, carried 12,168 passengers. Before long, it was estimated that the airline was amortising (paying off) one 707 per month. By October 1959, the 707s of all airlines had carried their first million passengers.

Until the 1980s, international air fares were regulated by the International Air Transport Association (IATA). More correctly it could be said that IATA kept fares artificially high by restricting the availability of discounted seats to small numbers per flight. Just after the war, a transatlantic fare was $700 coach class, but even at that price, passenger growth was 15 per cent per year. By 1951 the market was almost saturated and growth fell to 6 per cent per annum. Juan Trippe and Pan Am introduced the first tourist-class fares in 1951, reducing a New York–Paris flight to $487 and growth rocketed beyond 17 per cent by 1953. By April 1958, the fare had dropped only modestly to $450, but this was the point that air passenger numbers exceeded those of sea travellers for the first time across the Atlantic. The arrival of jets with their much better costs per seat-mile continued the trend of (slowly) declining fares and (rapidly) rising demand, paving the way for the 'jumbos' of the 1970s and beyond.

OPPOSITE ABOVE: The nose from the forward bulkhead to behind the forward passenger door was one of four sections that made up the fuselage of the 707/720. In the centre is a nose for Qantas. The placard indicates the block number, which in this case indicates -138 VH-EBB. At one time used by Michael Jackson, it was burnt out by saboteurs in Nigeria in 1998. *Boeing via the Aviation Picture Library*

ABOVE: Early 707s come together at Renton. By 1966 the average time it took to build a 707 was seventeen months. Partly owing to efficiencies brought about during the initial 747 sales crisis, building time dropped to eleven months by 1972. *Boeing via the Aviation Picture Library*

OPPOSITE BELOW: The nose and forward fuselage of the second 707 destined for Pan Am makes progress at Renton. PA002 became N707PA and was rolled out in February 1958 and delivered in December. Its first services were actually for National Airlines, which leased it for New York–Miami services in early 1959. *Aeroplane*

Aircraft in the following tables are listed by Boeing Construction Number (e.g. 17956). Gaps in the sequence are for other jetliners built at Renton, mainly 727s. Line numbers are the construction order of the 707s/720s. Model numbers starting with zero (as in 047B) indicate 720s. A B-suffix indicates turbofan (JT3D) power; C indicates convertible or cargo.

Abbreviations used in the production tables:

AF	Air force	DMAFB	Davis-Monthan Air Force Base, Arizona
AL	Air line(s)	Isr	Israeli
C	Current (in service)	Mil.	Military
Cvt	Converted	Regn	Registration
Del	Delivery	Scr.	Scrapped
		W/O	Written off

ABOVE: The 'joining line' at Boeing's Renton plant, where wings and centre fuselages came together. This early photo shows the first production 707s with the second aircraft for Pan Am at the top. In the bay to the left is the final assembly area for KC-135s. *Boeing via the Aviation Picture Library*

BELOW: A wet December night sees most models of the 707 family lined up at the factory. 707-220s for Braniff, a -300 for France, and -400s for Air-India and BOAC can be seen, headed by a United Airlines 720. *Boeing via the Aviation Picture Library*

Con. No.	L/n	Built as	Cvt to	1st Regn	For	Del date	Other Registrations	Last user	Fate	Location
17158	0	367-80	367-80B	N70700	Boeing, testbed	n/a	–	Boeing	Stored	For NASM, Seattle
17586	1	121	121B	N708PA	Pan Am	30.11.58	–	Pan Am	W/O	17.9.65 Montserrat, Antigua
17587	2	121	121B	N707PA	Pan Am	19.12.58	TC-JBA, HP-551, HP-780, N707PA	Int.Air Leases	Scr.	Miami 5.88
17588	3	121	–	N709PA	Pan Am	15.08.58	–	Pan Am	W/O	8.12.63 Elkton MD
17589	4	121	121B	N710PA	Pan Am	29.09.58	TC-JBB, HP-760, HP-792, HP-793	E-Systems Inc	Scr.	8.84 Taipei
17590	5	121	121B	N711PA	Pan Am	17.10.58	TC-JBC, N711, HP-807, N4593U	E-Systems Inc	Scr.	8.84 Taipei
17591	6	121	121B	N712PA	Pan Am	30.10.58	TC-JBD, HP-756, HP-793, HP-794	Air Asia	Scr.	4.84 Taipei
17592	13	321	–	N714PA	Pan Am	28.08.59	9M-AQD, N714PA, N714FC, N714PT, N714FC	Aeroamerica	Scr.	8.81 Seattle
17593	20	321	–	N715PA	Pan Am	19.07.59	TC-JAH, G41-174 , 9G-ACB, C9-ARF,	Tempair	Scr.	8.80 Brussels
17594	58	321	–	N716PA	Pan Am	22.08.59	TC-JAN, N716PA, N716HH	British Midland	Scr.	9.77 Stansted
17595	61	321	–	N717PA	Pan Am	01.09.59	–	IAI	Scr.	Marana, AZ
17596	62	321	–	N718PA	Pan Am	22.09.59	4X-BYZ, 4X-JYZ, 240	Isr AF	Der.	Tel Aviv
17597	68	321	–	N719PA	Pan Am	03.10.59	G-AYBJ, N431MA	Jet Power	Scr.	Sharjah after 1980
17598	70	321	–	N720PA	Pan Am	06.10.59	G-AYVG, N3791G	Jet Power Inc	Scr.	Miami after 1983
17599	71	321	–	N721PA	Pan Am	19.10.59	G-AYSL, N80703,	KIVU Cargo	Scr.	2.83 Lasham
17600	75	321	321F	N722PA	Pan Am	29.10.59	G-AZTG, N723PA,	Dan Air	Scr.	11.81 Lasham
17601	76	321		–	Pan Am	27.10.59	YU-AGA, N723PA, N711UT, 9Q-CRY, TC-JCF	Rashid Khan Air leased	Stored	1.80 Impounded, Ankara
17602	83	321	321F	N724PA	Pan Am	08.12.59	G-BAEL, N2276X, HK-2477, 9Q-CZK, 9Q-CGO, 9Q-CJW	Zairan AL	Stored	Kisangani, Zaire, bad condition
17603	84	321	–	N725PA	Pan Am	12.12.59	TC-JAJ, G41274, G-BCRS, 9G-ACD, N725CA,	General Air Serv	Scr.	1.84 Miami
17604	91	321	–	N726PA	Pan Am	13.01.60	RP-C7074	Air Manilla	Scr.	12.85 Manila
17605	98	321	321F	N727PA	Pan Am	28.01.60	G-AZWA, N70798, HK-2410	Aerotal	W/O	20.12.80 Bogota
17606	107	321	–	N728PA	Pan Am	06.03.60	N11RV, N99WT , N728PA, RP-C911	Marcos family, reg M. Cua	Stored	'Club 707' bar, Manila Airport
17607	121	321	–	N729PA	Pan Am	26.04.60	TC-JAM, N729JP, N731JP, N731, N731BA, N731JP, N427MA	Jet Power	Scr.	7.83 Miami
17608	122	321	321F	N730PA	Pan Am	28.04.60	G-AYXR, N37681, N707GE,	General Electric	Stored	Mojave, CA, CFM56-5B test bed
17609	25	124	–	N70773	Continental AL	19.04.59	–	Continental AL	W/O	01.7.65 Kansas City
17610	37	124	–	N70774	Continental AL	27.05.59	4X-BYA, 4X-JYA, 4X-JYB, N196CA, Is AF 009, HI-384HA	Hispaniola AL	Scr.	1982 Miami
17611	49	124	–	N70775	Continental AL	16.07.59	–	Continental AL	W/O	22.05.62 Unionville IA
17612	56	124	–	N70776	Continental AL	10.08.59	4X-JYE	Isr AF 001	Stored	Tel Aviv Ben Gurion by 94
17613	65	328	–	F-BHSA	Air France	21.10.59	–	Air France	W/O	27.7.61 Hamburg
17614	81	328	–	F-BHSB	Air France	12.12.59	N74615	Air France	Scr.	1.76 Paris Orly
17615	82	328	ELINT	F-BHSC	Air France	12.12.59	4X-BYV, 4X-JYV,	Isr AF 115	Stored	Tel Aviv by 1998
17616	93	328	–	F-BHSD	Air France	29.01.60	–	Air France	Scr.	3.76 Paris Orly
17617	110	328	–	F-BHSE	Air France	01.02.60	4X-BYW, 4X-JYW	Isr AF 116	Stored	Hatzerim for display
17618	111	328	–	F-BHSF	Air France	24.03.60	–	Air France	Scr.	Merville 1997 after instructional use
17619	126	328	–	F-BHSG	Boeing	13.5.60	N5093K, CN-RMD, 4X-JYN	Isr AF 119	DER	11.95 fire dump Tel Aviv
17620	138	328	–	F-BHSH	Air France	23.06.60	–	Air France	W/O	7.9.76 Corsica (blown up)
17621	139	328	–	F-BHSI	Air France	11.07.60	–	Air France	Scr.	9.77 Paris Orly
17622	151	328	–	F-BHSJ	Air France	01.08.60	–	Air France	Scr.	9.77 Paris Orly
17623	78	329	–	OO-SJA	Sabena	04.12.59	–	Sobelair	Scr.	1982 Nose pres. Brussels Mil. Museum
17624	92	329	–	OO-SJB	Sabena	15.01.60	–	Sabena	W/O	15.2.61 Brussels
17625	99	329	KC-707	OO-SJC	Sabena	13.02.60	4X-BYT, 4X-JYT Isr AF 137, 140	Isr AF 140	Der.	Tel Aviv
17626	118	329	–	OO-SJD	Sabena	10.04.60	–	Sobelair	Scr.	Brussels after 1981
17627	133	329	–	OO-SJE	Sabena	08.06.60	–	Sabena	W/O	15.2.78 Tenerife
17628	7	123	123B	N7501A	American AL	23.20.58	5B-DAM	Cyprus AW	W/O	19.8.79 Manama, Bahrain
17629	8	123	–	N7502A	American AL	23.01.59	–	American AL	W/O	28.1.61 off Long Island NY
17630	9	123	123B	N7503A	American AL	31.12.58	–	American AL	Scr.	10.77
17631	10	123	123B	N7504A	American AL	28.01.59	5B-DAL, EL-AJW, N2235W,	Omega Air	Stored	5.90 DMAFB, AZ
17632	11	123	123B	N7505A	American AL	31.01.59	G-BFMI, 5B-DAK,	Cyprus AW	Stored	Larnaca, Cyprus after 1983
17633	12	123	123B	N7506A	American AL	12.02.59	–	American AL	W/O	1.3.62 Jamaica Bay NY
17634	14	123	123B	N7507A	American AL	27.02.59	N707AR, N960CC	Skyways	Scr.	Amarillo, TX after 1995
17635	15	123	123B	N7508A	American AL	27.03.59	5B-DAP, EL-AJV, G-LIFT	Heavylift Cargo	Stored	DMAFB after 1990
17636	16	123	123B	N7509A	American AL	03.04.59	–	Tigerair	Stored	DMAFB after 1995
17637	17	123	123BF	N7510A	American AL	23.04.59	D-ALAM, N8418 , N7510A, HK-1818	Aerocondor	Scr.	Bogota 1988
17638	26	123	123B	N7511A	American AL	12.05.59	D-ALAL, N8420 , N7511A, HK-1802	Aerocondor	Scr.	Barranquilla after 1985
17639	30	123	123B	N7512A	American AL	21.05.59	N701PC,	Skyworld nn	Stored	Scrapped DMAFB after 1987
17640	31	123	123B	N7513A	American AL	28.05.59	G-TJAB, G-BHOX, N62TA	Tigerair	Stored	DMAFB for parts
17641	36	123	–	N7514A	American AL	05.06.59	–	American AL	W/O	15.8.59 nr Calverton, NY
17642	41	123	123B	N7515A	American AL	24.06.59	–	Boeing MAC	Scr.	11.85 Kingman
17643	42	123	123B	N7516A	American AL	29.06.59	HK-1942	Aerocondor	Scr.	Barranquila, Colombia, after 1990
17644	50	123	123B	N7517A	American AL	27.07.59	HZ-DAT, N2143H	Ess Jay Air Inc	Stored	San Antonio from 10.91
17645	51	123	123B	N7518A	American AL	31.07.59	N702PC	Skyworld	Scr.	1987 DMAFB
17646	52	123	123B	N7519A	American AL	24.08.59	PH-TVA, N29959, N519GA	Guy America	Scr.	1987 DMAFB
17647	53	123	123B	N7517A	American AL	27.07.59	C-GQBG, 5A-DHO, 5A-DHM, N3951A	Exelair	Scr.	8.84 Brussels, nose to Sinsheim Museum

ABOVE: 707s for Air France, Qantas and Pan Am are seen lined up on a Seattle night circa August 1959. Final completion work between roll-out and first flight could take up to two months. *Boeing via the Aviation Picture Library*

Con. No.	L/n	Built as	Cvt to	1st Regn	For	Del date	Other Registrations	Last user	Fate	Location
17648	63	123	123B	N7521A	American AL	14.09.59	N752TA	MRH Leasing	Scr.	4.82 Marana
17649	66	123	123B	N7522A	American AL	03.10.59	N751TA	Monarch AL	Scr.	1.82 Luton
17650	67	123	123B	N7523A	American AL	14.10.59	C-GQBH, N311AS	Aviation Sales	Pres.	St Lucia, sunk as diving attraction
17651	72	123	123B	N7524A	American AL	28.10.59	ST-AHG, 9G-ACO, G-TJAC, G-BHOY, N61TA	Computer Cosmopolitan leased	Stored	For KC-135 p arts DMAFB
17652	77	123	123B	N7525A	American AL	21.11.59	N5038, N731TW, F-BUZJ, 9Q-CBD, 9Q-CKP,	Dresser Industry	Stored	For KC-135 parts DMAFB
17653-57	–	–		Cancelled	American AL	29.04.60	–		–	–
17658	18	131	131F	N731TW	TWA	29.01.59	–	Omega Air	Scr.	1986 Shannon
17659	19	131	–	N732TW	TWA	17.03.59	–	TEA	Scr.	3.82 Brussels
17660	21	131	–	N733TW	TWA	30.03.59	–	Ramacor	Scr.	6.77 Tel Aviv
17661	22	131	–	N734TW	TWA	03.04.59	PI-C7071, N16648, 4X-AGT, 4X-JYI, N198CA, N6232G	Isr AF 007	Dest.	1994 Mojave for film 'Speed'
17662	23	131	–	N735TW	TWA	18.04.59	N735T	AeroAmerica	Scr.	Boeing Field
17663	24	131	–	N736TW	TWA	29.04.59	HS-VGC, N194CA	Rodman Aviation leased	Scr.	Mojave after 1993
17664	27	131	–	N737TW	TWA	10.05.59	I-SAVA	IAI Israel	Scr.	Tel Aviv after 1977
17665	28	131	–	N738TW	TWA	13.05.59	4X-ACN, OO-TED	TEA	Scr.	9.87 Brussels
17666	32	131	–	N739TW	TWA	28.05.59	HS-VGA, 4X-ACU, 4X-JYC, IsrAF 005, OO-TEE,	IAI Israel	Scr.	Laurinberg-Maxton AP, NC for KC-135 parts
17667	34	131	–	N740TW	TWA	03.05.59	4X-JYD, Isr AF 008, 4X-BYD	Stored	Pres.	Hatzerim
17668	38	131	–	N741TW	TWA	16.05.59	PIC7072, N16649, 4X-AGU, 4X-JYH, Isr AF 004, 4X-BYH, N195CA	FAA	Scr.	3.82 Atlantic City

Con. No.	L/n	Built as	Cvt to	1st Regn	For	Del date	Other Registrations	Last user	Fate	Location
17669	43	131	–	N742TW	TWA	03.06.59	–	TWA	W/O	6.11.67 Cincinnati
17670	46	131	–	N743TW	TWA	25.06.59	–	TWA	W/O	22.4.70 Indianapolis
17671	48	131	131F	N744TW	TWA	30.06.59	HB-IEG, N730JP, HK-1773, N730JP	LAB leased	W/O	13.10.76 Santa Cruz, Bolivia
17672	55	131	–	N745TW	TWA	01.08.59	N197CA	Charlotte Corp	Scr.	Tel Aviv
17673	69	331	–	N761TW	TWA	26.09.59	–	TWA	W/O	8.3.72 Las Vegas By bomb. Remains to Boeing
17674	73	331	–	N701PA	Pan Am	09.10.59	–	ATASCO Inc	Scr.	East Midlands
17675	74	331	–	N762TW	TWA	15.10.59	–	Caledonian AL	Stored	Dar-Es-Salaam
17676	79	331	–	N763TW	TWA	05.11.59	N763AB	Aviation Traders	Scr.	Stansted
17677	80	331	–	N702PA	Pan Am	10.11.59	N702TA, N702PT	Monarch Aviation	Scr.	3.80 Stansted
17678	86	331	–	N764TW	TWA	03.12.59	–	TWA	Scr.	1980 Kansas City
17679	88	331	–	N765TW	TWA	11.12.59	–	TWA	Scr.	1980 Damaged 1960. Scrapped Kansas City
17680	89	331	–	N703PA	Pan Am	11.12.59	PI-C7073, S2-ABM,	Air Manila	Scr.	1984 Manilla
17681	103	331	–	N766TW	TWA	11.02.60	–	TWA	Scr.	8.80 Kansas City
17682	104	331	–	N767TW	TWA	11.02.60	N767AB,	Aviation Traders	Scr.	5.81 Stansted
17683	116	331	–	N704PA	Pan Am	15.03.59	XV-NJD, N9230Z	Aerotron AC	Scr.	6.77 Long Beach
17684	117	331	–	N768TW	TWA	24.03.60	–	Allen AC Corp	Scr.	5.82 Kansas City
17685	123	331	–	N769TW	TWA	21.04.60	–	TWA	W/O	23.11.64 Rome
17686	124	331	–	N705PA	Pan Am	22.04.60	OO-SJP, 9Q-CMA,	C.F.Willis Comp leased	Scr.	Seized, preserved Malaysia. Later scrapped
17687	125	331	–	N770TW	TWA	26.04.60	–	TWA	Scr.	6.80 Kansas City
17688	135	331	–	N771TW	TWA	06.06.60	–	TWA	Scr.	6.80 Kansas City
17689	136	331	331F	N706PA	Pan Am	01.06.60	N706TA, N425MA	Jet Power	Scr.	10.83 Miami
17690	137	331	–	N772TW	TWA	13.06.60	–	Allen AC Corp	Scr.	5.82 Kansas City
17691	45	227	–	N7071	Boeing for Braniff	11.06.59	–	Boeing	W/O	19.10.59 Arlington WA
17692	87	227	227F	N7072	Braniff Airways	13.11.59	9Y-TDO, N64757, N811UT, N3842X,	Int Air Leas	Scr.	5.84 Miami
17693	96	227	–	N7073	Braniff Airways	08.01.60	9Y-TDR	IAI Israel	Scr.	1977 TelAviv
17694	97	227	–	N7074	Braniff Airways	15.01.60	9Y-TDP, N64740	–	Scr.	2.81 Moses Lake, WA
17695	102	227	–	N7075	Braniff Airways	01.02.60	9Y-TDQ	–	Scr.	1977
17696	29	138	138B	N31239	Boeing	20.03.59	VH-EBA, CF-PWV, C-FPWV, N138TA, N220AM, N138MJ, HZ-123	Saudi Government	Stored	Southend since 1999
17697	39	138	138B	VH-EBB	Qantas	20.05.59	N790SA, D-ADAP, TC-JBN, N790FA, N138SR	Jaffe Group	W/O	28.8.98 Port Harcourt, burnt on ground
17698	44	138	138B	VH-EBC	Qantas	08.06.59	N791SA	CP Air subleased	W/O	7.2.68 Vancouver, Canada
17699	54	138	138B	VH-EBD	Qantas	15.07.59	G-AVZZ, N500JJ	Sunnyside Hold.	Scr.	7.83 Paris
17700	59	138	138B	VH-EBE	Qantas	13.08.59	N793SA, N793SA, VP-BDE, N793NA	Av Technical Supp	Stored	For KC-135 parts DMAF
17701	60	138	138B	VH-EBF	Qantas	21.08.59	N792SA, D-ADAQ, N792SA, TC-JBP, N792SA	FBA Corp	Scr.	94 Marana
17702	64	138	138B	VH-EBG	Qantas	18.09.59	G-AWDG, N600JJ, N707KS, N707SK, 9Q-CLK	Republique du Congo	C	–
17703	35	436	–	N31241	Boeing for BOAC	09.05.60	G-APFB	BOAC	Scr.	79 Kingman
17704	101	436	–	N5088K	Boeing for BOAC	16.05.60	G-APFC	BOAC	Scr.	1980 Used for destructive tests
17705	112	436	–	N5091K	Boeing for BOAC	29.04.60	G-APFD, N888NW	BOAC	Scr.	8.86 Ft Lauderdale
17706	113	436	–	N5092K	Boeing for BOAC	13.05.60	G-APFE	BOAC	W/O	5.3.66 Mt Fuji
17707	127	436	–	G-APFF	BOAC	13.05.60	–	Boeing	Scr.	5.81 or later, Kingman
17708	128	436	–	N5094K	Boeing for BOAC	22.06.60	G-APFG	BOAC	Stored	Fuselage used for fire tests, Cardington
17709	144	436	–	G-APFH	BOAC	15.07.60	–	Boeing	Scr.	77 Marana after str. since 4.76
17710	145	436	–	G-APFI	BOAC	23.07.60	–	Boeing	Scr.	77 Marana after str. since 4.76
17711	163	436	–	G-APFJ	BOAC	22.09.60	–	British Airtours leased	Pres.	Since 6.81 Cosford Museum
17712	164	436	–	G-APFK	BOAC	29.09.60	–	British Airtours leased	W/O	17.3.77 Prestwick UK
17713	169	436	–	G-APFL	BOAC	14.10.60	9Q-CRW, 5X-CAU, G-APFL, N9194M, 5X-CAU	Uganda Government	Stored	Entebbe since 83. To become restaurant?
17714	170	436	–	G-APFM	BOAC	05.11.60	–	Boeing	Scr.	9.79 Kingman, str since 8.76
17715	171	436	–	G-APFN	BOAC	16.11.60	–	Boeing	Scr.	7.79 Kingman, str since 6.76
17716	175	436	–	G-APFO	BOAC	09.12.60	–	Boeing	Scr.	Kingman late 86. Str 3.81
17717	176	436	–	G-APFP	BOAC	22.12.60	–	Boeing	Scr.	Was preserved Philadelphia, scrapped 10.88
17718	90	430	–	N31240	Boeing for Lufthansa	24.02.60	D-ABOB, 9Q-CRT	Pearl Air	W/O	9.8.77 Sana'a, Yemen. Used for spares
17719	106	430	430F	D-ABOC	Lufthansa	10.03.60	N64739, EI-BFN, N90498, 5A-CVA	United African	Scr.	6.79 Trip, spares
17720	115	430	–	D-ABOD	Lufthansa	24.04.60	–	Lufthansa	Pres.	Hamburg Airport
17721	162	430	–	D-ABOF	Lufthansa	01.10.60	9G-ACK, N90498, 3C-ABI, EL-AJC	Liberian Overseas	Scr.	8.83 Bournem, str 7.83
17722	94	437	–	N5089K	Boeing for Air-India	18.02.60	VT-DJI	Air-India	W/O	23.1.71 Bombay
17723	100	437	–	VT-DJJ	Air-India	19.01.60	–	Air-India	W/O	22.6.82 Bombay
17724	105	437	–	VT-DJK	Air-India	07.03.60	–	Air-India	Scr.	12.84 Bombay
17903	108	139	139B	N74613	Boeing/Western	13.05.60	N778PA, TC-JBE, S2-AAL, 9G-AJC, G-TJAA, N778PA	Aerocar Aviation	Scr.	For KC-135 parts DMAFB
17904	119	139	–	N74614	Boeing/Western	04.05.60	N779PA	Pan Am	W/O	7.4.64 New York

Con. No.	L/n	Built as	Cvt to	1st Regn	For	Del date	Other Registrations	Last user	Fate	Location
17905	114	441	–	N5090K	Varig	07.06.60	PP-VJA, N59RD	BCF Aviation	Scr.	Houston after 4.90
17906	129	441	–	PP-VJB	Varig	16.06.60	–	Varig	W/O	27.11.62 Lima, Peru
17907	85	022	–	N7201U	United AL	01.10.60	–	Aviation Sales	Scr.	7.82 Luton
17908	95	022	–	N7202U	United AL	29.07.60	–	Aviation Sales	Scr.	12.76 Minneapolis
17909	109	022	–	N7203U	United AL	30.04.60	–	Aviation Sales	Scr.	12.76 Minneapolis
17911	131	022	–	N7205U	United AL	25.05.60	–	Aviation Sales	Scr.	12.76 Minneapolis
17912	132	022	–	N7206U	United AL	09.06.60	–	Aviation Sales	Scr.	12.76 Minneapolis
17913	141	022	–	N7207U	United AL	29.06.60	–	M M Landy	Scr.	6.83, Miami
17914	142	022	–	N7208U	United AL	26.06.60	–	Aviation Sales		12.76 Denver
17915	146	022	–	N7209U	United AL	27.07.60	N720CC, HI-372	Aeromar	Scr.	6.87 Miami
17916	147	022	–	N7210U	United AL	05.08.60	–	Aviation Sales	Scr.	12.76 Minneapolis
17917	148	022	–	N7211U	United AL	13.08.60	VP-HCP	Belize AW	Scr.	2.83 Miami
17918	152	328	–	N5095K	Boeing	19.08.60	N35634, F-BHSK	Air France	Scr.	9.77 Orly
17919	153	328	–	F-BHSL	Air France	20.08.60	–	Air France	Stored	AF Technical School, Vilgenis
17920	159	328	–	F-BHSM	Air France	21.09.60	–	Air France	W/O	3.6.62 Paris Orly
17921	160	328	RC-707	F-BHSN	Air France	18.09.59	OO-SBR, N90287, 4X-JYP	Isr AF 120	C	120 Sqn
17922	161	328	–	F-BHSO	Air France	16.09.60	TU-TBY, 4X-BYX, 4X-JYX	Isr AF 117	Stored	Ben Gurion
17923	167	328	–	F-BHSP	Air France	07.11.60	TU-TDC, F-BHSQ	Air France	Stored	Maxton NC, for fire training
17924	168	328	–	F-BHSQ	Air France	22.10.60	–	Air France	Scr.	9.77 Orly
17925	33	153	VC-137B	58-6970	USAF	04.05.59	–	USAF	Stored	Boeing Field for Museum of Flight
17926	40	153	VC-137B	58-6971	USAF	31.05.59	–	USAF	Pres.	Pima Air Museum
17927	47	153	VC-137B	58-6972	USAF	30.06.59	–	USAF	Stored	McConnell AFB KS
17928	134	344	–	ZS-CKC	South African	01.07.60	ZS-SAA, CC-CGM, CC-CGM, N90651	Columbia Pictures	Scr.	after burnt in film
17929	154	344	–	ZS-CKD	South African	22.08.60	ZS-SAB, EI-BFU, VN-A304,	HK Vietnam leased	Stored	3.80 Ho Chi Minh City
17930	155	344	–	ZS-CKE	South African	22.08.60	ZS-SAC, LX-LGW, OO-SBW, 9Q-CZF,	Air Region	Scr.	89 Kisangani
18012	57	124	–	N74612	Continental leased	17.03.60	4X-JYA Isr AF 006, 4X-BYA	Israel Airports	Scr.	Possibly extant as ground trainer
18013	120	023	023B	N7527A	American AL	30.07.60	G-BCBB, 60-SAU, C9-ARG, 4R-ACS, 4X-BMB, 4X-JYG/010	IAI Israel '010'	Stored	Hatzerim museum. IAI Lavi radar nose.
18014	143	023	023B	N7528A	American AL	24.07.60	G-BCBA, P2-ANG, G-BCBA, 4X-BMA, N341A	Omega Air	Scr.	For KC-135 parts DMAFB
18015	149	023	023B	N7529A	American AL	13.08.60	60-SAW, 60-SAW	Somali AL	Scr.	Mogadishu (badly corroded)
18016	150	023	023B	N7530A	American AL	22.09.60	A6-HHR, 70-ACP, N720AC	Air Crew Leasing	Scr.	DMAFB
18017	156	023	023B	N7531A	American AL	01.09.60	OD-AFP	MEA	W/O	12.6.82 Beirut by shelling
18018	157	023	023B	N7532A	American AL	08.09.60	OD-AFR	MEA	W/O	31.8.81 Beirut by bomb
18019	158	023	023B	N7533A	American AL	19.09.60	OD-AFS, N7533A, N18KM	Ten miles high	Scr.	7.86 Long Beach
18020	165	023	023B	N7534A	American AL	10.10.60	OD-AFT	MEA	W/O	1.1.76 Saudi Arabia by bomb explosion
18021	173	023	023B	N7535A	American AL	23.11.60	OD-AGB, C-FWXI, N720PW,	Pratt & Whitney Engine Svcs	C	Engine testbed for PW6000 and others
18022	174	023	023B	N7536A	American AL	03.12.60	N1R	Jetstar	Scr.	DMAFB after 95
18023	166	023B	–	N7537A	American AL	27.04.61	HK-1974	Air Trans	Scr.	3.81 Miami
18024	177	023B	–	N7538A	American AL	03.02.61	OD-AFQ, C-FETB	Pratt & Witney	C	2.97 based Montreal
18025	180	023B	–	N7539A	American AL	17.03.61	OD-AFZ	MEA	Stored	to be restaurant, Juniyah, Beirut
18026	181	023B	–	N7540A	American AL	17.02.61	OD-AFW	MEA	W/O	16.6.82 Beirut by shelling
18027	189	023B	–	N7541A	American AL	27.02.61	OD-AFM, C-FWXL	Pratt & Witney	Stored	Beirut
18028	193	023B	–	N7542A	American AL	29.03.61	HK-1974	Aerocondor	Scr.	Barranquila,Colombia by 87
18029	194	023B	–	N7543A	American AL	28.03.61	OD-AFU	MEA	W/O	16.6.82 Beirut by shelling
18030	195	023B	–	N7544A	American AL	10.04.61	OD-AFN, EL-AKD	Omega Air	Scr.	Fire practice Shannon, scrapped 96
18031	198	023B	–	N7545A	American AL	16.04.61	60-SAX	Somali AL	Scr.	Djibouti after 85
18032	199	023B	–	N7546A	American AL	19.04.61	70-ABQ	Alyemda	Scr.	Aden, Yemen, after 97
18033	206	023B	–	N7547A	American AL	23.05.61	N780PA, N780EC, HC-AZO , HC-BDP, N720BG	Int Air Leases	Stored	KC-135 parts, Phoenix
18034	207	023B	–	N7548A	American AL	12.05.64	OD-AFL,	MEA	W/O	21.8.85 Beirut by shelling
18035	214	023B	–	N7549A	American AL	09.06.61	OD-AFO	MEA	W/O	6.83 by shelling
18036	215	023B	–	N7550A	American AL	02.07.61	N781PA, N781PA, HC-AZP,	Commun Transport	Scr.	5.88 Marana, AZ
18037	220	023B	–	N7551A	American AL	21.07.61	N782PA, HC-AZQ, N782PA	Int Air Leases	Scr.	For KC-135 parts DMAFB
18038-40		153		Cancelled		–	–	–	–	–
18041	172	048	–	EI-ALA	Aer Lingus	25.10.60	N7083, LN-TUU, N734T, N1776Q	AeroAmerica	Scr.	7.78 Boeing Field
18042	182	048	–	EI-ALB	Aer Lingus	24.01.61	N7081, N303AS	AeroAmerica	Scr.	9.80 Boeing Field
18043	188	048	–	EI-ALC	Aer Lingus	07.04.61	N7082, 9Y-TCS, N8790R, LN-TUV, OO-TEB, 9Q-CFT	Fontshi Aviation	Stored	Mbuji-Maji
18044	178	022	–	N7212U	United AL	22.12.60	HP-685, N37777, N28JS,	US Global	W/O	22.4.76 near Barranquila, Colombia
18045	179	022	–	N7213U	United AL	19.12.60	VP-HCO	Belize AW	Scr.	1.83 Miami
18046	183	022	–	N7214U	United AL	14.01.61	VP-HCM	Belize AW	Scr.	3.83 Miami
18047	184	022	–	N7215U	United AL	27.01.61	–	Aviat Sales Comp	Scr.	12.76 Denver
18048	185	022	–	N7216U	United AL	02.02.61	–	Dolphin Aviat	Scr.	81, Hong Kong, impounded
18049	186	022	–	N7217U	United AL	13.02.61	N304AS, N421MA, HI-401	Hispaniola	Scr.	Puerto Plata after 85
18050	191	022	–	N7218U	United AL	06.03.61	–	Onyx Aviation	Scr.	12.83 Miami

Con. No.	L/n	Built as	Cvt to	1st Regn	For	Del date	Other Registrations	Last user	Fate	Location
18051-53	123B	–	–	-	American AL,	Cancelled	–	–	–	– –
18054	140	123B	–	N7526A	American AL	25.05.61	G-BGCT, 5B-DAO, YN-CCN	Aeronica leased	Stored	Managua, Nicuragua 98 for spares
18055	200	437	–	VT-DMN	Air-India	17.04.61	–	Air-India	W/O	24.1.66 Mt Blanc
18056	192	430	430F	D-ABOG	Lufthansa	17.03.61	N9985F	Air Sinai leased	Scr.	Ben Gurion, Israel. Nose attached to 18070
18057	190	030B	–	D-ABOH	Lufthansa	08.03.61	N783PA, HK-677	Aviation Sales	Scr.	St Petersburg 81
18058	202	030B	–	D-ABOK	Lufthansa	28.04.61	–	Lufthansa	W/O	4.12.61 near Ebersheim, West Germany
18059	203	030B	–	D-ABOL	Lufthansa	02.05.61	N784PA, HK-676, N3831X	Int Air Leases	Stored	For KC-135 parts DMAFB
18060	210	030B	–	D-ABOM	Lufthansa	03.06.61	N785PA, YA-HBA, N3746E, HK-2558	Aerotal	Scr.	Miami FL
18061	197	047B	–	N93141	Western AL	07.04.61	HK-723	Avianca	W/O	16.8.76 Mexico City
18062	204	047B	–	N93142	Western AL	10.05.61	AP-AXQ	PIA	Scr.	3.77 Las Vegas
18063	213	047B	–	N93143	Western AL	07.06.61	9H-AAK, N110DS	AAR Allen	Stored	For KC-135 parts DMAFB
18064	187	027	–	N7076	Braniff	11.02.61	N736T	Aeroamerica	Scr.	83 Boeing Field
18065	196	027	–	N7077	Braniff	22.03.61	N734T	AeroAmerica leased	Scr.	81 Boeing Field
18066	208		–	N113	FAA	12.05.61	N23, N2679U, N833NA	NASA	W/O	1.12.84 Edwards AFB Deliberate test crash
18067	201	138B	–	N93134	Boeing, for Qantas	29.07.61	VH-EBH, 9Y-TDC, VR-CAN	Euro Air Fin	Stored	Marana since 10.81
18068	227	138B	–	VH-EBI	Qantas	16.08.61	N105BN, OE-IRA, OE-URA, SU-FAB, N245AC	Air Crew Leasing	Scr.	For KC-135 parts DMAFB
18069	228	138B	–	N93135	Boeing	24.08.61	VH-EBJ, N106BN, OE-INA, OE-UNA,	Misrair nn	Stored	12.87 Cairo

BELOW: At Renton 707 production proceeded in parallel with KC-135s (background). The 707 in the centre became N734TW for TWA and later 4X-JYI with the Israeli Air Force. After further owners it met its end at Mojave when a bomb-laden bus was crashed into it – all part of the film *Speed*. *The Aviation Picture Library*

Con. No.	L/n	Built as	Cvt to	1st Regn	For	Del date	Other Registrations	Last user	Fate	Location
18070	205	458	–	4X-ATA	El Al	22.04.61	–	El Al	Stored	Cabin trainer. Original nose to Intrepid Mus. NYC
18071	216	458	–	4X-ATB	El Al	07.06.61	N32824, N130KR	Boeing, donated to LH	Preserved	Berlin-Tegel
18072	252	022	–	N7219U	United AL	01.12.61	HI-415, XA-SDL	SA de Cargo Express	C	–
18073	253	022	22F	N7220U	United AL	14.12.61	OO-VGM, N64696	G.T.Baker school	Stored	Miami static training airframe
18074	259	022	–	N7221U	United AL	21.12.61	VP-HCN	Belize AW	Scr.	83 Miami
18075	260	022	–	N7222U	United AL	10.01.62	TF-VVB	Air Viking	Scr.	6.76 Fire practice Reykjavik
18076	261	022	–	N7223U	United AL	17.01.62	VP-HCQ	Belize AW	Scr.	4.83 Miami
18077	265	022	–	N7224U	United AL	10.04.62	–	360 Corp	Scr.	For KC-135 parts DMAFB
18078	267	022	–	N7225U	United AL	24.04.62	9Q-CTM	Air Charter Serv	Stored	Kinshasa for spares
18079	278	022	–	N7226U	United AL	08.05.62	–	Aviation Sales	Scr.	12.76 Minneapolis St Paul
18080	284	022	–	N7227U	United AL	15.05.62	N62215	Caledonian AL	Stored	Kilimanjaro, Kenya
18081	297	022	–	N7228U	United AL	01.06.62	–	CAAC	Stored	Peking, Static trainer
18082	298	022	22F	N7229U	United AL	12.06.62	TF-VVA, N417MA, N419MA	Indian Govt confisc	Scr.	8.96 Bombay
18083	209	321	–	N757PA	Pan Am	16.05.61	G-AYVE, N757PA, N432MC	Jet Power	Scr.	8.83 Miami
18084	212	321	–	N758PA	Pan Am	23.05.61	G-AYRZ, VP-BDG, C6-BDG, N433MA, N707HD, TY-AAM, TY-BBW		Stored	Wetteren, Belgium, for restaurant?
18085	217	321	–	N759PA	Pan Am	13.06.61	G-AYAG, G14372, VP-BDF, N435MA	Mr McEvaddy	Scr.	7.84 Dublin
18086	245	059B	–	HK-724	Avianca	08.11.61	N4451B	Avianca	Scr.	11.85 Miami
18087	249	059B	–	HK-725	Avianca	16.11.61	–	Avianca	W/O	27.1.80 Quito
18154	226	026	–	N7078	Braniff AW	09.08.61	N730T	Aeroamerica	Scr.	83 Boeing Field
18155	225	025	–	N8701E	Eastern AL	14.08.61	OO-TEA	TEA	Scr.	10.80 Brussels
18156	232	025	–	N8702E	Eastern AL	25.08.61	N10VG	AmTransair	Scr.	78 Indianapolis
18157	233	025	–	N8703E	Eastern AL	02.02.62	OY-DSK, N3124Z	Al Muraibid Lsing	Scr.	85 Luton, impounded
18158	234	025	ASW test	N8704E	Eastern AL	20.09.61	LN-TUW, N8704E, N3183B, N40102	Boeing	Scr.	8.77 Kingman AZ
18159	235	025	–	N8705E	Eastern AL	27.09.61	OY-DSL, N7229L, VT-ERS	Continental Aviation	Stored	Nagpur
18160	236	025	–	N8706E	Eastern AL	17.10.61	HL7402	Korean AL	Stored	Seoul, cabin trainer
18161	239	025	–	N8707E	Eastern AL	17.10.61	OY-DSM	Conair	Scr.	7.84 Copenhagen
18162	240	025	–	N8708E	Eastern AL	08.11.61	D-ACIP, VP-YNL, 9Q-CTD	New ACS nn	Stored	Kinshasa for parts
18163	241	025	–	N8709E	Eastern AL	23.10.61	D-ACIQ, N15VG, N8709E, TF-VVE, TF-VLA	Eagle Air	Scr.	78 Keflavik
18164	242	025	–	N8710E	Eastern AL	23.10.61	HL7403	Boeing	Scr.	80 Kingman, AZ
18165	250	068B	–	N93136	Boeing, to Saudia	20.12.61	HZ-ACA, N2628Y	Sonico Inc	Scr.	10.82 Moses Lake
18166	251	068B	–	HZ-ACB Distribution	Saudia	29.12.61	–	Overseas Int	Scr.	DMAFB
18167	221	047B	–	N93144	Western AL	11.07.61	9H-AAL, N210DS,	AAR Allen AC	Scr.	88 Marana
18240	246	025	–	N8711E	Eastern AL	09.01.62	D-ACIR,	AT Dominicana leased	Stored	Port-au-Prince, derelict
18241	247	025	–	N8712E	Eastern AL	13.11.61	OY-DSP	Conair	Scr.	Danmarks Flygvermuseum, before 97
18242	248	025	–	N8713E	Eastern AL	22.11.61	D-ACIS, VP-YNM	Air Zimbabwe nn	Stored	Harare Cabin Trainer
18243	254	025	–	N8714E	Eastern AL	08.12.61	OY-DSR	Conair	W/O	13.9.74 Copenhagen
18244	255	025	–	N8715E	Eastern AL	16.12.61	D-ACIT, VP-YNN, Z-YNM	Air Charter Zaire	Scr.	88/89 spares at Harare
18245	264	328	–	N93138	Boeing, to Air France	01.02.62	F-BHSR, F-BHSR	Air France	Scr.	4.77 Orly
18246	269	328	–	F-BHSS	Air France	16.02.62	4X-BYK, 4X-JYK	Israeli Air Force 118	Derelict	Dumped beside Route 90, Israel
18247	274	328	–	F-BHST	Air France	09.03.62	–	Air France	W/O	22.6.62 Guadeloupe
18248	258	030B	–	D-ABON	Lufthansa	05.01.62	N786PA, HK-749	SAM leased from Avianca	Pres.	Bogota Museo de Los Ninos
18249	262	030B	–	D-ABOP	Lufthansa	12.01.62	–	Lufthansa	W/O	15.7.64 near Ansbach, West Germany
18250	263	030B	–	N93137	Boeing for LH	23.03.62	D-ABOQ, N787PA, JY-ADS, AP-AZP	PIA	Stored	Funfair Chilton Beach, Karachi
18251	273	030B	–	D-ABOR	Lufthansa	26.02.62	N788PA, JY-ADT, 9L-LAZ, N720BC	Boreas Corp	Scr.	For KC-135 parts DMAFB
18334	229	138B	–	VH-EBK	Qantas	29.08.61	9Y-TDB, N58937, CN-ANS	Moroccan Air Force	Stored	Rabat
18335	268	321B	–	N760PA	Pan Am	15.06.62	RP-C7076, N4605D	E-Systems	Scr.	6.85 Taipei
18336	270	321B	–	N761PA	Pan Am	13.06.62	RP-C7075, N944JW	Int Air Leases	Stored	For KC-135 parts DMAFB
18337	276	321B	–	N762PA	Pan Am	12.04.62	HL7430, N762TB,	Aviation Systems	Scr.	10.84 Marana used for spares
18338	287	321B	–	N763PA	Pan Am	01.06.62	N763W, N111MF, N98WS, HZ-TAS	Prince Turki	Scr.	Manston after 90
18339	292	321B	–	N764PA	Pan Am	01.06.62	N764SE, OE-IEB, N897WA,	Omega Air	Stored	For KC-135 parts DMAFB
18351	211	051B	–	N721US	Northwest	22.06.61	18351	Taiwan Gvmt	Pres.	Kangshan AB Museum
18352	218	051B	–	N722US	Northwest	22.06.61	SX-DBG	Olympic AW	Scr.	81 Athens
18353	219	051B	–	N723US	Northwest	11.07.61	SX-DBH	Olympic AW	Scr.	81 Athens
18354	224	051B	–	N724US	Northwest	26.07.61	–	Northwest	W/O	12.2.63 Near Miami
18355	231	051B	–	N725US	Northwest	31.08.61	SX-DBI	Omega Air	Scr.	7.85 Shannon
18356	238	051B	–	N726US	Northwest	05.10.61	SX-DBK	Olympic AW	Scr.	81 Athens
18357	272		–	4X-ATC	El Al	13.02.62	9Q-CPM, 9Q-CWR	Wolf Aviation	Scr.	86 Kinshasa
18358-59	463	–	–	–	Ghana Airways, cancelled			–	–	–
18372	271	465	–	VR-BBW	Cunard Eagle	27.02.62	G-ARWD	Boeing	Scr.	Kingman AZ
18373	302	465	–	G-ARWE	BOAC/Cunard	07.07.62	–	BOAC	W/O	8.4.68 London Heathrow
18374	283	329	ELINT	OO-SJF	Sabena	16.04.62	OE-LBA, 4X-BYL, 4X-JYL	Israeli Air Force 128	Stored	Tel Aviv

Con. No.	L/n	Built as	Cvt to	1st Regn	For	Del date	Other Registrations	Last user	Fate	Location
18375	293	328	–	F-BHSU	Air France	11.05.62	CN-RMA, N707RZ	Gateway AC LC	Scr.	3.85 Ft Lauderdale
18376	279	062	–	N720V	Pacific Northern	23.03.62	N301AS	Aviat Sales Comp	Scr.	1.84 Miami
18377	285	062	–	N720W	Pacific Northern	18.04.62	N302AS	AeroAmerica	Scr.	11.78 Berlin-Tempelhof
18378	257	040B	–	AP-AMG	PIA	21.12.61	9H-AAM	Air Malta	Burnt	Fire practice, Luqa, Malta
18379	321	040B	–	AP-AMH	PIA	19.10.62		PIA	W/O	20.5.65 Cairo
18380	324	040B	–	AP-AMJ	PIA	29.11.62	9H-AAN, N5487N	Int Air Leases	Scr.	For KC-135 parts DMAFB
18381	222	051B	–	N791TW	TWA	23.07.61	N730US, G-AZFB, N2464C	Jet Charter Service	Scr.	For KC-135 parts DMAFB
18382	223	051B	–	N792TW	TWA	02.08.61	N731US, G-AZKM, N2466K	Jet Charter Service	Scr.	For KC-135 parts DMAFB
18383	230	051B	–	N793TW	TWA	27.08.61	N732US, G-AZNX, N24666	Jet Charter Service	Scr.	For KC-135 parts DMAFB
18384	237	051B	–	N794TW	TWA	30.09.61	N733US, OY-APZ, OO-TYA, N720GT, N720H	Honeywell Int	C	Fitted with AS 977 (RJX) engine
18385	277	131B	–	N746TW	TWA	29.03.62	–	TWA	Scr.	For KC-135 parts DMAFB
18386	280	131B	–	N747TW	TWA	10.04.62	–	TWA	Scr.	For KC-135 parts DMAFB
18387	286	131B	–	N748TW	TWA	30.04.62	–	TWA	Scr.	For KC-135 parts DMAFB
18388	291	131B	–	N749TW	TWA	18.05.62	–	TWA	Scr.	For KC-135 parts DMAFB
18389	294	131B	–	N750TW	TWA	23.05.62	–	TWA	Scr.	For KC-135 parts DMAFB
18390	296	131B	–	N751TW	TWA	31.05.62	–	TWA	Stored	For KC-135 parts DMAFB
18391	299	131B	–	N752TW	TWA	16.06.62	–	TWA	Stored	For KC-135 parts DMAFB
18392	301	131B	–	N754TW	TWA	28.06.62	–	TWA	Scr.	For KC-135 parts DMAFB
18393	306	131B	–	N755TW	TWA	23.07.62	–	TWA	Scr.	For KC-135 parts DMAFB
18394	308	131B	–	N756TW	TWA	02.08.62	–	TWA	Stored	For KC-135 parts DMAFB
18395	309	131B	–	N757TW	TWA	01.08.62	–	TWA	W/O	16.1.74 Los Angeles. Dismantled for spares
18396	311	131B	–	N758TW	TWA	21.08.62	–	TWA	Stored	For KC-135 parts DMAFB
18397	312	131B	–	N759TW	TWA	29.08.62	–	TWA	Scr.	For KC-135 parts DMAFB
18398-99			–	N760TW	TWA CANC 131B		–	–	–	–
18400	313	131B	–	N781TW	TWA	31.08.62	–	TWA	Scr.	For KC-135 parts DMAFB
18401	315	131B	–	N782TW	TWA	21.09.82	–	TWA	Scr.	For KC-135 parts DMAFB
18402	316	131B	–	N783TW	TWA	26.09.62	–	TWA	Scr.	For KC-135 parts DMAFB
18403	317	131B	–	N784TW	TWA	28.09.62	–	TWA	Stored	For KC-135 parts DMAFB
18404	318	131B	–	N785TW	TWA	12.10.62	–	TWA	Scr.	For KC-135 parts DMAFB
18405	305	331B	–	N773TW	TWA	11.03.63	–	TWA	Stored	For KC-135 parts DMAFB
18406	320	331B	–	N774TW	TWA	01.11.62	–	TWA	Stored	For KC-135 parts DMAFB
18407	323	331B	–	N775TW	TWA	23.01.63	–	TWA	Stored	For KC-135 parts DMAFB
18408	326	331B	–	N776TW	TWA	23.01.63	N28714	TWA	Scr.	For KC-135 parts DMAFB
18409	331	331B	–	N778TW	TWA	21.02.63		TWA	Stored	For KC-135 parts DMAFB
18410	331	331B	–	–	TWA CANC	–	–	–	–	–
18411	266	436	–	G-ARRA	BOAC	16.02.62	N4465D	Coastal AW	W/O	13.10.83 Perpignan
18412	330	436	–	G-ARRB	BOAC/Cunard	12.02.63		Boeing	Scr.	9.79 Kingman, AZ
18413	334	436	–	G-ARRC	BOAC/Cunard	15.03.63	N4465C, 9Q-CTK	New ACS	Scr.	For KC-135 parts DMAFB
18414	275	437	–	VT-DNY	Air-India	07.03.62	–	Allen AC	Scr.	Either cabin trainer Bombay or Scr (see 18415)
18415	282	437	–	VT-DNZ	Air-India	12.04.62	–	Air-India	Scr.	Either cabin trainer Bombay or Scr (see 18414)
18416	288	024B	–	N57201	Continental AL	30.04.62	–	Allen AC	Scr.	Miami after 3.76
18417	295	024B	–	N57202	Continental AL	27.05.62	ET-EFK, N550DS	AAR Corp	Scr.	For KC-135 parts DMAFB
18418	300	024B	–	N57203	Continental AL	20.06.62	ET-AFA, N769BE	Boeing	Scr.	For KC-135 parts DMAFB
18419	304	024B	–	N57204	Continental AL	09.07.62	ET-AFB, N770BE	Boeing	Scr.	For KC-135 parts DMAFB
18420	243	051B	–	N727US	Northwest AL	25.10.61	SX-DBL	Olympic AW	Stored	81 Athens
18421	244	051B	–	N728US	Northwest AL	15.11.61	OY-APY, G-BHGE, TF-AYC		Stored	For KC-135 parts DMAFB
18422	256	051B	–	N729US	Northwest AL	13.12.61	OY-APW, TF-AYB	AirXport	Scr.	For KC-135 parts DMAFB
18423	289	027	–	N7079	Braniff	10.05.62	N731T, N321E	Eastern Orient AL	Scr.	4.82 Bournemouth
18424	281	058B	058BF	4X-ABA	El Al	23.06.62	N8498S	USAF	Stored	DMAFB complete
18425	290	058B	–	4X-ABB	El Al	30.04.62	N8498T, N4228G	Boeing Military	Scr.	For KC-135 parts DMAFB
18451	307	047B	–	N93145	Western AL	27.07.62	HZ-NAA, N2143J, N720JR	JAR Air Services	C	Operated for Mali Government
18452	310	047B	–	N93146	Western AL	08.08.62	N92GS	F.P.M&G,Miami	Scr.	11.96 Miami
18453	314	047B	–	N93147	Western AL	28.08.62	HZ-KA4	Sheikh K.Adham	C	–
18454	319	060B	–	ET-AAG	Ethiopian AL	02.11.62	–	MEA leased	W/O	9.1.68 Beirut
18455	322	060B	–	ET-AAH	Ethiopian AL	30.11.62	N330DS	AAR Allen AC	Stored	For KC-135 parts DMAFB
18456	325	328B	–	F-BHSV	Air France	15.12.63	4X-ATE	TEA	Scr.	11.89 Brussels
18457	327	328B	–	F-BHSX	Air France	17.01.63	TU-TXA, TU-TXB	TRATCO	Scr.	5.83 Luxembourg
18458	329	328B	–	F-BHSY	Air France	17.02.63	TU-TXF, TU-TXJ	TRATCO	Scr.	9.83 Luxemburg
18459	335	328B	–	F-BHSZ	Air France	30.03.63	–	TRATCO	W/O	4.12.69 Caracas
18460	328	329	EC-707	OO-SJG	Sabena	19.01.63	4X-BYM, 4X-JYM	Israeli Air Force 137	Stored	Tel Aviv
18461	303	353B	VC-137	62-6000	USAF	09.10.62	–	USAF 89AW	Pres.	USAFM, Dayton Ohio
18462	333	330B	–	D-ABOS	Lufthansa	28.02.63	D-ABOV, CC-CCG	LAN Chile	Pres.	Museo Nacional de Aeronautica Chile
18463	363	330B	–	D-ABOT	Lufthansa	05.03.63	–	Lufthansa	W/O	20.12.73 New Delhi
18579	332	321C	–	N765PA	Pan Am	07.06.63	G-BEBP	Dan Air/IAS Cargo	W/O	14.5.77 Lusaka, Zambia
18580	336	321C	–	N766PA	Pan Am	02.05.63	5X-UAL	Ronair/Uganda AL	W/O	1.4.79 Entebbe, Uganda by invading troops
18581	347	027	–	N7080	Braniff AW	12.05.76	N733T	AeroAmerica	Scr.	6.81 Boeing Field

ABOVE: A line-up of 707-131s from TWA's February 1956 order are shown lined up during final completion nearly three years later. Most of these aircraft were sold on in the early 1970s and passed through the hands of Israel Aircraft Industries at one time or another. *The Aviation Picture Library*

Con. No.	L/n	Built as	Cvt to	1st Regn	For	Del date	Other Registrations	Last user	Fate	Location
18582	344	373C	–	N373WA	World Airways	12.05.76	HZ-ACE	Saudia	Stored	Damaged, Jeddah, since 79
18583	346	373C	–	N374WA	World Airways	22.08.63	HZ-ACF, D2-TAG, D2-TOG	Angola Air Chart	Scr.	2.93 Manston
18584	342	351B	–	N351US	Northwest Orient	05.06.63	VR-HGH, CC-CCX	LAN Chile	W/O	3.8.78 Buenos Aires-Ezeiza
18585	343	351B	–	N352US	Northwest Orient	19.06.63	VR-HGI, G-BFBZ	Angola Air Chart	Scr.	Lasham
18586	345	351B	–	N353US	Northwest Orient	30.07.63	VR-HGO, VR-CAO, N651TF, N351SR, EL-SKD, G-BSZA, VR-BMV, VR-BOR, HZ-SAK1, P4-FDH, N707CA	Omega Air	Stored	Southend
18587	340	024B	–	N351SR	Continental AL	30.07.63	–	Allen AC Corp	Scr.	before 3.76
18588	337	047B	–	N93148	Western AL	03.04.63	5Y-BBX	Kenya AW	Stored	Ground trainer, Nairobi
18589	338	047B	–	N93149	Western AL	24.04.63	AP-BAF	PIA	Scr.	82 Karachi
18590	339	047B	–	N93150	Western AL	02.05.63	AP-AXK	PIA	W/O	8.1.81 Quetta, Pakistan
18591	341	321C	–	N767PA	Pan Am	07.06.63	G-BEAF, LV-MSG	TAR leased	Scr.	91 Buenos Aires
18592	–	–	–	–	Pan Am, cancelled	–	–	–	–	–
18685	359	328B	–	F-BLCA	Air France	13.01.64	–	TRATCO	Scr.	11.83 Luxembourg
18686	360	328B	–	F-BLCB	Air France	30.01.64	TU-TXI, TU-TXM, 5R-MFK, 5A-DLT, SU-DAJ, N83658	Boeing Military	Scr.	For KC-135 parts DMAFB
18687	351	051B	–	N734US	Northwest	22.10.63	SX-DBM	Olympic AW	Scr.	81 Athens
18688	361	051B	–	N735US	Northwest	23.01.64	SX-DBN, YN-BYI, G-BRDR, N8215Q	Air Crew Leasing	Stored	For KC-135 parts DMAFB
18689	354	323C	–	N7555A	American AL	19.11.63	G-WIND, J6-SLF, N902RQ, EL-JNS, EL-ALI	Daallo AL	C	–
18690	356	323C	–	N7556A	American AL	13.12.63	G-SAIL	Tradewinds AW	Stored	Lasham, UK
18691	357	323C	–	N7557A	American AL	20.12.63	5X-UWM, G-BFEO	Tradewinds	Stored	For KC-135 parts DMAFB
18692	358	323C	–	N7558A	American AL	31.12.63	N309EL, CP1365	LAB	W/O	31.8.91 Dothan AL in hangar fire

Con. No.	L/n	Built as	Cvt to	1st Regn	For	Del date	Other Registrations	Last user	Fate	Location
18693	348	351B	–	N354US	Northwest Orient	09.09.63	VR-HGN, G-BFBS	Midair	Scr.	1.83 str Lasham
18694	353	441	–	PP-VJJ	Varig	12.11.63	N58RD, 9Q-CMD	Blue AL	Stored	Goma, Zaire
18707	349	373C	–	N375WA	World AW	26.09.63	G-AYSI, N3751Y, HK-2401	TAMPA Colombia ls	W/O	14.12.83 Medellin
18708	375	337B	–	VT-DPM	Air-India	25.05.64	TF-IUE, N8880A	Omega	Stored	For KC-135 parts DMAFB
18709	350	373C	–	N789TW	TWA	18.11.63	HK-2606, HP1027, HC-BLY	SAETA	Scr.	7.93 Quito
18710	352	351B	–	N355US	Northwest Orient	13.10.63	B-1828, G-BCLZ, B-1828	Allen AC Corp	Scr.	6.85 Taipei
18711	370	331C	–	N786TW	TWA	25.04.64	N700FW, CC-CER, PP-PHB, OB-1696, PT-MST	Skymaster	W/O	7.3.01 Sao Paulo
18712	373	331C	–	N787TW	TWA	20.05.64	–	TWA	W/O	26.7.69 Ponoma NJ
18713	378	331C	TC-18E	N788TW	TWA	12.06.64	N131EA, 84-1398	USAF	Stored	Based Tinker AFB, OK
18714	362	321C	–	N790PA	Pan Am	27.02.64	HK-1718, TF-AEA, N228VV, HK-3333,	TAMPA leased	Scr.	WHERE
18715	364	321C	–	N791PA	Pan Am	20.03.64	TC-JCC, N791PA, ST-ALX	Golden Star	W/O	24.3.92 near Athens
18716	365	321C	–	N792PA	Pan Am	27.03.64	JY-AED, JY-CAB, 4YB-CAB, J6-SLR, TF-AYE, CX-CPQ, HI596CA, N66651, HR-AMX	Atlantic AC LC	Scr.	Manaus
18717	366	321C	–	N793PA	Pan Am	03.04.64	G-BGIS, G-TRAD, HK-3232, D2-FAV	Air Nacoia	C	–
18718	368	321C	–	N794PA	Pan Am	30.04.64	N794EP, N794RN, G-BFZF, G-BNGH, 5N-MAS	Kabo Air Cargo	W/O	31.3.92 Istres France
18737	377	348C	–	EI-AMW	Aer Lingus	10.06.64	LX-LGV, EI-AMW, 7O-ACJ	Alyemda	Stored	Restaurant no wings, Damascus
18738	355	373C	–	N790TW	TWA	23.12.63	–	TWA	W/O	30.11.70 Tel Aviv
18739	385	138B	–	VH-EBL	Qantas	19.08.64	N107BN, PK-MBA, N-46D	Omega Air	Scr.	1993 Shannon
18740	388	138B	–	VH-EBM	Qantas	10.09.64	N108BN, N707XX, N707JT	John Travolta	C	–
18745	380	040B	–	N68646	Boeing	28.04.65	AP-ATQ	ATASCO	Scr.	1986
18746	367	351B	–	N356US	Northwest Orient	09.04.64	CF-PWJ, OO-ABA, C-GRYO, 5A-DIZ, 5Y-AXC, N8163G, TF-ANC, 9G-RCA, 9G-RBO	Gas Air Nigeria leased	W/O	29.4.92 Lagos
18747	369	351C	–	N357US	Northwest Orient	18.04.64	VR-HHB, 5X-UAC, N21AZ, CC-CDI, Z-WST	Grecoair	Stored	Johannesburg
18748	379	351C	–	N358US	Northwest Orient	29.03.74	VR-HHD, VR-CAR, 3X-GAZ, N18AZ, CC-CCE, D2-TOR, N18AZ	David Tokoph	Stored	Addis Ababa
18749	374	047B	–	N93151	Western AL	21.05.64	AP-AXM	ATASCO Leasing	Preserved	Karachi Planetarium
18756	383	331C	–	N791TW	TWA	06.08.64	N5791	Boeing Military	Scr.	For KC-135 parts DMAFB
18757	387	331C	–	N792TW	TWA	29.08.64	T.17-2	Spanish Air Force	C	451 Esc. Grupo 45
18758	391	131B	–	N795TW	TWA	29.10.64	–	TWA	Stored	For KC-135 parts DMAFB
18759	392	131B	–	N796TW	TWA	13.11.64	–	TWA	Scr.	For KC-135 parts DMAFB
18760	393	131B	–	N797TW	TWA	10.11.64	–	TWA	Stored	San Francisco for fire department
18761	395	131B	–	N798TW	TWA	31.12.64	–	TWA	Scr.	For KC-135 parts DMAFB
18762	396	131B	–	N799TW	TWA	23.12.64	–	TWA	Scr.	For KC-135 parts DMAFB
18763	382	024B	–	N57206	Continental AL	23.07.64	–	Allen AC Corp	Scr.	After 3.76
18764	399	331B	–	N779TW	TWA	15.01.65	–	TWA	Stored	For KC-135 parts DMAFB
18765	371	321C	–	N795PA	Pan Am	30.04.64	N795RN, G-BEZT, SU-BAG, 5A-DHL	Jamahiriya AT nn Libyan Arab mgd	Scr.	Tripoli after 1988
18766	372	321C	–	N796PA	Pan Am	09.05.64	HK-1849, N865BX, HR-AMZ, CX-BSB, P4-CCG, CX-BSB	Transcontinental Sur leased	Stored	Montevideo
18767	376	321C	–	N797PA	Pan Am	21.05.64	JY-AEE	Alia	W/O	3.8.75 near Agadir
18790	394	321C	–	N798PA	Pan Am	03.12.64	–	Pan Am	W/O	12.6.68 Calcutta
18792	381	051B	–	N736US	Northwest Orient	26.06.64	OY-APU, G-BBZG, TF-AYA	AirXport	Stored	For KC-135 parts DMAFB
18793	384	051B	–	N737US	Northwest Orient	27.06.64	OY-APV, TF-AYD, N771BE	Boeing Military	Scr.	22.2.92 Everett
18808	404	338C	–	VH-EBN	Qantas	09.02.65	9V-BFW, N707GB, HK-3030, PT-WSZ	Skymaster AL	C	–
18809	407	338C	–	VH-EBO	Qantas	05.03.65	9V-BFN, N4225J, 5N-ARQ	WHO	Scr.	Manston 01
18810	438	338C	–	VH-EBP	Qantas	11.08.65	N14791, SU-BBA	Farner Air Service	Pres.	Restaurant, Movenpick Hotel Cairo Airport
18818	390	047B	–	N93152	Western AL	25.09.64	AP-AXL	PIA	Pres	Pres. 8.86, fuselage only Lahore/not seen
18819	398	330B	–	D-ABOX	Lufthansa	10.01.65	VP-WKR, Z-WKR, 5Y-AXM	Seagreen/African International	Stored	Nairobi
18820	401	047B	–	N93153	Western AL	21.01.65	TF-VLC	Aer Lingus	Scr.	6.80 Stansted
18824	397	321C	–	N799PA	Pan Am	31.12.64	–	Pan Am	W/O	26.12.68 Elmendorf AFB, Alaska
18825	386	321C	–	N17321	Continental AL	21.08.64	B-1832, N987AA, 5X-DAR	DAS Air Cargo	W/O	25.11.92 Port Harcourt, Nigeria
18826	389	321C	–	N17322	Continental AL	17.09.64	CF-PWZ	Pacific Western	W/O	2.1.73 near Edmonton
18827	410	047B	–	N3154	Western AL	10.03.65	TF-VLB	Eagle Air	Scr.	12.82 Shannon
18828	423	047B	–	N3155	Western AL	19.05.65	OD-AGG	MEA	W/O	1.8.82 Beirut
18829	427	047B	–	N3156	Western AL	02.06.65	CX-BQG	RACE Avt	Stored	For KC-135 parts DMAFB
18830	429	047B	–	N3157	Western AL	17.06.65	OD-AGF	MEA	Stored	Beirut
18831	414	059B	–	HK-726	Avianca	08.04.65	N4450Z	Avianca	Scr.	For KC-135 parts DMAFB
18832	403	321B	–	N401PA	Pan Am	05.02.65	EI-BKO, VN-A305, VN-B1416, VN-81416, 5X-JCR	DAS Air Cargo	Scr.	For KC-135 parts DMAFB
18833	405	321B	–	N402PA	Pan Am	17.02.65		Navaero Avt Corp	Stored	For KC-135 parts DMAFB
18834	406	321B	–	N403PA	Pan Am	24.02.65	TC-JBS, N5519W	ATASCO Leasing	Scr.	For KC-135 parts DMAFB
18835	408	321B	–	N404PA	Pan Am	05.03.65	N2138T	Air Force Systems Cmd	Stored	–
18836	409	321B	–	N405PA	Pan Am	10.03.65	TC-JBT, N5519U	Boeing parts	Stored	For KC-135 parts DMAFB
18837	411	321B	–	N406PA	Pan Am	17.03.65	F-OGIV, F-BSGT, XT-ABZ, XT-BBH	Equator Bank	Stored	For KC-135 parts DMAFB
18838	412	321B	–	N407PA	Pan Am	26.03.65	–	Pan Am	W/O	17.12.73 Rome by terrorists

Con. No.	L/n	Built as	Cvt to	1st Regn	For	Del date	Other Registrations	Last user	Fate	Location
18839	417	321B	–	N408PA	Pan Am	16.04.65	N4408F, N470PC, N454PC, C5-GOC, HR-AMV, OM-UFB, EL-AKF, N454PC	Omega	Stored	Mojave
18840	418	321B	–	N409PA	Pan Am	21.04.65	F-OGIW, N707GE	Jet Charter S	Stored	For KC-135 parts DMAFB
18841	419	321B	–	N410PA	Pan Am	27.04.65	ZP-CCE	LAP	Stored	Asuncion
18842	421	321B	–	N412PA	Pan Am	21.05.65	TC-JBU, N5517Z	ATASCO	Scr.	For KC-135 parts DMAFB
18873	402	337B	–	N68655	Boeing to Air-India	12.3.65	VT-DSI, EL-AJS, N8870A	Omega	Stored	For KC-135 parts DMAFB
18880	413	348C	–	EI-ANO	Aer Lingus	13.04.65	N381F, 5A-DIX	Libyan Arab	Stored	Cairo
18881	436	328C	–	F-BLCC	Air France	05.08.65	TF-VLR, 5A-DIK, 5Y-BFC, D2-TOV	Angola A Chart leased	W/O	21.7.88 near Lagos
18882	420	123B	–	N7550A	American AL	27.05.65	–	American AL	Stored	For KC-135 parts DMAFB
18883	422	123B	–	N7551A	American AL	26.05.65	–	American AL	Scr.	For KC-135 parts DMAFB
18884	426	123B	–	N7552A	American AL	15.06.65	–	American AL	Scr.	For KC-135 parts DMAFB
18885	432	123B	–	N7553A	American AL	23.07.65	–	American AL	Scr	For KC-135 parts DMAFB
18886	430	324C	–	N17323	Continental AL	17.06.65	G-AZJM, N17323, HK-2600, HK-3355X	Air Nacoia	C	–
18887	431	324C	–	N17324	Continental AL	21.06.65	B-1834	China AL	W/O	11.9.79 near Taipei
18888	425	351C	–	N359US	Northwest Orient	22.05.65	VR-HHE, 5A-DJT	Libyan Arab	W/O	9.12.91 Tripoli
18889	428	351C	–	N360US	Northwest Orient	12.06.65	VR-HHJ, 5A-DJU	Libyan Arab	Scr.	12.91 Tripoli
18890	416	329C	–	OO-SJH	Sabena	17.04.65	–	Zaire Int Cargo leased	W/O	11.5.80 Douala 0(3)
18891	441	344B	–	ZS-DYL	South African	27.08.65	ZS-SAD, LX-LGR, VP-WKW, 3B-NAE, EL-AJT	Liberia World AW	Scr.	2.97 Manston
18913	400	331B	–	N760TW	TWA	29.01.65	–	TWA	Stored	For KC-135 parts DMAFB
18914	415	331B	–	N780TW	TWA	09.04.65	–	TWA	Stored	For KC-135 parts DMAFB
18915	424	331B	–	N793TW	TWA	25.05.65	–	TWA	Stored	For KC-135 parts DMAFB
18916	455	331B	–	N8705T	TWA	10.12.65	–	TWA	Scr.	For KC-135 parts DMAFB
18917	460	331B	–	N8715T	TWA	21.12.65	–	TWA	W/O	13.9.70 blown up, Dawson's Field, Jordan
18918	462	331B	–	N8725T	TWA	12.01.66	–	TWA	Stored	For KC-135 parts DMAFB
18921	440	351C	–	N361US	Northwest Orient	13.08.65	VR-HGR, S2-ACF, N8090P, OB1401	Aeronaves del Peru	Stored	Lima
18922	444	351C	–	N362US	Northwest Orient	15.09.65	VR-HGP, N82TF, 5N-ASY, 5N-JIL, HR-AME, EL-AKF, EL-AKL	Amed Air leased	Stored	Shannon
18923	435	330B	–	D-ABUB	Lufthansa	04.08.65	VP-WKS, G-ASZF, Z-WKS	Air Zimbabwe	Stored	Harare
18924	448	336C	–	N2978G	Boeing to BOAC/Cunard	19.12.65	G-ASZF, 5N-ARO	RN Cargo	W/O	25.9.83 Bomb explosion
18925	452	336C	–	G-ASZG	BOAC/Cunard	19.12.65	LX-FCV, XT-ABX, EL-AKI, PP-BRB	TRATCO	Stored	Sao Paulo. Parts for Brazil AF
18926	446	330B	Tanker	D-ABUC	Lufthansa	05.10.65	CC-CEA, 903	Chilean Air Force	C	Grupo 10
18927	454	330B	–	D-ABUD	Lufthansa	24.11.65	VP-WKV, Z-WKV, 5Y-AXI	African Int	Stored	Nairobi
18928	457	330B	–	D-ABUF	Lufthansa	28.12.65	N5381X, N88ZL	Lowa	C	–
18929	461	330B	–	D-ABUG	Lufthansa	07.01.66	VP-WKT, Z-WKT	Air Zimbabwe	Stored	11.88 Harare, for restaurant
18930	464	330B	–	D-ABUH	Lufthansa	19.01.66	VP-WKU, Z-WKU, 3D-WKU, 3D-AKU	Inter-Air	C	–
18931	482	330B	–	D-ABUK	Lufthansa	27.03.66	A6-UAE, ST-NSR	Sudan AW	Scr.	Khartoum by 3.95
18932	477	330C	–	D-ABUE	Lufthansa	11.03.66	PT-TCO	Transbrazil	W/O	11.4.87 Manaus
18937	451	330C	–	D-ABUA	Lufthansa	10.11.65	VR-HTC, VH-HTC, LZ-PVA, HC-BTB,	AECA	C	–
18938	434	323C	–	N7559A	American AL	30.07.65	OD-AGN	TMA	Stored	Beirut, damaged
18939	437	323C	–	N7560A	American AL	30.08.65	OD-AGD	TMA	C	
18940	439	323C	–	N7561A	American AL	27.08.65	PP-VLP, N108BV, 5N-MXX, 9G-LAD	Johnsons Air	C	Operated for Ethiopian AL
18941	471	328B	–	F-BLCD	Air France	09.02.66	–	Air France	Pres.	Le Bourget
18948	495	384C	–	SX-DBA	Olympic AW	11.05.66	JY-AEB, JY-AJK, YR-JCC, P4-JCC, ST-JJC	AZZA Transport Comp	C	–
18949	497	384C	–	SX-DBB	Olympic AW	21.05.66	JY-AEC, 66-30052	USAF-Joint Stars	Stored	DMAFB for E-8 conversion
18950	504	384C	–	SX-DBC	Olympic AW	18.06.66		Venezuela AF	C	GAT-6
18954	458	338C	–	VH-EBR	Qantas	28.12.65	9M-ATR, 9M-MCR, 6O-SBN, G-BMJE, N449J	Omega Air	Stored	For KC-135 parts DMAFB
18955	467	338C	–	VH-EBS	Qantas	03.02.66	9M-ASO, 9M-MCS, 5A-DJO	United African	W/O	14.3.83 Sebha, Libya
18956	466	321B	–	N414PA	Pan Am	29.01.66	–	Air Carrier Supply	Scr.	3.81 Miami
18957	472	321B	–	N415PA	Pan Am	15.02.66	ZP-CCF, FAP01	Paraguayan Govt	C	Esc. Presidencial
18958	475	321B	–	N416PA	Pan Am	25.02.66	EP-IRJ	Iran Air	W/O	22.9.80
18959	478	321B	–	N417PA	Pan Am	21.05.66	–	Pan Am	W/O	22.7.73 Papeete
18960	484	321B	–	N418PA	Pan Am	07.04.66	–	IAI Israel	Pres.	Nose only Weeks Museum Tamiami FL
18961	456	382B	–	CS-TBA	TAP	16.12.65	N45RT, 165342	US Navy E-6 train	Stored	DMAFB
18962	501	382B	–	CS-TBB	TAP	08.06.66	TF-VLV, N46RT, 165343	US Navy E-6 train	Stored	New Orleans
18963	433	047B	–	N3158	Western AL	21.07.65	OD-AGE	MEA	W/O	27.6.76 Beirut by shelling
18964	453	351C	–	N363US	Northwest Orient	15.11.65	VR-HGQ, TF-VLP, 5A-DJS, 5Y-BFB, D2-TOU	Equat/Angola A Ch	Stored	Fire dump, Manston
18975	445	349C	–	N322F	Flying Tiger	27.09.65	G-AWTK, G-BDCN, D2-TAC, D2-TOB, D2-TOI	TAAG Angola AL	W/O	2.88 Luanda, Angola
18976	449	349C	–	N323F	Flying Tiger	13.10.65	EI-ASN, 9J-ADY, ST-ALK	Trans Arabian AT	W/O	14.7.90 Khartoum
18977	442	060B	–	ET-ABP	Ethiopian AL	20.09.65	N440DS, N7381	Hughes AC Corp	Stored	Mojave
18978	465	331B	–	N18701	TWA	25.01.66	–	TWA	W/O	22.12.75 Milan
18979	468	331B	–	N18702	TWA	03.02.66	–	TWA	Scr.	For KC-135 parts DMAFB
18980	469	331B	–	N18703	TWA	05.02.66	–	TWA	Stored	For KC-135 parts DMAFB
18981	476	331B	–	N18704	TWA	05.03.66	–	TWA	Stored	For KC-135 parts DMAFB
18982	483	331B	–	N18706	TWA	04.04.66	–	TWA	Stored	For KC-135 parts DMAFB

Con. No.	L/n	Built as	Cvt to	1st Regn	For	Del date	Other Registrations	Last user	Fate	Location
18983	485	331B	–	N18707	TWA	04.04.66	–	TWA	Stored	For KC-135 parts DMAFB
18984	487	331B	–	N18708	TWA	20.04.66	–	TWA	Scr.	For KC-135 parts DMAFB
18985	496	331B	–	N18709	TWA	21.05.66	4X-ATD, N707HP	Hartford Power Sys	Stored	For KC-135 parts DMAFB
18986	479	131B	–	N6720	TWA	25.03.66	–	TWA	Scr.	For KC-135 parts DMAFB
18987	486	131B	–	N6721	TWA	16.04.66	–	Used in 'Airplane' flim	Scr.	For KC-135 parts DMAFB
18988	489	131B	–	N6722	TWA	28.04.66	–	TWA	Scr.	For KC-135 parts DMAFB
18989	492	131B	–	N6723	TWA	06.05.66	–	TWA	Scr.	For KC-135 parts DMAFB
18991	450	373C	–	N376WA	World AW	22.10.65	AP-AWU, 68-18991 (Pak AF)	PIA	Scr.	By 1994 at Karachi
19000	447	385C	–	N68657	Boeing demonstrator	13.09.65	CC-CEB, FAC905, 4X-JYI, 904	Chile AF	C	Grupo 10
19001	488	348C	–	EI-ANV	Aer Lingus	21.04.66	9G-ACR, 5A-DIY	Libyan Arab mgd	Stored	Cairo
19002	473	024B	–	N17207	Continental AL	16.02.66	–	Allen AC Corp	Scr.	After 3.76
19003	474	024B	–	N17208	Continental AL	19.02.66	–	Allen AC Corp	Scr.	After 4.76
19004	459	358B	–	4X-ATR	El Al	07.01.66	N317F, N53302, TF-AYG, TF-ACG		Stored	DMAFB
19034	463	351C	–	N364US	Northwest Orient	08.01.66	VR-HGU, RP-C1186	Jetran	Stored	For KC-135 parts DMAFB
19104	498	327C	–	N7095	Braniff AW	21.05.66	OD-AGX, N7096	TMA	C	–
19105	499	327C	–	N7096	Braniff AW	28.05.66	OD-AGY	TMA	C	–
19106	502	327C	–	N7097	Braniff AW	18.06.66	PP-VLJ	Varig	W/O	9.6.73 Rio De Janeiro
19107	507	327C	–	N7098	Braniff AW	29.06.66	PH-TRV, OD-AFX	TMA	W/O	23.7.79 Beirut
19108	511	327C	–	N7099	Braniff AW	27.07.66	OD-AFY	TMA ret	W/O	26.7.93 Amsterdam, cockpit preserved
19133	538	344B	–	ZS-EKV	South African	09.01.67	ZS-SAE, LX-LGU, 3B-NAF, N287G, TF-IUC, 5Y-AXS, TF-IUG, 5Y-LKL, N6598W	Omega Air	Stored	For KC-135 parts DMAFB
19160	470	047B	–	N3159	Western AL	26.01.66	OD-AGQ	MEA	W/O	21.8.85 Beirut by Israeli shelling
19161	481	047B	–	N3160	Western AL	12.03.66	OD-AGR	MEA	W/O	16.6.82 Beirut by Israeli shelling
19162	480	329C	–	OO-SJJ	Sabena	23.03.66	9Q-CVG	Katale Aero Transp	W/O	1.3.90 Goma, Zaire
19163	494	351C	–	N365US	Northwest Orient	17.05.66	SX-DBP, N65010	Aircrew Leasing	Stored	For KC-135 parts DMAFB
19164	505	351C	ELINT	N366US	Northwest Orient	24.06.66	SX-DBO, 4X-JYF, T.17-4	Spanish AF	C	451 Esc.
19168	508	351C	–	N367US	Northwest Orient	12.07.66	S2-ABN, 5N-AYJ	FastC/GAS Air	W/O	14.12.88 near Luxor
19177	513	324C	–	N17325	Continental AL	29.07.66	PP-VLN, N110BV, 5X-UCM, 73-601 (Yug AF), YA-GAF	Balkh AL	Stored	Ostend
19178	517	324C	–	N17326	Varig	23.08.66	B-1830	Allen AC Corp	Scr.	6.85 Taipei
19179	500	373C	–	N372WA	World AW	29.05.66	CS-TBJ, 9Q-CSB, 3D-CSB, 3C-GIG	Trade Winds Air Cargo	IMP	Impounded Southend 10.01 drug smuggling
19185	490	123B	–	N7554A	American AL	30.04.66	–	Boeing	Scr.	For KC-135 parts DMAFB
19186	491	123B	–	N7570A	American AL	04.05.66	–	Boeing/American Trans Air	Scr.	For KC-135 parts DMAFB
19187	493	123B	–	N7571A	American AL	12.05.66	–	American AL	Stored	For KC-135 parts DMAFB
19188	506	123B	–	N7572A	American AL	30.03.66	–	American AL	Scr.	For KC-135 parts Tuscon
19207	512	047B	–	N3161	Western AL	29.07.66	–	Wicklund Aviation	Stored	For KC-135 parts DMAFB
19208	514	047B	–	N3162	Western AL	29.07.66	–	Wicklund Aviation	Stored	For KC-135 parts
19209	510	351C	–	N368US	Northwest Orient	20.07.66	9Y-TED, N29796, N144SP	Burlington Expr leased	W/O	13.4.87 Kansas City
19210	515	351C	–	N369US	Northwest Orient	12.08.66	YU-AGI, N152LM, CX-BPZ, N152LM, HR-ANG, HP1235CTH, N777FB, EL-AJB	Shuttle Air Cargo	Stored	Liege, Belgium
19211	518	329C	–	OO-SJK	Sabena	30.08.66		Sabena	W/O	13.7.68 Lagos
19212	588	331C	–	N5771T	TWA	18.06.67	EI-BER, LX-FCV, CX-BJV, LX-BJV, 5A-DJV, 9G-ACY, 9G-MAN, N227VV, N730FW, N851MA, N202DJ	Jetlease	Scr.	Miami 1995
19213	613	331C	–	N7552T	TWA	29.08.67	OD-AGT	Golden Sun AC leased	W/O	23.10.81 Tokyo Narita
19214	626	331C	–	N5773T	TWA	29.09.67	OD-AGS	TMA	C	–
19215	530	131B	–	N6724	TWA	12.11.66	–	TWA	Stored	For KC-135 parts DMAFB
19216	558	131B	–	N6726	TWA	08.03.67	–	TWA	Scr.	For KC-135 parts DMAFB
19217	564	131B	–	N6727	TWA	02.04.67	–	TWA	Scr.	For KC-135 parts DMAFB
19218	567	131B	–	N6728	TWA	29.03.67	–	TWA	Stored	For KC-135 parts DMAFB
19219	569	131B	–	N6729	TWA	14.04.67	–	TWA	Scr.	For KC-135 parts DMAFB
19220	573	131B	–	N6763T	TWA	22.04.67	–	TWA	Scr.	For KC-135 parts DMAFB
19221	577	131B	–	N6764T	TWA	13.05.67	–	TWA	Scr.	For KC-135 parts DMAFB
19222	583	131B	–	N6771T	TWA	27.05.67	–	TWA	Scr.	For KC-135 parts DMAFB
19223	598	131B	–	N6789T	TWA	13.07.67	–	TWA	Stored	For KC-135 parts DMAFB
19224	559	331B	–	N18710	TWA	15.03.67	–	TWA	Stored	For KC-135 parts DMAFB
19225	568	331B	–	N18711	TWA	04.04.67	–	TWA	Stored	For KC-135 parts DMAFB
19226	585	331B	–	N18712	TWA	31.05.67	–	Air Trans	Stored	For KC-135 parts DMAFB
19227	607	331B	–	N18713	TWA	06.08.67	–	TWA	Stored	For KC-135 parts DMAFB
19235	519	323C	–	N7562A	American AL	31.08.66	PP-VLU	Varig	W/O	30.1.79 near Tokyo
19236	521	323C	–	N7563A	American AL	28.09.66	81-0897	USAF	Scr.	Greenville, TX
19237	523	323C	–	N7564A	American AL	30.09.66	–	Boeing	Stored	For KC-135 parts DMAFB
19238	528	387B	–	LV-ISA	Aerolineas Argentinas	23.11.66	T-96	Argentine AF	W/O	31.1.93 Recife
19239	542	387B	–	LV-ISB	Aerolineas Argentinas	16.12.66	CX-BNU, PP-LBN	Pluna	Scr.	8.96 Galeao AB AFB Rio

Con. No.	L/n	Built as	Cvt to	1st Regn	For	Del date	Other Registrations	Last user	Fate	Location
19240	543	387B	–	LV-ISC	Aerolineas Argentinas	22.12.66	CX-BOH	Pluna leased	Scr.	2.93 Ezeiza
19241	555	387B	–	LV-ISD	Aerolineas Argentinas	24.02.67	T-95	Argentine AF	C	–
19247	520	337B	–	VT-DVA	Air-India	12.10.66	EL-AJR, N8840A	Omega Air	Stored	For KC-135 parts DMAFB
19248	549	337B	ELINT	VT-DVB	Air-India	12.02.67	K2900	Indian Air Force	C	Air Development and Research Centre
19263	516	351C	–	N370US	Northwest Orient	19.08.66	9J-AEB, EI-ASM, N720FW	Florida West	Scr.	1990s Miami
19264	527	321B	–	N419PA	Pan Am	06.11.66	ZP-CCG	LAP	Stored	Asuncion since 4.92
19265	529	321B	–	N420PA	Pan Am	09.11.66	HC-BCT	AECA AL	Stored	Guayaquil, Ecuador, since 94
19266	531	321B	–	N421PA	Pan Am	29.11.66	HK-2070, 9Q-CBL	Aviat Systems	Stored	DMAFB?
19267	541	321B	–	N422PA	Pan Am	15.12.66	EP-IRK	Iran Air	C	–
19268	544	321B	–	N423PA	Pan Am	21.12.66	–	Pan Am	W/O	22.4.74 Bali
19269	570	321C	–	N447PA	Pan Am	28.06.67	OD-AGO	TMA	C	3.97 Orly
19270	572	321C	–	N448PA	Pan Am	08.05.67	N448M, TF-VLL, G-BMAZ, N863BX, N705FW, 5N-EEO	Air Atlantic Cargo	Stored	Lagos since 99
19271	574	321C	–	N449PA	Pan Am	15.05.67	G-BEVN, N707HT, TC-JCF	SAVA PT leased	Stored	Roswell, NM
19272	578	321C	–	N450PA	Pan Am	23.05.67	YR-ABM	Air Afrique		TAROM W/O 15.1.93 Abidjan
19273	580	321C	–	N451PA	Pan Am	31.05.67	N451RN, HC-BGP	AECA AL	C	–
19274	594	321C	–	N452PA	Pan Am	22.06.67	OD-AGP	TMA	C	–
19275	590	321B	–	N422PA	Pan Am	28.06.67	–	Int Air Leases	Scr.	9.84 Miami
19276	592	321B	–	N423PA	Pan Am	30.06.67	HK-2016	AVIANCA	W/O	25.1.90 Long Island, New York
19277	603	321B	–	N424PA	Pan Am	23.07.67	HC-BFC, 4X-ATF	Pan Am	Stored	Tel Aviv. Partly dismantled
19278	605	321B	–	N425PA	Pan Am	29.07.67	–	Aviation Traders	Scr.	84 Stansted
19284	509	340C	–	AP-AUN	PIA	23.07.66	YU-AGE	JAT	Stored	Zagreb
19285	524	340C	–	AP-AUO	PIA	22.10.66	YU-AGG	JAT	Scr.	Zagreb
19286	625	340C	–	AP-AUP	PIA	21.09.67	YU-AGF	PIA	Scr.	dismantled by 12.93
19291	536	328B	EC-707	F-BLCE	Air France	07.03.67	TU-TXL, 3X-GCC, OO-TYC, N2090B, 4X-BYC, 4X-JYC/258	Israeli Air Force	C	Possibly withdrawn
19292	560	328C	–	F-BLCF	Air France	15.03.67	9XR-JA, 9XR-VO, P4-ESP	Espace Aviation	C	–
19293	546	338C	E-8	VH-EBT	Qantas	28.01.67	G-BFLE, N861BX, 94-0284	USAF-Joint Stars	C	93rd ACW
19294	550	338C	E-8	VH-EBU	Qantas	08.03.67	P2-ANH, N707MD, 9Q-CDA, N707HW, OBT1264, B-2426, G-EOCO, 93-0597/WR	USAF-Joint Stars	C	93rd ACW
19295	617	338C	E-8	VH-EBV	Qantas	06.09.67	9J-AEL, ST-ALP, N4115J, 92-3290	USAF-Joint Stars	C	93rd ACW
19296	630	338C	E-8	VH-EBW	Qantas	10.10.67	G-BDEA, EL-AKH, PT-TCT, EL-AKH, N6546L, 93-1097	USAF-Joint Stars	C	93rd ACW
19297	636	338C	–	VH-EBX	Qantas	23.10.67	G-BCAL, LV-MZE	Royal Air Maroc	Scr.	Miami mid 1990s
19315	545	330B	–	D-ABUL	Lufthansa	31.12.66	6O-SBS, EL-AJU	Skyways/TAR	Stored	Shannon KC-135 spares
19316	547	330B	–	D-ABUM	Lufthansa	30.01.67	6O-SBT	Somali AW	W/O	17.5.89 Nairobi
19317	557	330C	–	D-ABUI	Lufthansa	06.03.67	PT-TCM, PP-BSE	Beta Cargo	C	–
19320	522	341C	–	PP-VJR	Varig	28.12.66	–	Varig	W/O	7.9.68 in fire, Rio De Janeiro
19321	532	341C	–	PP-VJS	Varig	28.12.66	N107BV, 4K-AZ3, N8190U	ALG Inc, Kansas City	Stored	1999 Impounded Southend
19322	561	341C	–	PP-VJT	Varig	22.03.67	–	Varig	W/O	11.6.81 Manaus
19323	526	123B	–	N7573A	American AL	11.11.66	–	Boeing/American Trans Air	Scr.	For KC-135 parts DMAFB
19324	533	123B	–	N7574A	American AL	19.12.66	–	American AL	Scr.	For KC-135 parts DMAFB
19325	535	123B	–	N7575A	American AL	05.01.67	–	American AL	Scr.	For KC-135 parts DMAFB
19326	539	123B	–	N7576A	American AL	24.01.67	–	American AL	Stored	For KC-135 parts DMAFB
19327	562	123B	–	N7577A	American AL	04.04.67	–	American AL	Stored	For KC-135 parts DMAFB
19328	565	123B	–	N7578A	American AL	23.03.67	–	American AL	Stored	For KC-135 parts DMAFB
19329	571	123B	–	N7579A	American AL	14.04.67	–	American AL	Stored	For KC-135 parts DMAFB
19330	575	123B	–	N7580A	American AL	28.04.67	–	American AL	Stored	For KC-135 parts DMAFB
19331	579	123B	–	N7581A	American AL	08.05.67	–	American AL	Stored	For KC-135 parts DMAFB
19332	586	123B	–	N7582A	American AL	26.05.67	–	American AL	Stored	For KC-135 parts DMAFB
19333	589	123B	–	N7583A	American AL	06.06.67	–	Guy America AW	Stored	For KC-135 parts DMAFB
19334	591	123B	–	N7584A	American AL	16.06.67	–	American AL	Stored	For KC-135 parts DMAFB
19335	593	123B	–	N7585A	American AL	20.06.67	–	Transair Cargo	C	–
19336	595	123B	–	N7586A	American AL	27.06.67	–	Guy America AW	Scr.	For KC-135 parts DMAFB
19337	600	123B	–	N7587A	American AL	07.07.67	–	American AL	Scr.	For KC-135 parts DMAFB
19338	602	123B	–	N7588A	American AL	06.07.67	–	Guy America AW	Stored	For KC-135 parts DMAFB
19339	604	123B	–	N7589A	American AL	20.07.67	–	Boeing EqHC	Scr.	For KC-135 parts DMAFB
19340	622	123B	–	N7590A	American AL	15.09.67	–	American AL	Scr.	For KC-135 parts DMAFB
19341	682	123B	–	N7591A	American AL	02.03.68	–	American AL	Scr.	For KC-135 parts DMAFB
19342	787	123B	–	N7592A	American AL	12.03.69	–	American AL	Stored	For KC-135 parts DMAFB
19343	794	123B	–	N7593A	American AL	28.03.69	–	American AL	Scr.	For KC-135 parts DMAFB
19344	801	123B	–	N7594A	American AL	22.04.69	–	American AL	Stored	For KC-135 parts Marana, AZ
19345 to 19349			–	N7594 to N7599A	American AL	Cancelled	–		–	–
19350	537	324C	–	N17327	Continental AL	02.12.66	PP-VLO, G-HEVY, EL-LAT, YA-PAM, 9G-OLD		C	–
19351	552	324C	–	N17328	Continental AL	01.02.67	9V-BEW, TF-VLJ, N419B	Boeing parts	Scr.	For KC-135 parts DMAFB

Con. No.	L/n	Built as	Cvt to	1st Regn	For	Del date	Other Registrations	Last user	Fate	Location
19352	576	324C	–	N17329	Continental AL	21.04.67	9V-BEX, N707JJ, B-2423, N707PM, HK-3604X, PT-WUS	Skymaster AL	C	–
19353	587	324C	–	N47330	Continental AL	27.05.67	9V-BEY, N707SH, B-2422, N707HG, N750FW, JY-AJL, 5N-ONE, 9G-JNR	Jason Air	Stored	Lagos
19354	503	349C	–	N324F	Flying Tiger	21.06.66	EI-ASO, VH-EBZ, G-BAPW, 9J-AEC, S2-ACG, N324F, PT-TCS	Transbrazil	W/O	21.3.89 Sao Paulo
19355	553	349C	–	N325F	Flying Tiger	06.02.67	G-AWWD, D2-TAD, D2-TOC, D2-TOJ,	TAAG Angola	Stored	Damaged, Luanda
19361	618	321B	–	N426PA	Pan Am	08.09.67	HK-2015, N707LE	Air Taxi Int	Scr.	1996 Miami
19362	620	321B	–	N427PA	Pan Am	14.09.67	–	Aviation Traders	Scr.	Stansted
19363	623	321B	–	N428PA	Pan Am	21.09.67	–	ATASCO leased to Korean AL	W/O	2.4.78 Murmansk, forced down by fighter
19364	628	321B	–	N433PA	Pan Am	29.09.67	–	Aviation Traders	Scr.	82 Stansted
19365	631	321B	–	N434PA	Pan Am	12.10.67	–	Aviation Traders	Scr.	Stansted, after 1981
19366	633	321B	–	N435PA	Pan Am	13.10.67	HL7435, 5Y-AXW	African AL Int	C	–
19367	637	321C	–	N457PA	Pan Am	27.10.67	G-BPAT, 9J-AEQ, ST-ALM, VR-HKL, ST-AMF	TAAT	Stored	Manston
19368	640	321C	–	N458PA	Pan Am	07.11.67		Pan Am	W/O	3.11.73 Boston
19369	648	321C	–	N459PA	Pan Am	27.11.67	HL7431, TF-IUB, 9G-ACZ, 5Y-AXG, 9G-ADL, 9G-ADM	Continental Cargo	C	–
19370	651	321C	–	N460PA	Pan Am	30.11.67	F-BYCN, N720GS	Pan Aviation	Scr.	Miami
19371	653	321C	–	N461PA	Pan Am	30.11.67			W/O	25.7.71 Manila
19372	655	321C	–	N462PA	Pan Am	12.12.67	HL7427, TF-IUE, 5N-AWO, 9G-ESI, 9G-EBK, 9G-SGF, HS-TFS	Thai Flying Svcs	Stored	Southend
19373	656	321C	–	N463PA	Pan Am	11.12.67	F-BYCO, N422GS	Millon Air	Stored	Derelict, Miami
19374	658	321B	EW	N453PA	Pan Am	19.12.67	CC-CEK, 904 (Chile AF), CC-CYO, 901, CC-PBZ, D2-MAY	LR Aviation Technology	Stored	Tel Aviv, destined Angola AF
19375	662	321C	–	N473PA	Pan Am	09.01.68	N473RN, HK-2473, OBR1243, N864BX, 5N-TAS, 9Q-CSW, EL-AKJ, PP-BRR, N2NF	Omega Air Inc	Stored	Southend
19376	661	321B	–	N454PA	Pan Am	20.12.67			W/O	30.1.74 Pago Pago
19377	666	321C	–	N474PA	Pan Am	17.01.68	F-BYCP, EL-AJA, N5366Y, N721GS, ST-SAC	Sudania Air Cargo	W/O	4.12.90 Nairobi
19378	672	321B	–	N455PA	Pan Am	06.02.68	OO-PSI, OO-PST, 5A-DJM, SU-BLK	National Overseas AL	Stored	Cairo
19379	677	321C	–	N475PA	Pan Am	21.02.68	YR-ABN	Air Afrique		TAROM W/O 17.8.95 N'Djamena, Chad
19380	525	323C	TC-18E	N7565A	ATASCO Leasing	23.12.76	81-0898	USAF	C	–
19381	610	323C	EC-18D	N7566A	American AL	12.10.66	81-0895	USAF	C	–
19382	627	323C	EC-18B	N7567A	American AL	02.10.67	81-0892	USAF	C	–
19383	641	323C	–	N7568A	American AL	02.11.67	–	Boeing	Stored	For KC-135 parts DMAFB
19384	647	323C	TC-18E	N7569A	American AL	21.11.67	81-0893	USAF	C	–
19410	599	348C	–	EI-APG	American AL	01.07.67	N8789R, CF-TAI, EI-APG, ST-AIM	DAS Air Cargo	W/O	10.9.82 Khartoum
19411	540	351C	–	N371US	Northwest Orient	30.09.67	N371US, YU-AGJ, N740FW, N851MA, 5X-JET	DAS Air Cargo	C	–
19412	563	351C	–	N372US	Northwest Orient	06.12.66	N372US, 9Y-TEE, 8P-CAC, N707DY, ST-APY	Trans Arabian AT	W/O	3.2.00 Lake Victoria
19413	581	047B	–	N3163	Western AL	13.05.67	–	Wicklund Aviation	Scr.	For KC-135 parts Van Nuys
19414	597	047B	–	N3164	Western AL	28.06.67	–	Wicklund Aviation	Scr.	For KC-135 parts Van Nuys
19415	601	399C	–	G-AVKA	Caledonian AW	13.07.67	N319F, CS-TBH, N106BV, 4K-AZ4, 9G-ALG, 9G-OOD, 5Y-BOR	First International AW	C	–
19416	556	365C	–	N737AL	Airlift Int	14.04.67	PH-TRW, G-ATZC, C-GFLG, PT-TCP	AeroBrasil	W/O	26.11.92 Manaus
19417	582	355C	–	N525EJ	ExecJet/Airlift	19.05.67	G-AYEX, N525EJ, N707HL, 67-19417	USAF	C	–
19433	534	385C	–	N8400	IntAirBahama leased	06.12.66	PP-VLI, N109BV, ET-AJZ	Ethiopian AL	W/O	25.3.91 Asmara by shelling
19434	566	351C	–	N373US	British Caledonian	20.03.67	C-GTAI, S2-ACA, N8090Q, OB-1400	E-Systems	Stored	Lima
19435	629	331C	–	N5774T	American AL	12.10.66	CC-CAF, CX-BPL, YV-671C, P4-OOO,	First International AW	W/O	24.1.97 Kinshasa
19436	606	131B	–	N6790T	TWA	01.08.67	–	TWA	Scr.	For KC-135 parts DMAFB
19438	615	047B	–	N3165	Western AL	18.08.67	–	Wicklund Aviation	Scr.	For KC-135 parts Van Nuys
19439	621	047B	–	N3166	Western AL	07.09.67	–	Western AL	W/O	31.3.71 Ontario, CA
19440	554	327C	–	N7100	Western AL	17.02.67	OD-AGW	TMA	W/O	7.7.81 Beirut wrecked by bomb
19441	548	373C	–	N371WA	Braniff AW	22.12.66	AP-AWV, S2-ABQ	TMA	W/O	4.4.80 Singapore
19442	609	373C	E-8	N370WA	World AW	03.08.67	OO-SBU, N760FW, 67-30054, 94-0285/WR	USAF Joint Stars	C	93rd ACW
19443	611	351C	–	N374US	Northwest Orient	15.04.71	CC-CCK, 902 Chile AF	Chilean AF	C	Grupo 10
19498	645	336C	–	G-ATWV	BOAC	12.08.67	9G-ACX, N14AZ, 5Y-BNJ	Aero Zambia	Stored	Johannesburg
19502	551	358B	–	4X-ATS	El Al	02.02.67	N898WA	Omega Air	Stored	DMAFB
19515	608	323C	–	N7595A	American AL	15.08.67	OD-AHD	Air Gulf Falcon	Stored	Damaged, Beirut
19516	612	323C	–	N7596A	American AL	23.08.67	OD-AHE	Air Gulf Falcon	Stored	Athens
19517	614	323C	–	N7597A	American AL	28.08.67	PT-TCL, 4X-AOY, 7P-LAN, N29AZ, CC-CDI, N29AZ, ZS-IJI	Inter-Air leased	C	–
19518	616	323C	EC-18B	N7598A	American AL	31.08.67	81-0891	USAF	C	Edwards AFB
19519	619	323C	–	N7599A	American AL	11.09.67	PT-TCK, N5065T, 3D-ASB, 9G-OLU, 9Q-CKB, EL-RDS, 9G-AYO, HS-TFS, TN-AGO	Trans World Leasing	Stored	Lubumbashi, Congo, damaged
19521	584	328C	–	F-BLCG	Air France	03.06.67	SU-DAB, ST-AKR, XT-BBF, HB-IEI, 5B-DAZ, 4K-BEK, 9G-ROX	Avistar	W/O	7.2.99 Bratislava

Con. No.	L/n	Built as	Cvt to	1st Regn	For	Del date	Other Registrations	Last user	Fate	Location
19522	596	328C	–	F-BLCH	Air France	29.06.67	AF615/ZS-LSI	South African AF	C	60 Sqn
19523	624	047B	–	N3167	Western AL	20.09.67	5V-TAD, N3833C	Togo Govmt	Scr.	Tuscon by 1996
19529	632	327C	–	N7102	Braniff AW	10.10.67	9M-AQB, N707AD, PT-TCJ, 80065	USAF	C	–
19530	635	327C	–	N7103	Braniff AW	18.10.67	9V-BDC, N707ME, B-2424, CC-CYA, YR-JCA	JARO (Comtran)	C	–
19531	646	327C	–	N7104	Braniff AW	20.11.67	OD-AGZ, ET-AIV, 9Q-CGC	Congo Govt	W/O	14.4.00 Kinshasa by explosion
19566	717	331C	TC-18E	N15710	TWA	26.06.68	N132EA, 84-1399	USAF	Stored	
19567	720	331C	–	N15711	TWA	27.06.68	–	TWA	Stored	For KC-135 parts DMAFB
19568	669	131B	–	N16738	TWA	11.03.68	–	TWA	Scr.	For KC-135 parts DMAFB
19569	680	131B	–	N16739	TWA	08.03.68	–	TWA	Scr.	For KC-135 parts DMAFB
19570	674	331B	–	N28724	TWA	16.02.68	N7232X, OK-XFJ, LZ-PVB, N7232X	IAL AS ret Florida	Scr.	c. 1996 Tuscon
19571	685	331B	–	N28726	TWA	27.03.68	–	Av Technical Supp	Scr.	4.84 Waco
19572	687	331B	–	N28727	TWA/ARAMCO	22.03.68	N7231T	IAL/Independent Air	W/O	8.2.89 Santa Maria, Azores
19573	704	331B	–	N28728	TWA	07.05.68	–	Av Technical Supp	Scr.	4.84 Waco
19574	710	323C	E-8	N8411	TWA	21.05.68	N707MR , 86-0417	USAF/Army Joint St	Scr.	Melbourne FL by 2000
19575	714	323C	–	N8412	American AL	04.06.68	HK-2842X, HP-1028, FAP319	Peru Air Force	C	–
19576	719	323C	–	N8413	American AL	17.06.68	AP-BBK	PIA	Stored	Karachi
19577	722	323C	–	N8414	American AL	26.06.68	ZS-LSH, 9Q-CSZ, 9Q-CKK	Zaire AL	Stored	Damaged, Kinshasa since 1997
19578 to 19580		323C	–	N8415 to N8417	American AL, cancelled	–	–	–	–	
19581	638	323C	EC-18B	N8401	American AL	31.10.67	81-0896	USAF	C	Edwards AFB
19582	639	323C	–	N8402	American AL	27.10.67	EL-GNU, N751MA	N751MA	W/O	22.10.96 Manta, Ecuador
19583	650	323C	–	N8403	American AL	31.10.67	81-0894	USAF	C	–
19584	663	323C	–	N8404	American AL	27.10.67	4K-401	Azerbaijan AL	W/O	30.11.95 Baku, Azerbaijan
19585	668	323C	–	N8405	American AL	28.11.67	P4-CCC, XA-MAS, XA-ABU	Mexicargo	Stored	Tuscon
19586	670	323C	–	N8406	American AL	11.01.68	CP-1698, PP-BRG	Beta Cargo	C	–
19587	686	365C	–	N8408	American AL	26.02.68	N705PC, F-GHFT, 9G-ADS	Mexicargo	C	–
19588	692	338C	–	N8409	American AL	26.02.68	OD-AHB	MEA	W/O	8.1.87 Beirut by mortars
19589	701	338C	–	N8410	American AL	15.03.68	OD-AHC	USAF	Stored	–
19590	654	338C	–	G-ATZD	British Eagle Int	04.04.68	VR-BCP, 5A-DJV, SU-DAI, 5N-AOO, OO-CDE, JY-AJM, LV-WXL	Argentine AF	C	–
19621	652	338C	E-8	VH-EAA	Qantas	26.04.68	OO-YCK, P2-ANB, TF-AEB, 5Y-AXA, N733Q, N526SJ, 90-0175	USAF	C	93rd ACW
19622	660	338C	E-8	VH-EAB	Qantas	21.12.67	OO-YCL, P2-ANA, TF-AEC, SU-DAE, ST-ALL, 5B-DAY, N4131G, 92-3289/WR	USAF Joint Stars	C	93rd ACW
19623	671	338C	E-8	VH-EAC	Qantas	08.12.67	G-BDKE, C-GRYN, A20-623	USAF	C	93rd ACW
19624	689	338C	E-8	VH-EAD	Qantas	10.01.68	A20-624	USAF	C	93rd ACW
19625	693	338C	–	VH-EAE	Qantas	05.02.68	G-BFLD, N862BX, 5N-BBD	Oil Prod Maint	Scr.	Manston
19626	703	338C	E-8	VH-EAF	Qantas	27.03.68	HL7432, N770JS, 86-0416	USAF/Grumman	C	Demonstrator
19627	707	338C	–	VH-EAG	Qantas	04.04.68	A20-627	RAAF	Stored	33 Sqn, Richmond
19628	716	338C	–	VH-EAH	Qantas	04.05.68	HL7433, TF-IUD, 5A-DTF	Uganda AL	Stored	Tripoli
19629	737	338C	–	VH-EAI	Qantas	16.05.68	G-BDLM, A20-629	RAAF	C	33 Sqn, Richmond
19630	746	338C	–	VH-EAJ	Qantas	12.06.68	N376US, 9Y-TEK, 8P-CAD, N707KV, 5X-ARJ, ST-ANP	TAAT	W/O	17.10.88 Rome
19631	634	351C	–	N375US	Northwest Orient	22.08.68	5Y-BBJ	Botswana Govt	Stored	Derelict, Manston
19632	649	351C	–	N376US	Northwest Orient	21.11.67	5Y-BBI	TAAT	C	8.99 Damaged Sudan
19633	690	351C	–	N377US	Northwest Orient	14.10.67	AP-BAA, 6819635 (Pak. AF)	Pakistan AF	Stored	Police ground trainer, Botswana
19634	695	351C	–	N378US	Northwest Orient	21.11.67	AP-AZW	PIA	Stored	Nairobi
19635	706	351C	–	N379US	Northwest Orient	26.03.68	PH-TRF, N526EJ, G-AXRS, 5N-AOQ, TF-VLX, 5N-VRG	IAT Cargo	C	–
19636	731	351C	–	N380US	Northwest Orient	29.03.68	CC-CEJ, N1181Z	PIA	Scr.	Karachi by 12.93
19664	643	355C	–	N526EJ	Executive Jet	10.05.68	–	Summit Aviation (lsd)	W/O	14.11.98 Ostend
19693	673	321B	–	N491PA	Pan Am	24.07.68	N498GA, N808ZS	Jet Cargo Liberia	Scr.	For KC-135 parts DMAFB
19694	678	321B	–	N492PA	Pan Am	09.11.67	–	Pan Am	Scr.	12.84 New York
19695	684	321B	–	N493PA	Pan Am	08.02.68	–	Jet Cargo	Stored	Monrovia, Liberia
19696	688	321B	–	N494PA	Pan Am	22.02.68	–	Pan Am	W/O	12.12.68 nr Caracas, Venezuela 51(i) cr into sea
19697	694	321B	–	N495PA	Pan Am	14.03.68	–	Ledbetter PA Leasing	Scr.	For KC-135 parts DMAFB
19698	697	321B	–	N496PA	Pan Am	28.03.68	–	Ledbetter PA Leasing	Stored	For NASM At Pima, AZ
19699	699	321B	–	N497PA	Pan Am	09.04.68	–	Ledbetter PA Leasing	Scr.	For KC-135 parts DMAFB
19705	675	344C	–	ZS-EUW	South African AW	17.04.68	–	SAA	W/O	20.4.68 Windhoek
19706	691	344C	ELINT	ZS-EUX	South African AW	24.04.68	ZS-SAF, LX-LGT, OO-SJR, JY-AFR, ZS-LSL, 3D-ASC, AF623	SAAF	C	60 Sqn
19715	642	373C	–	N369WA	World AW	22.02.68	AP-AWE, N369WA, HL7412	Korean AL	W/O	2.8.76 near Teheran
19716	644	373C	–	N368WA	World AW	02.04.68	AP-AWD, HL7425, FAC1201	Colombian AF	C	Presidential squadron
19723	665	328C	Tanker	F-BLCI	Air France	07.11.67	–	SAAF	C	60 Sqn
19724	667	328C	–	F-BLCJ	Air France	13.11.67	ZS-LSJ, AF-617	Air France	W/O	5.3.68 Guadeloupe
19736	696	360C	–	ET-ACD	Ethiopian AL	17.01.68	–	Ethiopian AL	W/O	19.11.77 Rome
19737	713	312B	–	9V-BBA	Malaysia-Singap	24.01.68	4R-ALB	Tradewinds	Scr.	3.82 Shannon
19738	725	312B	–	9M-AOT	Malaysia-Singap	08.04.68	9V-BFB, 4R-ALA	GPA	Scr.	8.83 Shannon
19739	765	312B	–	9V-BBB	Malaysia-Singap	28.05.68	N600CS, 5V-TAG	Togo Govt	W/O	21.9.00 Niamey, Niger

Con. No.	L/n	Built as	Cvt to	1st Regn	For	Del date	Other Registrations	Last user	Fate	Location
19740	676	382B	–	CS-TBC	TAP	03.07.68	MM62148, (14-01)	Italian AF	C	8°Gruppo
19741	681	359B	–	HK-1402	Avianca	09.12.68	–	Avianca	Scr.	23.6.93 Miami
19760	715	384C	–	SX-DBD	Olympic AW	19.02.68		Venezuelan AF	C	–
19767	659	399C	–	G-AVTW	Caledonian AW	07.03.68	CS-TBI, HI-442, HI-442CT, N382US	Dominicana	Derelict	Santo Domingo
19773	705	351C	–	N382US	Northwest Orient	05.06.68	CN-RMB, N149DM, PT-WSM	Skymaster AL	Stored	Sao Paulo Viracopos
19774	708	351C	–	N383US	Northwest Orient	29.12.67	CN-RMC, XA-TDZ, PT-WSY, N677R, PP-BRH	Omega	C	–
19775	729	351C	–	N384US	Northwest Orient	03.05.68	SU-BAO, SU-EAA	Misrair Overseas	Stored	Cairo
19776	732	351C	–	N385US	Northwest Orient	14.05.68	S2-ACE, N8091J, PP-BRI	Beta Cargo	Stored	Sao Paulo Viracopos
19777	740	351C	–	N386US	Omega Air	18.07.68	7O-ABY	Alyemda	Stored	Aden
19789	698	311C	–	CF-FAN	Wardair	29.07.68	9K-ACX, N524SJ, N715FW	Florida West AL	Scr.	96 Miami
19809	657	368C	–	HZ-ACC	Saudia	14.05.68	N1486B, A20-809	Boeing Military	Stored	RAAF Richmond for spares
19810	664	368C	–	HZ-ACD	Saudia	17.04.68	N1763B	Boeing Military	Scr.	For KC-135 parts DMAFB
19820	709	379C	–	ET-ACQ	Ethiopian AL	08.01.68	–	Ethiopian AL	W/O	25.7.90 Addis Ababa
19821	718	379C	–	G-AWHU	Varig	19.01.68	9Q-CKI, VNB3415 , VN83415, 5X-JEF, ST-GLD, 9G-OLF, 9G-ONE, 9G-WON, 5X-JEF, 5X-GLA	Great Lakes AW	C	–
19822	726	379C	–	PP-VJK	Varig	20.05.68	–	Varig	W/O	3.1.87 Abidjan, Ivory Coast
19840	679	345C	–	N7321S	Seaboard World	27.06.68	PP-VJY, FAB2401	Brazil AF	C	–
19841	683	345C	–	N7322S	Seaboard World	04.11.68	PP-VJZ	Varig	W/O	11.7.73 Paris
19842	712	345C	–	PP-VJX	Varig	26.02.68	FAB2402	Brazil AF	C	–
19843	735	336C	–	G-AVBP	BOAC	06.03.68	SU-DAC, SU-PBA	Air Memphis	W/O	10.3.98 Mombassa
19844	744	366C	–	SU-AOU	United Arab AL	06.08.68	9Q-CJM, 9Q-CRA, 9Q-CKG	Congo AL	C	–
19845	809	366C	–	SU-AOW	United Arab AL	13.08.68	–	Egyptair	W/O	5.12.72 near Cairo, by missile?
19866	738	340C	–	AP-AVL	PIA	26.02.68	YU-AGD, AP-AWY, 68-19866	Pakistan Air Force	C	5.96
19869	700	324C	–	N47331	Continental AL	26.05.69	PP-VLM, N112HM, S7-2HM, TC-GHA, N707EL, D2-TOK	Angola Air Charter	Stored	Luanda
19870	702	324C	–	N47332	Continental AL	26.08.68	PP-VLK, FAB2404	Brazil AF	Stored	Rio-Gallegos
19871	711	324C	–	N67333	Continental AL	18.04.68	PP-VLL, N114HM, S7-4HM, TC-GHB, D2-TON	Angola Air Chart	Stored	Luanda
19872	742	351B	–	N381US	Northwest Orient	24.04.68	5Y-BBK	Kenya AW	W/O	11.7.89 Addis Ababa
19916	762	328C	–	F-BLCK	Air France	16.05.68	SU-DAA, SU-PBB	Air Memphis	C	–
19917	763	328C	Tanker	F-BLCL	Air France	28.08.68	ZS-LSK, AF619	South African AF	C	60 Sqn
19961	754	387C	–	LV-JGR	Aerolineas Argentinas	04.12.68	–	Aerolineas Argentinas	W/O	27.1.86 Buenos Aires
19962	755	387C	–	LV-JGP	Aerolineas Argentinas	10.12.68	TC-93, VR-21	Argentine AF	Stored	10.96 El Palomar AB
19963	723	347C	–	N1501W	Western AL	04.11.68	D2-TOL	Angola Air Chart	Stored	Luanda
19964	733	347C	–	N1502W	Western AL	04.11.68	TF-VLG, N1502W, EI-BLC, N707PD, B-2425, TT-WAB, TT-EAP, HR-AMA, 9J-AFT, ZS-NLJ, EL-AKU	Impala Cargo, Occidental AL leased	Scr.	2001 Manston
19965	734	347C	–	N1503W	Western AL	22.06.68	D2-TOM	TAAG Angola	W/O	10.10.88 Luanda
19966	743	347C	–	N1504W	Western AL	25.07.68	OD-AGU, C5-MBM, C5-MBM	Mahfooz Avtn	C	–
19967	745	347C	–	N1505W	Western AL	29.07.68	OD-AGV, SU-PBC	Air Memphis	C	–
19969	751	382B	–	CS-TBD	TAP	10.09.68	9T-MSS	Zaire Gvmt	Stored	Lisbon
19986	730	355C	E-8	F-BJCM	Air France	19.09.68	N723GS, EL-AIY, N707MB, 97-0100	USAF-Joint Stars	C	–
19988	736	337C	–	VT-DXT	Air India	14.10.68	K-2899	Indian AF	C	Air Research and Development unit
19996	748	329C	–	OO-SJL	Sabena	12.12.68	N3238N, LX-N19996	NATO	Scr.	12.98
19997	747	307C	–		West German AF	19.08.68	LX-N19997	NATO	C	NATO AFW Force
19998	750	307C	E-8		West German AF	30.09.68	99-0006	USAF-Joint Stars	Stored	For conversion
19999	756	307C	–		West German AF	30.09.68	3D-SGF, 5Y-GFF, ST-AQI, 3D-JAA	Air Gulf Falcon	C	–
20000	759	307C	–		West German AF	15.10.68	LX-N20000	NATO	C	NATO AFW Force
20008	739	320C	–	N707N	Boeing, to Varig	31.10.68	PP-VJH, FAB2403	Brazil AF	C	–
20016	752	321C	–	N870PA	Pan American	18.11.68	9K-ACS, N146SP, N527SJ, 68-11174, 95-0121	USAF-Joint Star	C	–
20017	753	321C	E-8	N871PA	Pan American	03.10.90	JY-AES, N710FW, N202DJ, N710FW, N517MA, PT-MTE, OB-1716	Cielos del Peru	C	–
20018	761	321C	–	N872PA	Pan American	12.12.68	9K-ACU, S2-ACK, PT-TCR	Transbrazil	Stored	For KC-135 parts DMAFB
20019	767	321B	–	N880PA	Pan American	25.10.68	–	Pan American	Stored	For KC-135 parts DMAFB
20020	768	321B	–	N881PA	Pan American	22.11.68	–	US Leasing Corp	Scr.	For KC-135 parts DMAFB
20021	769	321B	–	N882PA	Pan American	10.12.68	CC-CEI	LAN Chile	W/O	23.6.90 CAM Benitez Airport Santiago
20022	774	321B	–	N883PA	Pan American	13.12.68	N730Q, CC-CYB, YR-JCB, JY-JAA	Jordan Avtn	C	–
20023	775	321B	–	N884PA	Pan American	17.12.68	–	Aviation Traders	Scr.	Stansted after 12.82
20024	776	321B	–	N885PA	Pan American	18.12.68	N728Q, N707KS, D2-MAN	US Leasing Corp	Stored	For KC-135 parts DMAFB
20025	780	321B	–	N886PA	Pan American	08.01.69	N728Q, N707KS, D2-MAN	British Columbia Mngmt	C	–
20026	781	321B	–	N887PA	Pan American	10.01.69	N160GL	Global Int AL	Stored	For KC-135 parts DMAFB
20027	782	321B	–	N890PA	Pan American	24.01.69	9Y-TEX, N2213E	Omega Air	Scr.	For KC-135 parts DMAFB
20028	783	321B	–	N891PA	Pan American	31.01.69	9Y-TEZ, N3127K, VR-CBN, N320MJ	Omega Air	W/O	20.9.90 Marana, AZ

Con. No.	L/n	Built as	Cvt to	1st Regn	For	Del date	Other Registrations	Last user	Fate	Location
20029	790	321B	T/T	N892PA	Pan American	06.02.69	N729Q, EL-AKS, N707AR	Omega Air	C	Tanker/transport
20030	791	321B	–	N893PA	Pan American	06.02.69	–	CAAC	Stored	Tianjin, China ground trainer
20031	792	321B	–	N894PA	Pan American	04.03.69	N731Q	Jetran	Scr.	2.88 Philadelphia
20032	793	321B	–	N895PA	Pan American	14.03.69	N895SY	Jetran	Scr.	82
20033	797	321B	–	N896PA	Pan American	23.06.69	HC-BHY	AECA AL	Stored	San Antonio
20034	798	321B	–	N897PA	Pan American	14.03.69	N732Q	JARO leased	Stored	Quito
20035	770	384B	–	SX-DBE	Olympic AW	23.06.69	N6504K, EL-AKB	Guyana AW leased	Stored	to be scrapped
20036	778	384B	–	SX-DBF	Olympic AW	31.03.69	N7158T	Omega Air	Stored	For KC-135 parts DMAFB
20043	786	396C	–	N1786B	Boeing, to Wardair	19.12.68	CF-ZYP, OE-IDA, 85-6973	USAF-Joint Stars	C	–
20056	771	131B	–	N86740	TWA	23.01.69	–	Montana Flug	Scr.	5.96
20057	777	131B	–	N86741	TWA	23.06.69	–	TWA	Stored	For KC-135 parts DMAFB
20058	766	331B	–	N8729	TWA	08.01.69	–	TWA	Stored	For KC-135 parts DMAFB
20059	772	331B	–	N8730	TWA	23.01.69	–	TWA	Stored	For KC-135 parts DMAFB
20060	773	331B	–	N8731	TWA	12.12.68	N708A, N275B, T.17-1	Spanish Air Force	C	451 Esc.
20061	784	331B	–	N8732	TWA	15.01.69	–	TWA	Stored	For KC-135 parts DMAFB
20062	785	331B	–	N8733	TWA	03.03.69	–	Carefree/Worldwd	Stored	For KC-135 parts DMAFB
20063	789	331B	–	N8734	TWA	07.03.69	–	TWA	W/O	8.9.74 Aegean Sea by bomb
20064	799	331B	–	N8735	TWA	02.04.69	–	Carefree/Worldwd	Scr.	For KC-135 parts DMAFB
20065	802	331B	–	N8736	TWA	07.04.69	–	TWA	Stored	For KC-135 parts DMAFB
20066	810	331B	–	N8737	TWA	01.05.69	–	Chopper Air	Scr.	For KC-135 parts DMAFB
20067	812	331B	–	N8738	TWA	07.05.69	–	TWA	Stored	For KC-135 parts DMAFB
20068	814	331C	–	N15712	TWA	12.06.69	–	TWA	W/O	14.9.72 San Francisco
20069	815	331C	–	N15713	TWA	17.06.69	N345FA, CC-CUE, N234FA, TC-GHA, PP-AJP, P4-YYY, 9G-FIA	First International AW	C	–
20076	721	372C	–	N738AL	Airlift Int	02.07.69	LV-LGO, TC-94 (Arg. AF), TC-93, LV-LGO	LADE	Stored	Buenos Aires
20077	728	372C	–	N739AL	Airlift Int	16.07.69	LV-LGP, TC-92,	Argentine Air Force	W/O	23.10.96 Buenos Aires
20084	758	369C	–	9K-ACJ	Kuwait AW	14.06.68	N525SJ, N851JB, OB-1699, PT-MTR	Skymaster AL	C	–
20085	760	369C	–	9K-ACK	Kuwait AW	11.07.68	N147SP, N720FW, N528SJ, 5N-TNO	Air Atlantic Cargo	Stored	Miami
20086	764	369C	–	9K-ACL	Kuwait AW	04.11.68	ST-AIX	Sudan AW	Scr.	–
20087	724	323C	–	N8415	American AL	14.11.68	SU-FAC	Misrair Overseas	Stored	Cairo
20088	727	323C	–	N8416	American AL	25.11.68	PT-TCN, PP-BRR	BETA Cargo	C	–
20089	741	323C	–	N8417	American AL	05.07.68	G-AYZZ, N8417	Red Apple Aviation Services	Stored	For KC-135 parts DMAFB
20097	779	358B	Tanker	4X-ATT	El Al	17.07.68	TF-AYF	Jet Av Comp & AC	Stored	For KC-135 parts DMAFB
20110	800	344C	–	ZS-SAG	South African	30.08.68	VP-WGA, 4X-BYQ, 4X-JYQ, 242	Israel AF	C	120 Sqn
20122	807	358C	–	4X-ATX	El Al	22.01.69	9Q-CVG	Congo AL	Scr.	Kinshasa
20123	788	330C	–	D-ABUJ	Lufthansa	17.04.69	A6-DPA, P4-AKW, ST-AKW	AZZA Transport	C	–
20124	806	330C	707RE	D-ABUO	Lufthansa	15.05.69	N707HE	Omega Air	C	With JT8D-219s
20136	803	382B	–	CS-TBE	TAP	27.02.69	D2-TOP	TAAG Angola	Stored	Luanda
20170	795	323B	–	N8431	American AL	08.05.69	N708PC, OD-AHF, 5Y-GFH	Air Gulf Falcon	C	–
20171	796	323B	–	N8432	American AL	28.04.69	N910PC	Ports of Call	Scr.	9.86 Waco, TX
20172	804	323B	–	N8433	American AL	09.04.69	N161GL, N711PC, C5-BIN	Bin Mahfooz Avtn	C	–
20173	805	323B	–	N8434	American AL	16.04.69	–	Global Int leased	W/O	4.12.82 Brasilia
20174	808	323B	–	N8435	American AL	30.04.69	N145SP, 4X-ATG	Seagreen AT	Stored	El Paso
20175	811	323B	–	N8436	American AL	09.05.69	N709PC	Aviation Consultants	Derelict	Shannon
20176	817	323B	–	N8437	American AL	23.05.69	N712PC, C5-AMM	Dala Air Services	C	–
20177	818	323B	–	N8438	American AL	13.06.69	N706PC, EL-AKC, C5-GOA, HR-AMW, EL-AKK, N706PC	Omega Air	Stored	Mojave
20178	820	323B	–	N8439	American AL	31.07.69	N457PC	Florida West AL	Scr.	94 Miami
20179	821	323B	–	N8440	American AL	19.08.69	S7-LAS, 5Y-BFF, N7158Z	Omega Air	Stored	For KC-135 parts DMAFB
20198	813	329C	–	OO-SJM	Sabena	09.09.69	PH-TVK, LX-N20198	NATO	Stored	Naples for scrapping
20199	816	329C	–	OO-SJN	Sabena	22.07.69	N3238S, LX-N20199	NATO	C	–
20200	828	329C	–	OO-SJO	Sabena	17.06.69	9Q-CBS, 9Q-CBW	Scibe Airlift	Stored	Southend
20224	749	3B4C	–	OD-AFB	MEA	22.07.69	–	MEA	W/O	12.6.82 Beirut by military action
20225	757	3B4C	–	OD-AFC	MEA	03.12.69	–	MEA	W/O	28.12.68 Beirut by military action
20230	819	344C	Phalcon	ZS-SAH	South African AW	18.11.68	4X-BYS, 4X-JYS/246	Israeli Air Force	Stored	Tel Aviv
20259	822	3B4C	–	OD-AFD	MEA	18.11.68	–	Air Gulf Falcon	C	–
20260	823	3B4C	–	OD-AFE	MEA	28.08.69	SU-BMV	Luxor Air	W/O	23.3.01 Monrovia, Liberia
20261	827	309C	–	B-1824	China AL	01.10.69	N707ZS, EL-ZGS	Jet Cargo	Stored	Dubai
20262	830	309C	–	B-1825	China AL	28.10.69	G-AZPW, AP-AWZ	China AL	W/O	27.2.80 Manila
20275	844	340C	–	AP-AWB	PIA	07.11.69	LX-LGS, JY-AFQ, ZS-LSF, EL-TBA, AF-621	PIA	W/O	26.11.79 near Jeddah
20283	831	344C	–	ZS-SAI	South African AW	18.12.69	N105BV, 85-6974	South African AF	Scr.	60 Sqn, reported for sale
20287	832	386C	–	EP-IRL	Iran Air	31.12.69	EP-IRL	Iran Air	C	–
20288	839	386C	–	EP-IRM	Iran Air	17.03.70	–	Iran Air	C	–
20297	836	382B	C-137C	CS-TBF	TAP	13.02.70	N105BV, 85-6974	USAF	Scr.	For parts 98
20298	840	382B	T/T	CS-TBG	TAP	25.03.70	MM62149 (14-02)	Italian AF	C	8° Gruppo
20301	835	358C	–	4X-ATY	El Al	26.01.70	N707WJ, OB-1592, ARC-001	Colombian AF	C	Colombian AF seized
20315	824	CC-137	347C	13701	Canadian Air Force	25.02.70	N803CK, HR-AMN, N108RA, CX-BSI, XA-ABG	Mexicargo	Stored	Tuscon

Con. No.	L/n	Built as	Cvt to	1st Regn	For	Del date	Other Registrations	Last user	Fate	Location
20316	825	CC-137	E-8C	13702	Canadian Air Force	28.02.70	N1785B, HR-AMF, 96-0043	USAF	C	USAF Joint-STARS
20317	826	CC-137	E-8C	13703	Canadian Air Force	04.03.70	97-0200	USAF	C	USAF Joint-STARS
20318	829	CC-137	E-8C	13704	Canada Air Force	10.03.70	97-0201	USAF	C	USAF Joint-STARS
20319	833	CC-137	E-8C	13705	Canada Air Force	11.05.70	96-0042	USAF	C	Under conversion, Melbourne FL
20340	842	359B	–	HK-1410	Avianca	24.04.70	N22055	Enterprise Air	Scr.	7.94 Bogota
20341	834	366C	–	SU-APD	United Arab AL	16.01.70	–	Egyptair	C	–
20342	837	366C	–	N4094B	United Arab AL	24.03.70	SU-APE	Egyptair	W/O	17.10.82 Geneva
20374	838	336C	–	G-AXGW	BOAC	06.03.70	7O-ACO	Yemenia	Scr.	5.96 Aden
20375	841	336C	–	G-AXGX	BOAC	25.03.70	A7-AAC, VR-BZA	–	C	USAF Joint-Stars
20395	848	330C	–	D-ABUY	Lufthansa	16.10.70	–	Lufthansa	W/O	26.7.79 Brazil
20428	845	331C	KC-707	N1793T	TWA	23.07.70	4X-BYY, 4X-JYY/250	Israeli Air Force	C	120 sqn
20429	846	331C	KC-707	N794TW	TWA	25.08.70	4X-BYB, 4X-JYU/248	Israeli Air Force	C	120 sqn
20439	–	-320B	–	–	Cancelled	–	–	–	–	–
20456	851	336B	–	G-AXXY	BOAC	18.02.71	4X-BMC, N343A, PT-TCQ	Transbrazil	Stored	DMAFB for KC-135 parts
20457	853	336B	–	G-AXXZ	BOAC	17.04.71	9G-ADB, TY-BBM, TY-BBR	Libyan Arab Airlines	W/O	13.6.85 Sebha, Libya
20474	843	3F9C	–	5N-ABJ	Nigeria AW	11.05.71	–	Equador Leasing	Scr.	98 Shannon
20477-79	–	-303C	–	–	Caribair	Cancelled	–	–	–	–
20487	847	340C	–	AP-AVZ	PIA	15.10.70	–	–	W/O	15.12.71 Urumchi, China
20488	849	340C	340C(Q)	AP-AWA	PIA	23.12.70	AP-AXG, G-AZRO	PIA	Stored	Karachi
20494	850	3D3C	–	JY-ADO	Alia Jordanian	08.04.72	JY-ADO	Alia Jordanian	W/O	22.1.73 Kano, Nigeria
20495	852	3D3C	–	JY-ADP	Alia Jordanian	31.10.73	71-1841, 95-0122	USAF-Joint Stars	C	–
20514	857	3F5C	T/T	CS-DGI	Portugal Govt.	23.09.71	8801 (Port. AF), CS-TBT, MM62150 (14-03)	Italian AF	C	8° Gruppo
20515	859	3F5C	T/T	CS-DGJ	Portugal Govt.	14.12.71	8802 (Port. AF), CS-TBU, MM62151(14-04)	Italian AF	C	8° Gruppo
20516	–	3F5C	–	–	Portugal Govt.	Cancelled	–	–	–	–
20517	854	336C	–	G-AYLT	BOAC	28.05.71	9Q-CLY, SU-DAD, VR-HHK, 9G-TWO, 5Y-SIM, 3D-SGG, 5Y-GFG	Air Gulf Falcon	Stored	Sharjah
20518	856	EC-137D	E-3A	71-1407	Boeing	18.02.72	–	AWACS test	REBUILT	rebuilt as 898
20518	898	E-3A	E-3C	71-1407	USAF	23.10.78	–	USAF	C	3rd Wg
20519	858	EC-137D	E-3A	71-1408	Boeing	23.2.72	–	AWACS test	REBUILT	rebuilt as 920
20519	920	E-3A	E-3C	71-1408	USAF	15.12.78	–	USAF	C	552 ACW
20522	855	3B5C	–	HL7406	Korean AL	06.08.71	–	–	W/O	29.11.87 by bomb
20546	860	369C	–	9K-ACM	Kuwait AW	15.01.72	N523SJ, 5X-JON	Air Afrique leased	W/O	30.6.96 Bamako, Mali
20547	861	369C	–	9K-ACN	Kuwait AW	25.02.72	7O-ACS, EL-ALG, EL-ACP, CC-?	Pacific AL Chile	C	–
20629	863	3H7C	–	TJ-CAA	Cameroon AL	20.11.72	4X-BYR, 4X-JYB/255	Israeli Air Force	C	–
20630	862	VC-137B	–	72-7000	USAF	09.08.72	N8459	USAF	Stored	For museum, Santa Barbara, CA
20669	864	3F9C	–	5N-ABK	Nigeria AW	16.01.73	–	–	W/O	19.12.94 Hadejia Town, Nigeria
20714	869	3J6B	–	B-2402	CAAC	23.08.73	–	China Southwest	W/O	2.10.90 Canton by crashing 737
20715	870	3J6B	VIP	B-2404	CAAC	17.09.73	D2-TPR	–	C	–
20716	880	3J6B	–	B-2406	CAAC	15.04.74	4X-BYN, 4X-JYN/260	Israeli Air Force	C	–
20717	882	3J6B	–	B-2408	CAAC	10.05.74	N717QS	Quiet Skies	C	–
20718	872	3J6C	–	B-2410	CAAC	12.11.73	B-513L, A6-ZYD	Air Gulf Falcon	C	–
20719	873	3J6C	E-8	B-2412	CAAC	22.11.73	N719QS	USAF	Stored	Burbank for E-8 conversion
20720	874	3J6C	–	B-2414	CAAC	13.12.73	JY-AJN	Royal Jordanian	C	–
20721	875	3J6C	–	B-2416	CAAC	14.01.74	4X-JYH/264	Israeli AF	C	–
20722	877	3J6C	–	B-2418	CAAC	26.02.74	B-606L, 5X-TRA	Triangle AL	C	–
20723	879	3J6C	–	B-2420	CAAC	19.03.74	JY-AJO	Royal Jordanian	C	–
20741	866	386C	–	N1785B	Boeing, for Iran Air	01.05.73	EP-IRN	Iran Air	C	–
20760	865	366C	–	SU-AVX	Egyptair	30.03.73	–	Egyptair	W/O	22.8.96 Istanbul
20761	867	366C	–	SU-AVY	Egyptair	29.05.73	9Q-CKK, 9Q-CKB	Congo AL	C	–
20762	868	366C	–	SU-AVZ	Egyptair	29.06.73	–	Air Memphis	C	–
20763	871	366C	–	SU-AXA	Egyptair	20.09.73	–	Egyptair	W/O	25.12.76 Bangkok
20803	878	3K1C	–	YR-ABA	Tarom	21.02.74	–	–	C	–
20804	883	3K1C	–	YR-ABB	Tarom	03.06.74	–	Romavia	C	–
20805	884	3K1C	–	YR-ABC	Tarom	03.06.74	–	Tarom	C	–
20830	876	3J9C	–	N1790B	Boeing for Iran AF	29.05.74	5-241, 5-8301	Iran Air Force	C	13 TS
20831	881	3J9C	–	5-242	Iran Air Force	10.05.74	5-8302	Iran Air Force	C	13 TS
20832	886	3J9C	–	5-243	Iran Air Force	26.07.74	5-8303	Iran Air Force	C	13 TS
20833	890	3J9C	–	5-244	Iran Air Force	30.09.74	5-8304	Iran Air Force	C	13 TS
20834	894	3J9C	–	5-245	Iran Air Force	17.11.74	5-8305, EP-NHW	Iran Air Force	C	13 TS
20835	895	3J9C	–	5-246	Iran Air Force	16.12.74	5-8306, EP-SHP	Saha AL	C	–
20889	889	370C	–	YI-AGE	Iraqi AW	27.08.74	–	–	C	–
20890	891	370C	–	YI-AGF	Iraqi AW	23.09.74	JY-CAC, 4YB-CAC, 1002	Iran AF	C	13 TS
20891	892	370C	–	YI-AGG	Iraqi AW	07.10.74	–	–	Stored	Amman, Jordan
20897	885	3J8C	–	ST-AFA	Sudan AW	17.06.74		Sudan AW	C	–
20898	887	3J8C	–	ST-AFB	Sudan AW	10.07.74		Sudan AW	C	–

Con. No.	L/n	Built as	Cvt to	1st Regn	For	Del date	Other Registrations	Last user	Fate	Location
20919	888	366C	–	SU-AXJ	Egyptair	21.08.74		Egyptian Gvmt	C	–
20920	893	366C	–	SU-AXK	Egyptair	15.11.74	–		Scr.	–
21046	901	E-3A/B	E-3C	73-1674	Boeing	28.04.94			C	last 707 del, still based Seattle Boeing Field
21047	902	E-3A	–	75-0556	USAF	05.05.78			C	18th Wing
21049	896	3L6B	–	9M-TDM	Boeing, to Av Serv & Support	08.01.75	N62393, A6-HPZ, P4-TBN, 5V-TGE	Togo Govt.	C	–
21070	897	387B	387C	T-01	Argentine AF	11.06.75	TC-91	Argentine AF/LADE	C	–
21081	903	368C	–	HZ-HM1	Saudi Arab Govt.	25.09.75	HZ-HM2	Saudi Arab Govt.	C	–
21092	899	3M1C	–	PK-PJQ	Pelita AS	25.09.75	A-7002, PK-GAU	Indonesian AF	C	–
21096	900	3L6C	VIP	9M-TMS	Boeing	09.06.75	N48055, G-CDHW, A6-HRM, P4-MDJ, 4X-JYV/272	Israel AF	Scr.	–
21103	905	368C	–	HZ-ACG	Saudia	14.10.75	N1987B, A20-103	Australian Air Force	W/O	29.10.91 Bridgetown, NSW
21104	906	368C	–	HZ-ACH	Saudia	18.12.75	ST-DRS, N707MJ, P4-DRS	Comtran International	C	
21123	908	3J9C	–	5-247	Iran Air Force	27.02.76	5-8307, EP-SHF, EP-NHA	Saha AL	C	
21124	910	3J9C	–	5-248	Iran Air Force	14.06.76	5-8308	Iran Air Force	C	13 TS
21125	912	3J9C	–	5-249	Iran Air Force	18.06.76	5-8309, EP-SHG	Saha AL	C	
21126	914	3J9C	–	5-250	Iran Air Force	31.08.76	5-8310	Iran Air Force	C	13 TS
21127	915	3J9C	–	5-211	Iran Air Force	27.09.76	5-8311, EP-SHJ	Saha AL	C	
21128	917	3J9C	–	5-212	Iran Air Force	19.11.76	5-8312, EP-SHE, EP-SHK	Saha AL	C	
21129	918	3J9C	–	5-213	Iran Air Force	14.12.76	5-8313	Iran Air Force	W/O	
21185	904	E-3A	E-3B	73-1675	USAF	18.08.78	–	USAF	Stored	to 3rd wing 2002?
21207	907	E-3A	E-3B	75-0557	USAF	23.03.77	–	USAF	C	552 ACW
21208	909	E-3A	E-3B	75-0558	USAF	29.05.77	–	USAF	C	552 ACW
21209	913	E-3A	E-3B	75-0559	USAF	21.10.77	–	USAF	C	552 ACW
21228	911	3L5C	–	5A-DAK	Libyan Arab	19.07.76	–	Libyan Arab	C	
21250	916	E-3A	E-3B	75-0560	USAF	22.11.77	–	USAF	C	552 ACW
21251	919	368C	–	HZ-ACI	Saudia	23.12.76	N7486B, A20-261	Australian Air Force	C	33 Sqn
21334	923	3P1C	–	A7-AAA	Qatar Govt.	28.07.77		Israel Air Force	C	
21367	922	368C	–	HZ-ACJ	Saudia	04.04.77	N7667B, T.17-3	Spanish Air Force	C	451 Esc
21368	925	368C	–	HZ-ACK	Saudia	27.06.77	HZ-HM3	Saudi Arabian Govt.	C	
21396	928	386C	–	EP-HIM	Iranian Gvmt	03.05.78	1001, EP-NHY	Iran Air Force	C	13 TS
21428	929	3F9C	–	5N-ANO	Nigeria AW	30.01.78	–	Nigeria AW	Scr.	99 Dublin
21434	921	E-3A	E-3B	76-1604	USAF	19.01.78	–	USAF	C	552 ACW
21435	924	E-3A	E-3B	76-1605	USAF	25.05.78	–	USAF	C	552 ACW
21436	926	E-3A	E-3B	76-1606	USAF	22.06.78	–	USAF	C	552 ACW
21437	927	E-3A	E-3B	76-1607	USAF	29.09.78	–	USAF	C	552 ACW
21475	936	3J9C	–		Iran Air Force	20.12.78	2342787	Iran Air Force	C	13 TS
21551	930	E-3A	E-3B	77-0351	USAF	29.09.78	–	USAF	C	18th Wing
21552	931	E-3A	E-3B	77-0352	USAF	20.11.78	–	USAF	C	552 ACW
21553	932	E-3A	E-3B	77-0353	USAF	19.12.78	–	USAF	C	552 ACW
21554	933	E-3A	E-3B	77-0354	USAF	19.01.79	–	USAF	W/O	22.9.95 Elmendorf AFB
21555	934	E-3A	E-3B	77-0355	USAF	16.03.79	–	USAF	C	3rd Wing
21556	935	E-3A	E-3B	77-0356	USAF	22.05.79	–	USAF	C	552 ACW
21651	938	3K1C	-	YR-ABD	Romanian Gvmt	30.03.79	–	Tarom	W/O	10.1.91 Bucharest
21752	937	E-3A	E-3B	78-0576	USAF	14.09.79	–	USAF	C	552 ACW
21753	939	E-3A	E-3B	78-0577	USAF	20.12.79	–	USAF	C	552 ACW
21754	940	E-3A	E-3B	78-0578	USAF	03.06.80	–	USAF	C	552 ACW
21755	942	E-3A	E-3B	79-0001	USAF	18.09.80	–	USAF	C	552 ACW
21756	943	E-3A	E-3B	79-0002	USAF	19.12.80	–	USAF	C	552 ACW
21757	944	E-3A	E-3B	79-0003	USAF	19.03.81	–	USAF	C	552 ACW
21956	941	-700	-3W6C, KC-707	N707QT	Boeing CFM56 test	18.11.81	CN-ANR, CN-CCC, 4X-980, N707JU, 290/4X-980	Israel Air Force	C	–
22829	946	E-3A	E-3C	80-0137	USAF	10.03.82	–	USAF	C	552 ACW
22830	948	E-3A	E-3C	80-0138	USAF	04.12.81	–	USAF	C	552 ACW
22831	950	E-3A	E-3C	80-0139	USAF	06.04.82	–	USAF	C	552 ACW
22832	952	E-3A	E-3C	81-0004	USAF	23.07.82	–	USAF	C	552 ACW
22833	955	E-3A	E-3C	81-0005	USAF	19.10.82	–	USAF	C	18th Wing
22834	958	E-3C	–	82-0006	USAF	20.04.83	–	USAF	C	552 ACW
22835	960	E-3C	–	82-0007	USAF	29.07.83	–	USAF	C	552 ACW
22836	962	E-3C	–	82-0008	USAF	01.11.83	–	USAF	C	552 ACW
22837	965	E-3C	–	82-0009	USAF	18.04.84	–	USAF	C	552 ACW
22838	947	E-3A	–	79-0443	Boeing	19.06.84	LX-N90443	NATO	C	NATO AEW Force
22839	949	E-3A	–	79-0444	Boeing	19.05.82	LX-N90444	NATO	C	NATO AEW Force
22840	951	E-3A	–	79-0445	Boeing	19.08.82	LX-N90445	NATO	C	NATO AEW Force
22841	953	E-3A	–	79-0446	Boeing	12.11.82	LX-N90446	NATO	C	NATO AEW Force
22842	954	E-3A	–	79-0447	Boeing	10.03.83	LX-N90447	NATO	C	NATO AEW Force
22843	956	E-3A	–	79-0448	Boeing	05.06.83	LX-N90448	NATO	C	NATO AEW Force
22844	957	E-3A	–	79-0449	Boeing	27.06.83	LX-N90449	NATO	C	NATO AEW Force
22845	959	E-3A	–	79-0450	Boeing	19.08.83	LX-N90450	NATO	C	NATO AEW Force
22846	961	E-3A	–	79-0451	Boeing	12.10.83	LX-N90451	NATO	C	NATO AEW Force

Con. No.	L/n	Built as	Cvt to	1st Regn	For	Del date	Other Registrations	Last user	Fate	Location
22847	963	E-3A	–	79-0452	Boeing	20.10.84	LX-N90452	NATO	C	NATO AEW Force
22848	964	E-3A	–	79-0453	Boeing	27.04.84	LX-N90453	NATO	C	NATO AEW Force
22849	966	E-3A	–	79-0454	Boeing	18.05.84	LX-N90454	NATO	C	NATO AEW Force
22850	967	E-3A	–	79-0455	Boeing	02.11.84	LX-N90455	NATO	C	NATO AEW Force
22851	968	E-3A	–	79-0456	Boeing	11.02.85	LX-N90456	NATO	C	NATO AEW Force
22852	969	E-3A	–	79-0457	Boeing	07.11.84	LX-N90457	NATO	W/O	17.7.96 Preveza AFB Greece
22853	970	E-3A	–	79-0458	Boeing	19.12.84	LX-N90458	NATO	C	NATO AEW Force
22854	971	E-3A	–	79-0459	Boeing	18.03.85	LX-N90459	NATO	C	NATO AEW Force
22855	945	E-3A	–	79-0442	Boeing	30.04.85	LX-N90442	NATO	C	Special NATO anniversary colours
23417	972	E-3A	–	82-0066	Boeing	22.01.82	–	Saudi Air Force	C	18 Sqn
23418	973	E-3A	–	82-0067	Boeing	31.10.86	–	Saudi Air Force	C	18 Sqn
23419	974	E-3A	–	82-0068	Boeing	29.08.86	–	Saudi Air Force	C	18 Sqn
23420	976	E-3A	–	82-0069	Boeing	29.06.86	–	Saudi Air Force	C	18 Sqn
23421	980	E-3A	–	82-0070	Boeing	23.12.86	–	Saudi Air Force	C	18 Sqn
23422	975	KE-3A	–	82-0071	Boeing	02.05.87	–	Saudi Air Force	C	18 Sqn
23423	977	KE-3A	–	82-0072	Boeing	24.06.87	–	Saudi Air Force	C	18 Sqn
23424	978	KE-3A	–	82-0073	Boeing	02.03.87	–	Saudi Air Force	C	18 Sqn
23425	979	KE-3A	–	82-0074	Boeing	16.06.87	–	Saudi Air Force	C	18 Sqn
23426	981	KE-3A	–	82-0075	Boeing	12.02.87	–	Saudi Air Force	C	18 Sqn
23427	982	KE-3A	–	82-0076	Boeing	08.07.87	–	Saudi Air Force	C	18 Sqn
23428	984	KE-3A	RE-3A	83-0510	Boeing	11.06.87	1817, 1901	Saudi Air Force	C	19 Sqn
23429	985	KE-3A	–	83-0511	Boeing	16.09.87	–	Saudi Air Force	C	18 Sqn
23430	983	E-6A	–	162782	US Navy	13.08.87	–	US Navy	C	VQ-3
23889	986	E-6A	–	162783	US Navy	18.03.92	–	US Navy	C	VQ-3
23890	987	E-6A	–	162784	US Navy	07.09.89	–	US Navy	C	VQ-3
23891	988	E-6A	–	163918	US Navy	02.08.89	–	US Navy	C	VQ-3
23892	989	E-6A	–	163919	US Navy	02.08.89	–	US Navy	C	VQ-3
23893	990	E-6A	E-6B	163920	US Navy	01.10.89	–	US Navy	C	VQ-3
23894	991	E-6A	E-6B	164386	US Navy	18.12.89	–	US Navy	C	VQ-4
24109	993	E-3D	–	ZH101	Royal AF	13.07.90	–	Royal Air Force	C	Doc 8/23 Squadron
24110	996	E-3D	–	ZH102	Royal AF	22.05.91	–	Royal Air Force	C	Dopey 8/23 Squadron
24111	1004	E-3D	–	ZH103	Royal AF	25.03.91	–	Royal Air Force	C	Happy 8/23 Squadron
24112	1007	E-3D	–	ZH104	Royal AF	08.07.91	–	Royal Air Force	C	Sleepy 8/23 Squadron
24113	1010	E-3D	–	ZH105	Royal AF	19.09.91	–	Royal Air Force	C	Sneezy 8/23 Squadron
24114	1011	E-3D	–	ZH106	Royal AF	21.11.91	–	Royal Air Force	C	Grumpy 8/23 Squadron
24115	1000	E-3F	–	SDA201	French AF	09.03.92	F-ZBCA SDA 201	French AF	C	EDA-36
24116	1003	E-3F	–	SDA202	French AF	22.05.91	F-ZBCB SDA 202	French AF	C	EDA-36
24117	1006	E-3F	–	SDA203	French AF	23.07.91	F-ZBCC SDA 203	French AF	C	EDA-36
24499	1012	E-3D	–	ZH107	Royal AF	11.09.91	–	Royal AF	C	Bashful 8/23 Squadron
24500	992	E-6A	E-6B	164387	US Navy	12.05.92	–	US Navy	C	VQ-3
24501	994	E-6A	E-6B	164388	US Navy	12.04.90	–	US Navy	C	VQ-3
24502	995	E-6A	E-6B	164404	US Navy	29.08.90	–	US Navy	C	VQ-4
24503	1001	E-6A	YE-8B	88-0322	USAF	28.05.92	N707UM, 1902	Raytheon	C	
24504	997	E-6A	–	164405	US Navy	03.10.91	–	US Navy	C	VQ-4
24505	998	E-6A	E-6B	164406	US Navy	20.12.90	–	US Navy	C	VQ-4
24506	999	E-6A	–	164407	US Navy	25.04.91	–	US Navy	C	VQ-4
24507	1002	E-6A	E-6B	164408	US Navy	02.08.91	–	US Navy	C	NAWC-AD
24508	1005	E-6A	–	164409	US Navy	01.08.91	–	US Navy	C	VQ-4
24509	1008	E-6A	–	164410	US Navy	21.12.91	–	US Navy	C	VQ-4
24510	1009	E-3A	–	SDA204	French AF	15.02.92	F-ZBCD SDA 204	French AF	C	EDA-36

7 THE 707 TODAY

Within ten years of service entry, the 707 seemed a bit 'old hat' to some commentators. The Seattle *Register* wrote in 1969 that the Jet Stratoliner, 'the giant airplane that ushered in the Jet Age' was being 'superseded by giant air buses (*sic*) and supersonic transports just coming off the drawing boards'. Reports of the 707's demise were, needless to say, premature, although it was true that 747s would soon replace the smaller jet on major international routes with the main US and foreign carriers. Ironically, the *Register* article appeared next to one headlined 'Airport Officials Fear Boeing 747 Is Too Big', and the simple fact that the terminals and handling facilities (rather than the runways or ramps) remained inadequate for the 'jumbo' in many places kept the 707 in service for some time longer than anticipated, especially with the national airlines of less well-developed countries. The main threats to the 707 were in fact Boeing's own 727 and 737 as well as the Douglas DC-9, HS Trident and other short- to medium-range aircraft which offered jet speed and comfort at better seat-mile costs and lower purchase prices.

Twenty years after entry into service, many of the earliest 707-120s had been scrapped or were stored awaiting that fate, but a few had some life left in them. N711PA *Clipper Mayflower*, the first 707 to fly a revenue service on 26 October 1958, had been retired at Brussels, and its sister ship *Clipper Caroline*, which flew the second service the following day, was in a similar state in England. Both had logged 42,000 flying hours by that time. The number of 707s in US service was dropping rapidly by the late 1970s. In 1977 there were 219; five years earlier there had been 337.

Despite this, production of 707 airframes continued, albeit for military purposes. Finally in September 1991, Boeing announced that production was to come to an end after thirty-seven years with the delivery of the 1,010th airframe, an E-3D AWACS for the Royal Air Force, thus ending the longest continuous production run of any airliner airframe. The 840

BELOW: Since 1987, Allied Signal Aerospace has used this 720 (N720GT) as an engine testbed with a special mounting on the forward fuselage which keeps the fifth engine out of the influence of the airframe and vice versa. Engines tested to date include the Garrett TPF 351 and the TFE 731which is used on the Learjet 45. The 720 (c/n 18384) served with TWA, Northwest Orient, Maersk and Nigeria Airways in its time. *Peter J. Cooper*

Israel is the biggest user of the basic 707 for military duties, with aircraft in use as tankers, transports and for electronic intelligence (elint) missions. In 2002 plans were announced to equip most of the fleet with 'glass' cockpits. It also seems likely that the JT3D engines may be replaced by JT8D-219s engines supplied by the Seven Q Seven group. This aircraft was seen on a visit to RAF Waddington. *(Photo Graham Robson)*

BELOW: Omega Inc. operate the first and currently only commercially available aerial refuelling tanker on the market. N707AR is the former *Clipper Star King* and is seen here at Prestwick Airport in Scotland in June 2001, where it was supporting the USS *Enterprise* air wing in a Joint Maritime Course (JMC) exercise. This was the first time the US Navy had contracted a private company to provide such a service. Future conversions of some of Omega's many 707 airframes to tanker/transport configuration are likely. *Author*

ABOVE: Lasham, Southend and Manston airports in the UK have seen a number of 707s in short or long storage in recent years. Azerbijan Airlines stored two of the four 707s it acquired in the mid-1990s for some time at both Lasham and Southend. It was last seen operating for First International Airways as 9G-OOD. *Peter J. Cooper*

employees working on the AWACS programme were redeployed to other projects. Since 1991, the few large AWACS-type aircraft sold or ordered have been based on the 767 (Japan's E-767s) and 737 (Australia's 'Wedgetail' programme).

As the time came for many airlines to replace their 707s, Boeing was pressured into accepting the older airliners as trade-ins as part-payment for newer equipment. In 1982 they set up Boeing Used Aircraft and Sales in order to broker 707s and other obsolescent jetliners so that customers could purchase newer Boeings. Some of these aircraft were sold on to other operators, but most have found their way into a programme to extend the life of the 707's cousin, the KC-135 Stratotanker.

The search for a replacement for the many hundreds of KC-135s in USAF service was a troubled process in the 1970s and was only partially achieved by the 1977 decision to purchase sixty McDonnell Douglas KC-10s and to structurally upgrade 640 Stratotankers. Although the numbers involved have now fallen below 400 aircraft, the wing and tailplane modifications and the subsequent conversion to CFM-56 power of older KC-135s to create the KC-135R has resulted in a demand for common components from the 707 that could only be satisfied economically by buying and dismantling surplus airliners. As a result, the famous 'boneyard' at Davis Monthan AFB in Arizona, normally a home for dormant fighters and bombers, has seen dozens of 707s arrive since the early 1980s and slowly

come apart for components such as wing skins and control surfaces. Nearly 200 707s have met or await this fate at Davis Monthan or other locations under the USAF's KC-135 Re-engining and Spares Support Programme.

FILM PROPS

In addition to the many starring and cameo appearances in film and television the 707 made in its heyday, in more recent years it has proved useful to Hollywood producers looking for a 'modern' airliner, often to perform some indignity on. Credits include the original *Airport* film (1970) with N324F, a 707-349C (19354) of 'Trans Global Airlines' landing with bomb damage at a troubled airport, and the Chuck Norris pot-boiler *The Delta Force* filmed in Israel in 1985 with 'hijacked' 707-139B N778PA (17903) of 'American Travelways'. TWA loaned the makers of *Airplane* (1980) 707-131B N6721 to star as the 'Trans American' jet aboard which the flight crew all foolishly ate the fish. 'Hijacked' at least twice was N374WA (18583), once as a 'Global Airlines' jet in *Skyjacked* with Charlton Heston (1972) and later in Clint Eastwood's *Magnum Force* (1973) wearing 'Sovereign Airlines' titles. This film star among 707s also appeared in an episode of the *Charlie's Angels* TV series. Both 'Angel' Jaclyn Smith and a 707 appeared in the TV movie *Jacqueline Bouvier Kennedy*, the latter masquerading as a VC-137B. Several other 707s have briefly portrayed 'Air Force One' in various productions. Other roles include two 'BOAC' jets (G-BFBZ/18585 and G-BFBS/18693) in an episode of the British TV series *One By One* (*circa* 1986) and the film *Speed* (1994) in which 707-131 N6232G with dummy high-bypass fan engines and 'World Air Freight' colours is blown up by a runaway bus at Mojave Airport, standing in for Los Angeles International.

PRESERVATION

While there are many 707s around the world in various states of repair, only a small number have been actively preserved. The size of a 707 and the difficulties of moving and housing one, particularly at a non-airport location, have put off many private museums and groups from acquiring them, or other examples of the early jetliners. Several airframes that were preserved in parks and as ground trainers have been broken up in recent years as a result of corrosion or replacement by more modern aircraft.

While the 367-80 has found a secure place in the new Dulles Airport outstation of the National Air and Space Museum, efforts to save other early 707s for posterity have come to little. The first and third of Pan Am's -121s were lost in accidents but the second, N707PA *Clipper Maria* was stored at Miami from 1980 and offered perhaps the best chance of preserving a significant early 707. Despite plans to transfer it by barge to a museum in Connecticut, the financial problems of the sponsor, Pan Am, and other difficulties caused the dismantled airframe to be moved to 'Corrosion Corner' at Miami, and by 1988 it had been scrapped.

The possibility of restoring a 707-320 to flight condition and putting it on the airshow circuit, perhaps in the colours of a now-defunct airline such as Pan Am, has been considered, at least in theory, by enthusiasts. A group such as the Airline History Museum at Kansas City (also known as Save-A-Connie) who have already preserved a Super Constellation, Martin 4-0-4 and a DC-3 in flying condition would seem to be the ideal home for a flying 707, operated as a memorial to the beginnings of the jet age. The regular problems of space, money, labour and the need for a benefactor to donate a suitable airframe are likely to keep this idea but a dream for the foreseeable future.

ABOVE: Former El Al and Arika Israel Airlines 707-458 4X-ATB is now preserved at Berlin's Tegel Airport in *Lufthansa* colours as 'D-ABOC'. The real D-ABOC was scrapped at Tripoli in 1979. *Austin J. Brown, the Aviation Picture Library*

In 2001 there were estimated to be 185 707-300s, four 707-100s and five 720s in worldwide service, about seventy of them with airlines, the remainder with governments, engine manufacturers or in use as 'flying palaces' with Arab sheikhs and other wealthy owners. Perhaps the most famous 707 owner is the actor John Travolta, whose ex-Qantas 707-138B N707JT (18740) redefines the term 'business jet' and rattles the windows around its home at Van Nuys in greater Los Angeles, somewhat to the annoyance of the neighbours.

HUSHKITS

Increasing noise regulation forced large numbers of 707s from US skies from the mid-1980s. Re-engining 707 freighters was not seen as economic, especially as there were many stretched CFM-56-powered DC-8 freighters with more carrying capacity already out there. A cheaper alternative, although one that would only delay the inevitable as more stringent regulations were introduced, was to 'hushkit' the JT3Ds of most surviving 707s. Hushkits are modification packages, usually involving sound-deadening nacelle linings and lengthened exhaust ducts, that reduce the size of the aircraft noise 'footprint' measured around the airport. Comtran International of Texas offered the 'Super Q' conversion to allow 707s to meet Stage II/Chapter II regulations. Comtran has since joined with Rohr to develop a Stage III/Chapter III kit, as are the Quiet Technology Venture (QTV) company and Avacelle, the latter in association with Boeing. Delays in producing the Stage III hushkits have

ABOVE: This rather anonymous 707 (N88ZL) seen landing at Heathrow is a -330B belonging to Lowa, Inc., a Swiss-based company associated with Jet Aviation of Basel. This aircraft (now with Stage III hushkits) once flew with Lufthansa as D-ABUF Hanover. *Peter J. Cooper*

OPPOSITE ABOVE: Although there are a number of 707s in long-term storage in the UK, the only one actually preserved for display in the country is Conway-engined G-APFJ (c/n 17711) at the Royal Air Force Museum's Cosford outstation. Built for BOAC, it also served under the BOAC-Cunard, British Airways and British Airtours banners, as well as a period on lease to Malaysia-Singapore Airlines (MSA). In June 1981 it was delivered to Cosford's short runway and has been displayed outdoors ever since. British Airways contributes to the upkeep of 'FJ', a rare example of a major airline helping preserve its retired hardware. *John Myers*

OPPOSITE BELOW: Just like the previous generation of airliners, 707s retired by the major airlines have soldiered on as freighters, notably in South America and Africa. This 1968 model -323C went from American Airlines (as N8406) to Lloyd Aereo Boliviano as did two others. Seen at Miami in the early 1980s, CP-1698 was sold to Beta Cargo of Brazil and is still in service as PP-BRG. *Austin J. Brown, the Aviation Picture Library*

allowed 707 operators some dispensation to operate Stage II 707s until they can be converted.

Meanwhile, Omega Air, a joint US/Irish company, together with several other firms under the Seven Q Seven (SQS) banner has joined with Pratt & Whitney to offer the 707RE (Re-Engined). The prototype (N707HE/20124) flew at the end of July 2001 with four 21,000-lb st (93.4-kN) JT8D-219s, having previously tested a single engine alongside three JT3Ds. The new engine is that used on the MD-83 twinjet and is significantly cheaper than the 22,000-lb st (97.9-kN) CFM-56 and gives more power at altitude. The installation requires new pylons and cowl doors, which were supplied by Nordam. The result is an aircraft that meets Stage III requirements with a 10 DbA margin, has lower operating costs, lower emissions, improved fuel burn and less maintenance.

The 707RE was demonstrated to NATO leaders on a tour of Europe in late 2001. The consortium has high hopes that the conversion will be chosen for use on NATO and USAF E-3s, E-8s, RC-135s and older KC-135s as well as VIP and freighter 707s, a potential market of around 300 aircraft.

Omega Air today owns a fleet of over twenty 707s, although only a handful fly under the Omega name. Some are stored but most are leased out and operate under other banners. Omega's

best-known aircraft is N707AR (20029), once upon a time Pan Am's N892PA *Clipper Star King*. This 707-321B appeared at many international airshows as a concept demonstrator and 'flying hospitality chalet' for Omega's private tanker/transport conversion programme. Progressively modified with refuelling equipment, the 707AR (Airborne Refueller) was tested in its final configuration at Naval Air Station Patuxent River, Maryland in mid-2000 and cleared for use with all US Navy tactical aircraft. The refuelling system consists of two belly-mounted 95 ft (29 m) long hose and drogue units and a video monitoring system. The hose reels are installed in the standard rear cargo compartment and only one is used at any one time, the other being there as a back-up. In the cockpit the flight engineer has an extra panel that controls the reels and fuel

pumps. His view of the refuelling comes from one of two video camera lenses in the belly, one of which is relayed to a monitor on the refuelling panel and the other to a video recorder. Although the Omega 707 tanker can only refuel one receiver aircraft at a time, the greater length of the 707-300 airframe makes it a more stable platform than the KC-135, which also has to use a hybrid boom/drogue system for refuelling USN and most NATO aircraft.

The Omega tanker 707 was used for the first time to fill a commercial refuelling contract when it took part in a Joint Maritime Course (JMC) exercise in Scottish waters in June 2001, refuelling the aircraft of Air Wing 8 operating off the USS *Enterprise*. A typical mission in this exercise saw the 707 leave Prestwick Airport near Glasgow with about 160,000 lb (72,600 kg) of fuel, fly forty-five minutes to its refuelling station, spend four hours there, offload 74,000 lb (33,566 kg) of fuel to up to thirty F-14s and F/A-18s and return to base with two hours' reserve. All fuel is dispensed from the 707's own tanks. The main cabin is not encumbered by any fuel tanks or related systems and thus is free for use in the freight, trooping or VIP roles.

Omega has since won a contract to provide refuelling support for two Navy air wings on a longer-term basis. This use of contractorised, civilian-operated tankers (the first in the world) reduces the burden on Navy S-3 Vikings and Marine Corps KC-130s which can be better used in other roles, and on USAF tankers, which are not always available. It is likely that further

ABOVE: Air Malta was one of the last passenger operators in Europe to fly 707s or 720s. Seen climbing out of Heathrow in November 1987 is 720-047B 9H-AAO, a former Western Airlines aircraft. In 1989 it was sold to Race Aviation in 1989 and sent to Davis-Monthan AFB for KC-135 parts. *Austin J. Brown/The Aviation Picture Library*

BELOW: Looking slightly forlorn in a field next to the Museo Nacional de Aeronautica in Santiago, Chile, is 707-330B CC-CCG. One time Lufthansa D-ABOS and D-ABOV, the jet was sold to Lan Chile in 1974 and flew with them until 1986. It was semi-derelict for ten years before joining the museum collection. *Robert Hewson*

ABOVE AND BELOW: Many members of the 707 family have found their final resting place at Davis-Monthan AFB, Arizona, and in associated scrapyards. While only about 20 per cent of parts are common between the 707 and 717 (C-135 series), Boeing Military Airplane Company bought nearly 200 aircraft back over the years to supply components for the Stratotanker and its variants. Both -331B N779TW and -321B N497PA served all their careers with TWA and Pan Am respectively before slowly succumbing in the 1990s to the spares recovery teams. *Graham Robson (both)*

707AR conversions will be made, with or without JT9 engines.

And what of the Pan Am Clippers *Mayflower* and *Caroline*, stored in Europe twenty years after their pioneering transatlantic flights? Their lives were not yet over, as both were sold to Taiwanese operator Air Asia for a few more years of service. In 1983 they were sold to parent company Raytheon E-Systems and scrapped for E-6 Hermes/Mercury parts in Taipei. In some small way, the first transatlantic jetliners are flying on today, helping the US military carry out some of its important strategic missions.

Opposite is a list of known preserved 707s and 720s.

Preserved 707 and 720 airframes

c/n	Model	Registration	Location	Status/notes
17158	367-80	N70700	Boeing Field, Seattle	For NASM, Dulles Airport
17606	707-321	RP-C911	Manila, Philippines	Nightclub 'Club 707'
17623	707-329	OO-SJA	Musee Royal de l'Armee, Brussels, Belgium	Nose only preserved
17642	707-123B	N7515A	Deutches Museum, Germany	Nose only preserved
17647	707-123B	N3951A	Sinsheim Auto+Technik Museum, Germany	Nose only preserved
17667	707-131F	4X-JYD/008	Israel AF Museum, Hatzerim	On display
17711	707-436	G-APFP	RAF Museum, Cosford UK	On display, British Airways colours
17720	707-430	D-ABOD	Hamburg Airport, Germany	Apprentice trainer, Lufthansa colours
17919	707-328	F-BHSL	Vilgenis, France	Apprentice trainer
17926	C-137C	58-6971	Museum of Flight, Seattle	Preserved
18070	707-458	4X-ATA	Intrepid Air and Space Museum, New York	Nose only preserved
18071	707-458	N130KR	Berlin-Tegel Airport, Germany	On display as 'D-ABOC', Lufthansa colours
18073	720-022	N64696	George T. Baker Aviation School, Miami	Apprentice trainer
18084	707-321	TY-BBW	Wetteren, Belgium	Fuselage preserved
18241	720-025	OY-DSP	Danmarks Flygvemuseum	On display
18245	707-328	F-BHSR	Orly Airport, Paris	Front fuselage and wings preserved
18246	707-328	4X-JYK/118	Elifelet, Israel	Restaurant
18248	720-030B	HK-749	Museo del Los Ninos, Bogota, Colombia	On display
18250	720-030B	AP-AZP	Chilton Beach, Karachi, Pakistan	In fun park
18351	720-051B	18351	RoC Air Force Museum Kainshang, Taiwan	On display
18352	720-051B	SX-DBG	Fuselage used as nightclub 'Club 720', Acharnea, Greece	Fuselage preserved
18356	720-051B	SX-DBK	Fairground, Kifissa, Greece	Fuselage preserved
18390	707-131B	N751TW	Pima Air & Space Museum, Arizona	Fuselage on display
18461	C-137C	62-6000	US Air Force Museum, Dayton Ohio	On display
18462	707-330B	CC-CCG	Museo Nacional de Aeronautica, Santiago, Chile	On display
18737	707-348C	7O-ACJ	Bab Toma, Damascus, Syria	'Plane Restaurant'
18749	720-047B	AP-AXM	Karachi Planetarium, Pakistan	Fuselage preserved
18810	707-338C	SU-BBA	Movenpick Hotel, Cairo, Egypt	'Plane Restaurant'
18818	720-47B	AP-AXL	Museum, Lahore, Pakistan	Fuselage believed preserved
18941	707-328B	F-BLCD	Musée de L'Air, Le Bourget, Paris, France	On display, Air France colours
18960	707-321B	N418PA	Weeks Air Museum, Tamiami, FL (now closed)	Nose preserved
19108	707-327C	N7099	Amsterdam	Cockpit preserved
20630	C-137C	72-7000	For Reagan Library, Simi Valley, CA.	Stored Santa Barbara, CA.
?	707-328B	?	Musee de L'Air, Le Bourget, Paris, France	Nose only preserved
?	707-328B	?	Guadalajara Planetarium, Mexico	Nose only preserved

8 ACCIDENTS AND INCIDENTS

In all it is estimated that about 18 per cent of 707s and 15 per cent of 720s built were written off in accidents between 1958 and 2001. The accompanying table records over 180 accidents or major incidents involving 707s, 720s and E-3s, not all of which were write-offs. Many of these occurred long after the 707 had left regular passenger service, and over a career of over forty years this is not a remarkable figure, comparable with many other early jet airliners such as the DC-8 and VC-10 (both 14 per cent) but somewhat better than the Comet (23 per cent) and Convair 880 (26 per cent). The loss rate of more modern airliners such as the Airbus A300 (entered service 1974, 4 per cent lost) and Boeing 767 (less than 1 per cent since 1982) reflects advances in aircraft and engine design, navigation aids and crew training (source: Aviation Safety Network).

Unlike the previous generation of piston-engined airliners such as the Boeing Stratocruiser and Lockheed Constellation, the 707 was not plagued by fires caused by engines pushed to their limits, nor collisions caused by air traffic control based mainly on the concept of 'see and avoid'. None the less, there were many 707 accidents over the years, some of them with heavy loss of life, the inevitable result of the higher capacity of the new jetliners. Pan American was the major 707 user and this is reflected in the number of aircraft losses. Pan Am had seven major fatal accidents, TWA had two and American Airlines only one. Air France had four fatal accidents, losing two 707s to unrelated causes in July 1960 alone, with over 100 fatalities each.

BELOW: One of the most famous 707 crashes was that of G-APFE, which broke up in severe turbulence in the lee of Mt Fuji, Japan, on 5 March 1966. A violent gust collapsed the vertical fin and precipitated the failure of all four engine mounts. All 124 occupants were killed when the wreckage fell near Gotemba City. Although it was not thought to be a factor in this crash, the accident focused attention on the structural integrity of other 707s with over 1,800 flying hours. Over sixty were found to have significant cracks in the tail and Boeing introduced tail modifications and more frequent inspections. *John Stroud Collection/The Aviation Picture Library*

The spectres of terrorism and extortion, which had barely troubled the airlines of the 1940s and 1950s, were to change the nature of air travel and airports in the subsequent decades as desperate, deranged or greedy people used the civil airliner as a tool to achieve their nefarious objectives. A number of 707s were destroyed and others damaged by bombs and terrorist attacks over the years. Conflicts in the Middle East found numerous 707s often literally caught in the crossfire, notably those of Lebanese flag-carrier MEA.

THE FIRST

As with the first Lockheed Constellation accidents, the first 707s lost were on training flights and the investigations into these crashes led to modifications that made the aircraft safer in service. Two crashes in 1959 highlighted the problem of 'Dutch roll', which is a roll (as in a turn), combined with a yaw, that can lead in some circumstances (such as asymmetric power caused by engine shutdown) to the nose tucking under and a full roll developing. This is invariably fatal if insufficient altitude is available for recovery.

On 15 August 1959, American Airline's *Flagship Connecticut*, delivered but forty days previously, was on a training flight with a crew of five out of Calverton-Peconic River Airport on Long Island. After a practice aborted landing, the airliner was positioned for another approach, this time with the two starboard engines throttled back to simulate failure. As it rolled out of a left turn, a right yaw developed, which quickly

ABOVE: One of the few fatal accidents to occur at Heathrow Airport befell BOAC's 707-436 G-ARWE on 8 April 1966 when its No. 2 engine caught fire and fell off shortly after take-off. The fire spread after landing back at Heathrow and four passengers and a stewardess were killed. Five months before, the No. 4 engine had exploded while taxiing at Honolulu. The nose of 'RWE' was salvaged and used as an in-flight simulator attached to a Convair 240 owned by Tex Johnston's company. *The Aviation Picture Library*

OPPOSITE ABOVE: The coveted registration N7071 was only worn for a short time, for it was applied to the first of Braniff's JT-4-engined 707-227s which crashed on a training flight on 19 October 1959. The aircraft belonged to Boeing at the time of the crash, which occurred when a 'Dutch roll' occurred on a training flight and three engines were torn off. A crash landing on the banks of the Stilaguanish River killed four of the eight crew aboard. *The Aviation Picture Library*

OPPOSITE BELOW: Seen nearing completion at Renton in March 1961 with its weather radar and Conway engines exposed is 707-437 VT-DMN for Air-India. Named after Kanchenjunga (K-2) the world's second-highest mountain, it crashed into Mont Blanc, Europe's highest peak, on 24 January 1968, sixteen years after the crash of an Air-India Constellation near the same spot. *John Stroud Collection/The Aviation Picture Library*

turned into a Dutch roll and the aircraft crashed inverted, killing all aboard. The official accident summary stated: 'the crew failed to recognise and correct the development of excessive yaw which caused an unintentional rolling manoeuvre at an altitude too low to permit complete recovery.' Lack of crew co-ordination was given as the cause of this crash and training procedures were tightened, although shortly afterwards near disaster befell Pan Am and Air France aircraft which

performed full rolls and shed engines, fortunately at an altitude from which control could be recovered.

More serious was the crash of N7071, the first of five -220 models ordered by Braniff (and the only examples of this variant to be built) on 19 October 1959. On an acceptance flight before delivery, the aircraft entered a roll so violent that it flung off *three* engines. The Boeing pilot, Russell Baum, ordered the trainees not needed in the cockpit to the back of the aircraft, where they survived when the 707 crash-landed, in trees alongside a river north of Seattle. The four in the cockpit, including Baum, were killed and this time the accident could not be classified as the result of pilot inexperience. There was an inherent flaw in the design that revealed itself only when engine-out procedures were not followed to the letter.

The airlines and regulatory bodies, particularly in Britain, were alarmed and demanded a fix – this was supposed to be the most thoroughly tested airliner in history, and yet it was prone to sudden 'upsets' if not enough attention was paid during a (not uncommon) engine-out approach. Without admitting liability, Boeing designed some remedies to prevent 'Dutch roll' – hydraulically boosted rudder controls and a ventral fin for extra lateral stability. This latter modification was sometimes known as the 'ARB fin' after the UK regulatory authority the Airworthiness Registration Board, and was fitted to 707s from the -420 onwards with retrofitting to earlier aircraft. The ARB also required a taller fin and rudder and this was increased in height by 40 in (102 cm), a measure which improved the stability and performance of the 707 in general.

No 707 on a passenger flight was subsequently lost to 'Dutch roll'; the loss of American's *Flagship Oklahoma* off Montauk Point, New York in January 1961, again on a training flight, may have been another case, but an exact cause was never positively established.

THE WORST

The worst two 707 accidents in terms of fatalities both involved aircraft of Alia Royal Jordanian Airlines, although one was under charter to another airline at the time. JY-ADO was a 707-3D3C named *Petra* after the ancient city, and was carrying 202 people on a non-scheduled flight bringing Haj pilgrims back from Jeddah, Saudi Arabia to Lagos, Nigeria. Bad weather forced a diversion to Kano, where conditions were hazy with strong crosswinds. The pilot, an American, made a poor landing and the starboard maingear left the runway and was torn off in a depression. The 707 spun around and broke up, and 176 passengers and six crew members were killed in the crash and subsequent fire. The pilot, who survived, was given most of the blame, although the weather and runway conditions were certainly contributing factors.

Two and a half years later on 3 August 1975, Alia's 707-321C JY-AEE was under charter to Royal Air Maroc and

BELOW: JY-ADO of Alia Royal Jordanian Airlines crashed at Kano, Nigeria, with heavy loss of life in 1973. Sister ship JY-AEE was lost two years later in Morocco in the worst 707 accident in terms of fatalities. *The Aviation Picture Library*

ABOVE: This dramatic image shows the immediate aftermath of a runway undershoot at Manila Airport on 27 February 1980. The aircraft, a 707-309C of Taiwan's Air China made its approach at too high a rate of descent and suffered massive structural damage, leading to a fuel spill and subsequent fire. Amazingly, all 135 passengers and crew escaped from the wreck, but two passengers later died of burns. *Author's Collection*

was making a non-scheduled flight from Paris to Agadir's Inezgane Airport at night and in foggy conditions. The jet had been delivered to Alia in April that year after nine years of service as Pan Am's *Clipper Northwind*. Cleared to descend to the approach, JY-AEE went lower and struck the top of a 5,000 ft (1,500 m) mountain with its starboard outer engine, tearing it and the outer wing off. The rest of the aircraft carried on to crash in a ravine 5 miles (8 km) away. None of the 181 passengers and seven crew survived the crash, the most deadly to befall a 707, the reason for which could not be established with certainty.

The first US 707 accident with major loss of life was that of N7506A, a 707-123 destined for Los Angeles as American Flight 1, which took off from New York's Idlewild Airport on the sunny morning of 1 March 1962 but within two minutes was blazing on the surface of Jamaica Bay.

Immediately after take-off, the crew made the required 20-degree left heading change for noise abatement and then another turn towards its destination. At this point the 707 rolled inverted from 1,500 ft (450 m) and dived into the Pumpkin Patch channel of Jamaica Bay, which at low tide was barely covered by water in places. The crash killed all 87 passengers and eight crew instantly. Despite the extensive destruction of the aircraft, components of the rudder control system were reassembled by the investigators and tested. Wire chafing was found in the system and this was proved to be capable of causing a short circuit and a hard-over command to the rudder servo actuator. With the rudder at full deflection and the aircraft in a climb attitude, roll, sideslip and yaw were introduced and control was lost at a relatively low altitude. The idea that any one component failure could cause such a catastrophic loss of control was disputed by Boeing, which, like the Civil Aeronautics Board, conducted a series of flight tests to try and duplicate the sequence of events that preceded the crash.

As some parts of the servo-rate generator motors were found to be defective on aircraft still on the production line, an Airworthiness Directive (AD) was issued calling for the inspection of these parts on all 707s and 720s then in service.

TERRORISM AND WAR

Although it was not the first incidence of a bomb blast destroying an airliner, nor the first case of such an attack to claim an insurance payout, the explosion on board a Continental Airlines 707 on 22 May 1962 was probably the first case of suicide for insurance using an airliner as the method. Flight 11 was bound for Kansas City, Missouri, from Chicago and cruising at 37,000 ft (11,300 m) when, at about 9.15 p.m., an explosion in the right rear lavatory compartment, probably in a used towel bin, caused the crew to begin an emergency descent. No communications to air traffic control were made before the rear 38 ft (11.6 m) of fuselage separated from the aircraft and the bulk of the remains fell in an alfalfa field near Unionville, Iowa. Parts were scattered along a path up to 40 miles (65 km) long. The four engines were found in a relatively compact area beginning just over 1 mile (1.6 km) from the main wreckage, having

fallen vertically from some height.

Despite the presence of thunderstorms, which the 707, a -124 model registered as N70775, had been bypassing at the time of the explosion, it was relatively quickly established that dynamite had exploded within the aircraft. Parts identified as coming from the lavatory, together with human remains, were discovered some distance from the main wreckage, and reconstruction of parts of the aircraft on a frame pointed to an explosion emanating from the waste bin. A single passenger was found alive in the wreckage, but died about ninety minutes after rescue, bringing the death toll to forty-five persons, including eight crew. The FBI concluded that a passenger named Thomas G. Doty, who had taken out a $300,000 insurance policy, naming his wife as the beneficiary, had killed himself and all those aboard in an attempt to conceal the cause of his death as an accident. The Unionville tragedy was the last incident to date of a fatal bomb explosion on a US domestic flight.

Terrorism for political ends saw the destruction of several 707s and 720s. On 13 September 1970, near Zerqa, Jordan, at a desert airstrip known as Dawson's Field, three airliners that had been hijacked by PFLP terrorists were blown up in front of the

BELOW: Middle East Airlines (MEA) of Lebanon lost numerous 707s and 720s during that country's prolonged civil war. OD-AFP (foreground) was destroyed by Israeli shelling at Beirut, one of four MEA 720s lost that day. Fellow 'Cedarjet' OD-AFE (second in line) was damaged that month but served with MEA until 1997. OD-AFQ still flies today as an engine testbed with Pratt & Whitney of Canada. *The Aviation Picture Library*

ABOVE: United Arab Airlines was the predecessor of Egyptair and SU-AOW was one of nine 707-366Cs purchased from Boeing by the airline from 1968. While on a training flight near a military training area in December 1972, it crashed following separation of its No. 4 engine. It was rumoured that the aircraft was actually brought down by a wayward missile. *The Aviation Picture Library*

world's media. Among these were a Swissair DC-8, a BOAC VC-10 and TWA 707-331B N8715T. On the same day the attempted hijack of an El Al 707 was thwarted by the cockpit crew, who knocked down the hijackers by diving the aircraft and the cabin crew, who fought and subdued one. An air marshal shot the other. The passengers and crew were spared at Dawson's Field, which was not the case three years later at Rome's Leonardo da Vinci Airport when terrorists attacked the terminal and ran across the tarmac, throwing incendiary grenades into Pan Am's *Clipper Celestial* (N407PA), which was preparing to depart for Beirut. Thirty-two people were killed and the attackers hijacked a Lufthansa 737 to escape to Kuwait, where they surrendered the next day.

Middle East Airlines (MEA) of Lebanon operated thirty-two 707 and 720 'Cedarjets' from 1968 and lost at least fourteen of them. Only one loss was an accident, the rest being the result of civil war and regional strife. The first was destroyed in 1968 within six weeks of delivery by Israeli commandos who landed by Super Frélon helicopter at Beirut Airport and blew it up in a retaliatory raid for a terrorist attack on Israeli passengers at Athens. During the Israeli invasion of 1982, Beirut Airport was shelled heavily, and no less than six 707s and 720s were lost on 22 June of that year alone. With a much-reduced

fleet, no airport and not much of a country left, the battered but determined MEA continued in business by operating from France and by leasing many aircraft out.

KAL SHOOTDOWN

The shooting down of a Korean Air Lines Boeing 747 by Soviet fighters in September 1983 was headline news around the world, but the destruction of the off-course 'jumbo' was not the first time an airliner was brought down due to a Cold War navigation error and sequence of misunderstandings. On 20 April 1978, an incident occurred with many similarities to the later tragedy, also involving a Korean Air Lines Boeing and Sukhoi Su-15 'Flagon' interceptors, and also resulting in the airliner intruding into Soviet airspace, albeit at opposite ends of this giant nation. The aircraft involved was HL-7429, a former Pan Am 707-321B, recently purchased from ATASCO and operating as Flight 902 from Paris to Seoul via Anchorage with ninety-seven passengers and thirteen crew members.

ABOVE: HL-7406 was built for Korean Airlines in 1971. In 1978 it returned the passengers from HL-7429, brought down by Russian fighters near Murmansk, from Helsinki back to Seoul. On 29 November 1987 it was brought down by a bomb left aboard by two North Korean agents and crashed off the Western coast of Burma, killing all 115 aboard. The agents, a 24-year-old woman and a 70-year-old man were arrested in Bahrain, but the man committed suicide soon afterwards. The woman was convicted but later pardoned by the South Korean government.
The Aviation Picture Library

Heading over the polar route to Korea, somehow the airliner deviated from its planned course and penetrated Soviet airspace over the Barents Sea. For over an hour it continued until a pair of Su-15 interceptors arrived and tried to signal the airliner to land with flybys and tracer fire. The Korean pilot, Captain Kim Chang Kyu, reduced speed and activated his landing lights in a signal that he was prepared to follow the fighters and tried to raise them on the radio, but the Soviet pilots were ordered by their superiors to shoot down the 707, which they believed was an RC-135 'Rivet Joint' spyplane. A missile struck the left wing and shrapnel penetrated the fuselage, killing two passengers and injuring thirteen. With the aircraft depressurising, Captain Kim made an emergency descent from 35,000 to 3,000 ft (10,000 – 900 m), then sought somewhere to make a landing, which he skilfully achieved on a frozen lake near the port of Kem, 280 miles (448 km) south of Murmansk and more than 1,000 miles (1,600 km) off course. The aircraft stopped short of a stand of trees on the lakeshore and the surviving passengers were successfully evacuated. A chartered American flight was permitted to fly everyone except the pilot and navigator to

Helsinki after two days. After nine days of interrogations, the remaining crew were released and the Korean government was presented with a bill for $100,000 for rescuing, housing and feeding the passengers.

The final fate of the 707, which remained in the Soviet Union, is unclear, but it seems that the lesson of this incident, that an airliner blundering over the country was subject to attack with little, if any, warning was not learned in time to prevent the tragedy of KAL 007 in 1983 and the loss of 269 lives.

RECENT LOSSES

Although the 707 has all but completely left passenger service, numerous freight operators around the world continue to operate the type in ones and twos. They are often subject to poorer operating and maintenance standards than they enjoyed in their heydays as part of a large passenger fleet, and periodically, the numbers of 707s in service is reduced by a mishap to one in some far corner of the world. One of the most recent write-offs, fortunately without loss of life, occurred near Mwanza, Tanzania, in February 2000 and is not without its elements of comedy.

One-time Northwest Orient's N372US, 707-351C line number 563 had served with BWIA and seven other lesser operators before joining Trans-Arabian Air Transport (TAAT) in 1985. Registered ST-APY in April, 1998, and long since converted to freight configuration, the airliner was en route on a night flight from Khartoum, Sudan to Mwanza on the Tanzanian shore of Lake Victoria to pick up a 38-tonne load of

In 1984, NASA and the FAA conducted the only full-scale airliner crash test to date when 720 N833NA was flown by remote control into obstacles set up in the Mojave Desert. This spectacular fireball was the (unintended) consequence, but much useful data on airworthiness was obtained. *Aeropspace Publishing*

fish when the aircraft's instrument lighting failed. Mwanza airport's own lighting and landing aids had failed and efforts to start a back-up generator were underway when the 707 arrived over Lake Victoria in darkness. Although runway lights were powered up, the VOR, NDB and DME equipment was all out of service and the first officer, who was flying, made a visual approach while the radio altimeter was unlit and unreadable. The aircraft overshot and the captain took over to position the aircraft for a new approach. Making a tight 360-degree turn, the 707 was on the runway heading when it struck the surface of Lake Victoria, bounced two or three times, losing all four engines in the process, and came to a stop, happily floating about 3 miles (5 km) offshore. The external lights guided a fishing boat to the scene and the five crew were rescued uninjured. The next day the airliner was towed to the lakeshore, where it may remain as a visual beacon for some years to come, and ironically, a home for relatives of the fish it arrived to pick up.

THE 720

The Boeing 720 made a particular contribution to the safety of

air travellers when an example used by the FAA and NASA was destroyed in the 'controlled impact demonstration' test on 1 December 1984. N833NA was a 720-061 that had been used by the FAA for runway arrestor hook and other tests before being damaged in 1964 and later stored. By the time of its final flight it had only 20,000 flight hours. For the test it was flown by a ground controller to a specially set up impact area on the Rogers Dry Lake, part of Edwards AFB, California. A variety of obstacles were placed in the path of the jet, which only reached a height of 2,500 ft (750 m) in a flight lasting nine minutes and eleven seconds. The principal object of the exercise was to test the effectiveness of a fuel additive called anti-misting kerosene (AMK), which was claimed to prevent explosions in crash impacts, but many other safety aspects were tested at the same time. The cabin was occupied by seventy-five instrumented dummy 'passengers' to measure impact forces on the body and the cabin was outfitted with a variety of fabrics and plastics to test flammability. High-speed cameras monitored the spread of fire and smoke in the cabin. In order to ensure the spillage and likely ignition of fuel, the impact area was laid out with steel 'wing cutters' and gas flame jets. AMK was designed so that it did not form explosive vapours in the fuel tanks but only in the combustion chamber of the engine itself. Unfortunately, the 720 landed 500 ft (150 m) short and was not aimed precisely down the centre line of the impact area and one of the wing cutters split the No. 3 engine down the middle, stopping the turbine within a fraction of a revolution. The AMK fuel in the engine erupted in a spectacular fireball as

the starboard wing was torn off. The initial fire quickly dissipated, but spilled fuel continued to burn for two hours and the airframe was mostly burnt out. Although much useful data was gathered on the crash-worthiness of various seat-belts, seat-mountings, fabrics and plastics, it was widely regarded as a failure. Certainly, AMK was not adopted by the aviation industry which instead slowly switched to lower flash-point fuels instead.

ABOVE: After bomb threats were made about four TWA aircraft on 7 March 1972, an explosion early the following morning destroyed the cockpit of N761TW *London Town*, which was parked at Las Vegas' McCarran Airport. No money was paid out and no suspect arrested. The remains of the 707-331 were purchased back by Boeing and used for structural testing. *The Aviation Picture Library*

Date	Reg	Model	c/n + l/n	Operator	Aboard/killed (+ on ground)	Route	Location	Details
25/2/59	N810PA	-121	17586/1	Pan Am	?/0	Training flight	Chartres, France	Engine torn off during Dutch roll. Landed safely at Heathrow.
15/8/59	N7514A	-123	17641/36	American Airlines	5/5	Training flight	Calverton-Peconic River Apt, NY	Two engines shut down on practice approach. Dutch roll developed, hit ground.
19/10/59	N7071	-227	17691/45	Boeing/for Braniff	8/4	Training flight	Arlington, WA	Dutch rolled, three engines torn off in recovery. Crashlanded in trees.
28/1/61	N7502A	-123	17629/8	American Airlines	6/6	Training flight	Off Montauk Point, New York	Lost control and hit sea.
15/2/61	OO-SJB	-329	17624/92	Sabena	72/72+1	New York–Brussels	Near Brussels-Zaventem Apt	Crashed on go-around. Possibly asymmetric spoiler activation. Led to modifications.
27/7/61	F-BHSA	-328	17613/65	Air France	41/0	Hamburg–Anchorage	Hamburg-Fuhlsbuttel	Abandoned take-off, veered off runway and crashed in depression.
4/12/61	D-ABOK	030B	18058/202	Lufthansa	3/3	Frankfurt–Cologne	Near Ebersheim, Germany.	Dived into ground on training flight.
22/5/62	N70775	-124	17611/49	Continental Airlines	45/45	Chicago–Kansas City	6 miles (9.5 km) NNW Unionville, Missouri, USA	Dynamite bomb in toilets – man committed suicide for insurance.
3/6/62	F-BHSM	-328	17920/159	Air France	132/130	Paris–New York	Paris–Orly	Aborted take-off (elevator trim motor failed) ran off runway into buildings.
22/6/62	F-BHST	-328	18247/274	Air France	112/112	Paris–Pointe a Pitre	Pointe a Pitre, Guadaloupe	Hit mountain on approach in thunderstorm. Navigation aid failure and insufficient met information.
27/11/62	N7506A	-123B	17633/12	American Airlines	95/95	New York–Los Angeles	Jamaica Bay, NY	After take-off reached 1,500 feet, rolled inverted and crashed into bay. Rudder controls damaged during manufacture.
27/11/62	PP-VJB	-441	19706/129	Varig	97/97	Porto Alegre–Lima	La Cruz Peak, Lima, Peru	Overshot because too high, carried on into mountain. Possible misinterpretation of instruments.
12/2/63	N724US	051B	18354/224	Northwest Orient	43/43	Miami–Chicago	Near Miami	Entered thunderstorm and broken up by turbulence. Crew tried to maintain airspeed rather than attitude.
8/12/63	N709PA	-121	17588/3	Pan Am	81/81	Baltimore–Philidelphia	Elkton, MD	Lightning ignited fuel vapour. Led to fitting of static wicks to jetliners.
7/4/64	N779PA	-139	17904/119	Pan Am	145/0	San Juan, PR–New York	New York–JFK Airport	Touched down very long along runway and ran into bay.
15/7/64	D-ABOP	030B	18249/262	Lufthansa	3/3	Training flight	Near Ansbach, Germany	Performed roll on training flight, disintegrated attempting a second.
23/11/64	N769TW	-331	17685/123	TWA	73/50	Rome–Athens	Rome-Fiumicino	No.2 engine thrust reverser failed on aborted take-off, aircraft veered into steamroller.
24/11/64	N113	061	18066/208	FAA	?/0	Training flight	Oklahoma City	Landed short, struck approach lights.
20/5/65	AP-AMH	040B	18379/321	PIA	121/127 (or 119/125)	Karachi–Cairo	5 miles 8km from Cairo Airport	Flew into ground on night approach. Airport aids and procedure criticised.
28/6/65	N761PA	-321B	18336/270	Pan Am	153/0	San-Francisco–Honolulu	Travis AFB, Sacramento	Engine exploded after take-off, taking 1/3 of wing away. Made safe landing.
1/7/65	N70773	-124	17609/25	Continental	66/0	Los Angeles–Kansas City	Kansas City, MO	Hydroplaned on landing. Overran and broke in two.
17/9/65	N708PA	-121B	17586/1	Pan Am	30/30	Fort de France–St Johns, Antigua	Chances Mt, Monserrat	Crashed into 1,400 ft (422 m) hill 15 miles (24 km) from the runway threshold. Navaids, instruments faulty. Crew given poor met. Information.
4/12/65	N748TW	-131B	18387/4256	TWA	58/0+4	Boston–Newark	Carmel, New York	Collided with Eastern L-1049C N6218C. 707 lost 25 ft (8 m) of wing, landed safely, 4 killed on L-1049.
24/1/66	VT-DMN	-437	18055/200	Air-India	117/117	Bombay–Geneva	Mont Blanc, Switzerland	Struck mountain ridge. Off course, possible "white-out" a factor.
5/3/66	G-APFE	-436	17706/113	BOAC	124/124	Tokyo–Hong Kong	Gotemba City, nr Mount Fuji, Japan	Flew into lee wave of mountain, suffered structural failure.
6/11/67	N742TW	-131	17669/43	TWA	159/1	Cincinnati–Los Angeles	Cincinnati Int Airport	Aborted take-off due to suspected ground collision, overran runway and gear collapsed.
21/11/67	G-ARWE	-436	18373/302	BOAC	?/0	Honolulu–	Honolulu Airport, Hawaii	Engine exploded while taxiing. Six passengers injured.
9/1/68	ET-AAG	060B	18454/319	MEA	49/0	–Beirut	Beirut Airport, Lebanon	Landed nosegear first. Fire broke out and later destroyed the aircraft.
7/2/68	N791SA	-138B	17698/44	Canadian Pacific Air Lines –CPAL	61/1+1	Honolulu-Vancouver	Vancouver International Airport	Fog concealed ground just before touchdown. Overran, struck a DC-8 and buildings.
6/3/68	F-BLCJ	-328C	19724/667	Air France	63/63	Caracas–Pointe a Pitre	16 miles (25 km) from Pointe a Pitre, Guadaloupe	Pilot misidentified position before beginning approach, struck volcano at night.
8/4/68	G-ARWE	-436	18373/302	BOAC	127/5	London–Zurich	London-Heathrow Apt	No.2 engine caught fire on take-off and fell off before emergency landing, aircraft burned out.
20/4/68	ZS-EUW	-344C	19705/675	South African Airways - SAA	128/123	Windhoek–Luanda	3 miles (5km) from Windhoek Apt, Namibia	Crashed soon after night take-off. Probable pilot disorientation.
12/6/68	N798PA	-321C	18790/394	Pan Am	63/6	–Calcutta	Near Calcutta Airport	Hit tree and crashed in heavy rain 4,000 ft (1.2km) short of runway. Altimeter incorrectly set.
13/7/68	OO-SJK	-329C	19211/518	Sabena	7/7	Brussels–Lagos	8.5 miles (13.5 km) N of Lagos Airport	Descended below safe altitude and crashed into trees.
7/9/68	PP-VJR	-341C	19320/522	Varig	0/0	–	Rio de Janeiro-Galeao IAP	Destroyed in hangar fire.
19/11/68	?	?	?	Continental Airlines	70/0	Los Angeles–Denver	Near Gunnison, Colorado	Bomb exploded in toilet. Aircraft landed safely.
12/12/68	N494PA	-321B	19696/688	Pan Am	51/51	New York–Caracas	9.5 miles (15 km) offshore from Caracas Apt	Undershot at night. Possible pilot disorientation caused by town lights.
26/12/68	N799PA	-321C	18824/397	Pan Am	3/3	Anchorage–Tokyo	Anchorage-Elmendorf AFB, AK	Flapless take-off on freight flight, crashed.

Date	Reg	Model	c/n + l/n	Operator	Aboard/killed (+ on ground)	Route	Location	Details
28/12/68	OD-AFC	-3B4C	20225/757	MEA	0/0	–	Beirut IAP	Destroyed by Israeli commandos as part of retaliation for Athens attack.
11/3/69	?	?	?	Ethiopian Airlines	0/0	–	Frankfurt Airport, Germany	Severely damaged by explosions while parked.
26/7/69	N787TW	-331C	18712/373	TWA	5/5	Training flight	Atlantic City, NJ	Spoiler actuator failed while in asymetric condition. Lost control, crashed.
1/12/69	N892PA	-321B	20029/790	Pan Am	?/0		Kingsford-Smith Airport, Sydney	Multiple birdstrike, overran and seriously damaged. Repaired.
4/12/69	F-BHSZ	-328B	18459/335	Air France	62/62	Caracas–Guadaloupe	6 miles (10 km) from Maiguetia Apt, Guadaloupe	Dived into sea after take-off. Cause never determined.
22/4/70	N743TW	-131	17670/46	TWA	0/0	–	Indianapolis	Destroyed by fire on ground.
13/9/70	N8715T	-331B	18917/460	TWA	0/0	–	Zerqa, Jordan (Dawson's Field)	Blown up by PFLP after hijack.
30/11/70	N790TW	-373C	18738/335	TWA	3/0+2	Tel Aviv-	Tel Aviv-Ben Gurion Airport	Collided with IAF C-97 being towed across runway as 707 took off.
23/1/71	VT-DJI	-437	17722/94	Air-India	5/0	Training flight	Bombay Airport	Ran off runway and caught fire during 3-engined take-off.
31/3/71	N3166	047B	19439/621	Western Air Lines	5/5	Los Angeles–Ontario	Ontario, CA.	Rudder actuator failed, rolled and crashed after missed 3-engine approach.
25/7/71	N461PA	-321C	19371/653	Pan Am	4/4	Guam–Manila	Mt Kamunay, Philippines	Premature descent, struck mountain.
24/8/71	?	?	?	Alia Royal Jordanian	0/0	–	Madrid Airport, Spain	Severely damaged by bomb while parked.
15/12/71	AP-AVZ	-340C	20487/847	PIA	5/5	–Urumqi	Urumqi-Diwopu Airport, China	'Crashed'.
8/3/72	N761TW	-331	17673/69	TWA	0/0	–	Las Vegas-McCarran IAP, NV	Blown up by extortionist.
8/5/72	OO-SJG	-329	18460/328	Sabena	?/0+2	Vienna–Tel Aviv	Tel Aviv Airport	Two hijackers killed when commandos stormed aircraft.
14/9/72	N15712	-331C	20068/814	TWA	3/0	San Fransisco–	San Fransisco IAP, CA	Aborted take-off due to vibration. Overran into bay.
5/12/72	SU-AOW	-336C	19845/809	Egypt Air	6/6	Training flight	Beni Sueif, Egypt	No. 4 engine fell off, leading to crash. Missile strike?
12/12/72	N787TW	-331C	18713/378	TWA	3/0	Baltimore–New York	New York JFK Airport	Landed short. Lost engines and undercarriage in slide down runway. Repaired.
2/1/73	CF-PWZ	-321C	18826/389	Pacific Western Airlines	5/5	–Edmonton	Near Edmonton Airport	Crashed 2 miles (3 km) from airport in snow storm.
22/1/73	JY-ADO	-3D3C	20494/850	Alia Royal Jordanian Airlines	202/176	Jeddah-Kano	Kano, Nigeria	Diverted to Kano, landed badly in haze and crosswinds, crashed beside runway.
9/6/73	PP-VLJ	-327C	19106/502	Varig	4/2	–Rio de Janeiro	Rio de Janeiro-Galeao IAP	Inadvertent spoiler activation, pitched down into water.
11/7/73	PP-VJZ	-345C	19106/683	Varig	134/123	Rio de Janeiro–Paris	5 km from Paris Charles de Gaulle	Fire in aft lavatory spread to cabin. Force-landed and burnt out short of runway.
22/7/73	N417PA	-321C	18959/470	Pan Am	78/79	Papeete–Honolulu	3 km from Faaa Apt, Papeete	Crashed into sea after take-off, possible crew disorientation.
28/8/73	N8705T	-331B	18916/455	TWA	149/1	Honolulu–Los Angeles	near Los Angeles, California, USA	Porpoised for two minutes on descent. A passenger fatally injured.
3/11/73	N458PA	-321C	19368/640	Pan Am	3/3	New York–Prestwick UK	Boston, MA	Spillage of nitric acid in cargo caused uncontrollable fire.
17/12/73	N407PA	-321C	18838/412	Pan Am	177/32	Rome–Beirut	Rome-Fiumicino	Terrorists threw grenades into boarding aircraft.
20/12/73	D-ABOT	-330B	18463/363	Lufthansa	109/0	Bangkok–Delhi	Delhi Airport	Undershot and hit navaid building.
16/1/74	N757TW	-131B	18395/309	TWA	63/0	New York–Los Angeles	Los Angeles IAP, CA	Nosegear collapsed on landing.
30/1/74	N454PA	-321B	19376/661	Pan Am	101/97	Auckland–Pago Pago	Pago Pago, American Samoa	Crashed on approach due to excessive sink. Possible windshear. Most killed by fire.
22/4/74	N446PA	-321B	19268/544	Pan Am	107/107	Hong Kong–Denpasar	Mt Mesche, 42 miles (67 km) NW Denpasar	Non-precision approach when out of position. Struck mountain.
8/9/74	N8734	-331B	20063/789	TWA	88/88	Athens–Rome	58 miles (93 km) W Cephalonia	Bomb placed by Palestinian group damaged tail controls, aircraft spiralled to crash in sea.
13/9/74	OY-DSR	025	18243/254	Conair	?/0	–Copenhagen	Copenhagen, Denmark	Hard landing, damaged beyond repair, later scrapped.
3/8/75	JY-AEE	-321C	18767/376	Alia Royal Jordanian Airlines	188/188	Paris–Agadir	23 miles (37 km) NW Agadir, Morocco	Royal Air Maroc charter. Descended too low in bad weather. Wing hit mountain, aircraft crashed.
22/12/75	N18701	-331B	18978/465	TWA	125/0	New York–Milan	Milan-Malpensa Airport	Landed beside runway, struck landing aids. Undercarriage and engines torn off.
1/1/76	OD-AFT	032B	18020/165	MEA	81/81	Beirut–Dubai	25 miles (40 km) NW Al Qaysumah, Saudi Arabia	Bomb in forward cargo compartment caused aircraft break up.
18/2/76	4X-ABB	048B	18425/290	El Al	?/1	Zurich–Tel Aviv	Zurich Airport, Switzerland	Shot at by terrorists while taxiing. One crewmember killed.
22/4/76	N37777	022	18044/178	US Global	4/0	Bogota–Barranquilla	Near Cortissoz, Colombia	Crashed short of runway with cargo of flowers.
27/6/76	OD-AGE	047B	18963/433	MEA	4/2	–	Beirut Airport	Hit by rockets and shells just after passengers disembarked.
2/8/76	HL-7412	-373C	19715/642	Korean Air Lines	5/5	Tehran-Seoul	9 miles (14.5 km) WNW Tehran	Turned wrong way after take-off, hit mountain.
16/8/76	HK-723	47B	18061/197	Avianca	?/0	–Mexico City	Mexico City Airport	Landed in bad weather, lifted off again and stalled onto nosegear.
7/9/76	F-BHSH	-328	17620/138	Air France	0/0	–	Ajaccio, Corsica	Separatist group blew up aircraft on ground.
13/10/76	N730JP	-131F	17671/48	Lloyd Aéreo Boliviano – LAB	3/3+88	Santa Cruz-Viru	Santa Cruz, Bolivia	Failed to climb on take-off, struck houses and wound up on soccer field. Crew fatigue.
25/12/76	SU-AXA	-366C	20763/871	Egypt Air	52/52+19	Rome–Bangkok	Near Don Muang Apt, Thailand	Struck factory on approach in poor visibility.
17/3/77	G-APFK	-436	17712/164	British Airtours	4/4	Training flight	Prestwick, Uk	Engine nacelle struck ground on take-off, crashed on runway.
14/5/77	G-BEBP	-321C	18579/332	IAS Cargo	6/6	Nairobi–Lusaka	Near Lusaka	Right stabiliser separated, aircraft dived into ground from 800 ft (245 m).

Date	Reg	Model	c/n + l/n	Operator	Aboard/killed (+ on ground)	Route	Location	Details
9/8/77	9Q-CRT	-430	17718/90	Pearl Air	?/0	–Sana'a	Sana'a, Yemen	Nosegear damaged on first landing attempt. Landed safely.
19/11/77	ET-ACD	-360C	19736/696	Ethiopian Airlines	5/5	Rome-	Near Rome-Fiumicino Airport	Struck trees and crashed just after take-off.
15/2/78	OO-SJE	-329	17627/133	Sabena	196/0	Brussels–Tenerife	Tenerife Los Rodeos Airport	Undershot, caught fire.
20/4/78	HL-7429	-321B	19363/623	Korean Air Lines	109/2	Paris-Seoul	Near Murmansk	Attacked by Russian fighters when veered off course. Landed on frozen lake.
3/8/78	CC-CCX	-351B	18584/342	LAN Chile	63/0	Miami–Buenos Aires	Near Buenos Aires-Ezeiza Airport	Struck trees 1.5 miles (2.5 km) short of runway.
30/1/79	PP-VLU	-323C	19235/519	Varig	5/5	Tokyo–Rio de Janeiro	Pacific Ocean	Disappeared on freight flight.
19/2/79	C-GQBH	-123B	17650/67	Quebecair	171/0	Toronto–St Lucia	Vieux Fort-Hewanorra IAP	Windshear caused heavy landing and nosegear collapse.
1/4/79	5X-UAL	-321C	18580/336	Uganda Airlines	0/0	–	Entebbe Airport, Uganda	Destroyed on ground by Tanzanian forces.
23/7/79	OD-AFX	-327C	19107/507	TMA	6/6	Training flight	Beirut	Lost control after touch-and-go landing and crashed on runway.
26/7/79	D-ABUY	-330C	20395/848	Lufthansa	3/3	Rio de Janiero–Dakar	Petropolis, Brazil	Controllers failed to direct aircraft away from mountain.
19/8/79	5B-DAM	-123	17628/7	Cyprus Airways	66/0	–Bahrain	Bahrain IAP	Bounced on landing, nosegear collapsed and aircraft left runway.
11/9/79	B- 1834	-324C	18887/431	China Airlines	6/6	Training flight	In sea off Taipei	Crashed into sea after take-off.
26/11/79	AP-AWZ	-340C	20275/844	PIA	156/156	Jeddah–Karachi	90 miles (145 km) E Jeddah	Inflight fire, possibly caused by gasoline stove. Crew incapacitated.
30/11/79	HZ-ACE	-373C	18582/344	Saudia	?/0	–Jeddah	Jeddah, Saudi Arabia	Badly damaged in heavy landing.
27/1/80	HK-725	059B	18087/249	Avianca	?/0	–Quito	Quito-Mariscal, Ecuador	Landed too fast, overran and nosegear collapsed.
27/2/80	B-1826	-309C	20262/830	China Airlines	135/2	Taipei-Manila	Manila Airport	Undershot runway and crashed (have photo of accident).
3/4/80	S2-ABQ	-373C	19441/548	Bangladesh Biman	?/0	Singapore	Changi Airport, Singapore	Crashed back on runway after take-off. Written off.
4/4/80	S2-ABQ	-373C	19441/548	Biman Bangladesh Airlines	74/0		Singapore-Paya Lebar.	4 engines lost power, sank back to runway after take-off.
11/5/80	OO-SJH	-329C	18890/416	Zaire International Cargo	3/3	–Douala	Douala, Cameroon	Gear collapsed, two engines came off after landing.
30/11/80	N797TW	-131B	18760/393	TWA	133/0	St Louis–San Francisco	San Fransisco IAP, CA	Nosegear failed to lower before landing.
20/12/80	HK-2410X	-321F	17605/98	Aerotal Colombia	4/0	–Bogota	Bogota-Eldorado	Crashed on approach in heavy rain.
8/1/81	AP-AXK	047B	18590/339	PIA	79/0	–Quetta	Quetta, Pakistan	Nosegear collapsed, damaged beyond repair.
29/3/81	OO-SJA	-329	17623/78	Sobelair	118/0	Brussels–	Brussel-Zaventem Airport	No.3 engine fire, made overweight landing and veered off runway. W/0.
11/6/81	PP-VJT	-341C	19322/561	Varig	3/0	–Manaus	Manaus, Brazil	Aquaplaned, struck runway lights, right gear collapsed.
7/7/81	OD-AGW	-327C	19440/554	TMA	0/0	–	Beirut Airport	Destroyed by bomb on ground.
31/8/81	OD-AFR	023B	18018/157	MEA	?/0	Libya–Beirut	Beirut Airport	Destroyed by dynamite shortly after landing.
23/10/81	OD-AGT	-331C	19213/613	TMA	3/0	Tokyo–	Tokyo-Narita IAP	No.3 engine failed, made bad landing, ran off runway, nosegear collapsed. Not repaired.
16/12/81	HI-384HA	-124	17610/37	Hispaniola	5/0	–Miami	Miami IAP, FL	Right maingear failed on landing.
26/1/82	7O-ACJ	-348C	18737/377	Alyemda	0()	Libya–Damascus	Damascus	Attacked by Israeli or Iraqi fighters. Landed but DBR.
26/1/82	7O-ACJ	-348C	18737/377	Alyemda Yemen	?/0	Tripoli-Damascus	Near Damascus	Damaged by fighters on approach. Never flew again.
12/6/82	OD-AFP	023B	18017/156	MEA	0/0	–	Beirut Airport	Destroyed by Israeli shelling.
12/6/82	OD-AFU	023B	18029/194	MEA	0/0	–	Beirut Airport	Destroyed by Israeli shelling.
12/6/82	OD-AFW	023B	18026/181	MEA	0/0	–	Beirut Airport	Destroyed by Israeli shelling.
12/6/82	OD-AGR	047B	19161/481	MEA	0/0	–	Beirut Airport	Destroyed by Israeli shelling.
16/6/82	OD-AFB	-323C	18938/434	MEA	0/0	–	Beirut Airport	Destroyed in shelling of airport.
16/6/82	OD-AGN	-3B4C	20224/749	TMA	0/0	–	Beirut Airport	Destroyed in shelling of airport.
22/6/82	VT-DJJ	-437	17723/100	Air-India	111/17	Kuala Lumpur–Bombay	Bombay Airport	Made very heavy landing. Go-around attempted but crashed on runway.
1/8/82	OD-AGG	047B	18828/423	MEA	0/0	–	Beirut Airport	Destroyed by Israeli bombing.
10/9/82	ST-AIM	-348C	19410/599	Sudan Airways	11/0	Jeddah-Khartoum	3 miles (5 km) from Khartoum Airport	Landed in River Nile.
17/10/82	SU-APE	-336C	20342/837	Egypt Air	182/3	Cairo–Geneva	Geneva Airport	High and fast approach. Landed short, spun around and crashed.
4/12/82	N8434	-328B	20173/805	Global International	57/0	Brasilia–	Brasilia, Brazil	Struck ILS aerials on take-off, left gear torn off. Crashed on landing but repaired.
14/3/83	5A-DJO	-338C	18955/467	Jamahiriya	5/5	?	19 miles (30 km) N of Sabha, Libya	Crashed on positioning flight.
?/5/83	9Q-CMD	-441	18694/353	Blue Airlines	?/0	–Goma	Goma, Zaire	Engine exploded on landing, later written off.
1/6/83	OD-AFO	023B	18035/214	MEA	0/0	–	Beirut Airport	Damaged beyond repair by Israeli shelling.
25/9/83	5N-ARO	-336C	18924/448	RN Cargo	4/0	Lagos–Accra	Accra-Kotoka Airport	Caught fire after landing. Possible sabotage.
13/10/83	N4465D	-436	18411/266	Coastal Airways	0/0	–	Perpignan	Fire on ground.
14/12/83	HK-2401	-373C	18707/349	TAMPA Colombia	3/3+22	Medellin–Miami	Near Medellin, Colombia	No.3 engine failed, No.4 at idle, hit wires and buildings after take-off.
?/7/84	9Q-CWR	-458	18357/272	Wolf Aviation	?/0	–Isiro	Isiro, Zaire	Written off after hard landing.
1/12/84	N833NA	027	18066/208	NASA	0/0	–	Edwards AFB, CA	Destroyed in remotely-controlled crash test.
13/6/85	TY-BBR	-336B	20457/853	Benin Government	?/0	Sebha–	Sebha, Libya	Aborted take-off, destroyed by fire.
21/8/85	OD-AFL	023B	18034/207	MEA	0/0	–	Beirut Airport	Destroyed by Israeli shelling.
21/8/85	OD-AGQ	047B	19160/470	MEA	0/0	–	Beirut Airport	Destroyed by Israeli shelling.

Date	Reg	Model	c/n + l/n	Operator	Aboard/killed (+ on ground)	Route	Location	Details
27/1/86	LV-JGR	-387C	19961/754	Aerolineas Argentinas	5/0	–Buenos Aires	Buenos Aires Airport	Overran in heavy rain and hit hill.
3/1/87	PP-VJK	-379C	19822/726	Varig	51/50	Abidjan–Rio de Janeiro	Abidjan, Ivory Coast; 11 miles (18km) NE	Took off with No.1 engine on fire, crashed in jungle.
8/1/87	OD-AHB	-323C	19588/692	MEA	126/0	–	Beirut Airport	Destroyed after landing in shelling of airport.
11/4/87	PT-TCO	-330C	18932/477	Transbrasil	7/0	–Manaus	Manaus, Brazil	Landed beside runway in heavy rain. Right gear collapsed.
13/4/87	N144SP	-351C	19209/510	Burlington Air Express	4/4	Wichita–Kansas City	Near Kansas City, MO	Crashed short of runway in fog.
29/11/87	HL-7406	-3B5C	20522/855	Korean Air	115/115	Abu Dhabi–Bangkok	Andaman Sea off Burma	Bomb placed by North Korean agents.
8/2/88	D2-TOI	-349C	18975/445	TAAG Angola Airlines	9/0	–Luanda	Luanda Airport	Struck aerial on building. Overran and nosegear collapsed.
21/7/88	D2-TOV	-328C	18881/436	Angola Air Charter	6/6	Ostend–Lagos	Near Lagos	Crashed while lining up for approach.
10/10/88	D2-TOM	-347C	19965/734	TAAG Angola Airlines	3/0	–	Luanda	Fire in cargo hold.
17/10/88	5X-UBC	-338C	19630/746	Uganda Airlines	52/33	London–Rome	Near Rome-Fiumicino	Hit building on approach while making third landing attempt in fog.
15/11/88	Z-WKT	-330BA	18929/461	Air Zimbabwe	0	–	Harare–Charles Prince Apt	Destroyed in hanger fire.
13/12/88	5N-AYJ	-321C	19168/508	GAS Air Nigeria	8/8+1	Dar-es-Salaam–Cairo	Kom-Omran, Egypt	Ran out of fuel on diversion to Luxor. Hit houses.
8/2/89	N7231T	-331B	19572/687	Independent Air	144/144	Bergamo, Italy–Azores	6 miles (10 km) from Pico Alto, Azores, Portugal	Misunderstanding of descent altitude, hit mountain.
21/3/89	PT-TCS	-349C	19354/503	Transbrasil	3/3+22	Manaus–Sao Paulo	1.25 miles (2 km) from Sao Paulo-Guarulhos	Made over-steep approach, then stalled and crashed into houses.
17/5/89	6O-SBT	-330B	19316/547	Somali Airlines	70/0	Nairobi-	Nairobi	Aborted take-off and ran into rice field.
11/7/89	5Y-BBK	-351B	19872/742	Kenya Airways	76/0	Addis Ababa-	Addis Ababa, Ethiopia	Gear failed to retract, brakes failed on landing and overran.
25/1/90	HK-2016	-321B	19276/592	Avianca	158/73	Medellin–New York	Cove Neck, NY	Missed approach, ran out of fuel. Poor communication with ATC.
1/3/90	9Q-CVG	-329C	19162/480	Katale Aero Transport	3/0	–Goma	Goma, Zaire	Damaged beyond repair in landing accident.
23/6/90	CC-CEI	-321B	20021/769	LAN Chile	0/0	–	Santiago de Chile	Engine ripped off in towing accident.
14/7/90	ST-ALK	-349C	18976/449	TAAT	?/0	–Khartoum	Khartoum	Nosegear collapsed on landing.
25/7/90	ET-ACQ	-379C	19820/709	Ethiopian Airlines	4/0	Addis Ababa-	Addis Ababa-Bole Airport	Birdstrike, aborted runway and crashed down hill.
20/9/90	N320MJ	-321B	20028/783	Omega Air Inc.	3/2	Omega Air	Marana, AZ	Porpoised after take-off, cartwheeled and broke up. Pilot error.
2/10/90	B-2402	-3J6B	20714/869	China Southwest AL	1/1	–	Baiyun Airport, Canton	Struck by hijacked 737. Total of 132 incl 707 pilot killed.
3/12/90	ST-SAC	-321C	19377/666	TAAT	7/7	Kharthoum–Nairobi	Nairobi, Kenya	Hit pole 3 miles (5 km) from airport in fog.
10/1/91	YR-ABD	-3K1C	21651/938	Romavia	13/0	–Bucharest	Bucharest-Otopeni	Landed left wing low, two engines hit runway causing fire.
25/3/91	ET-AJZ	-385C	19433/534	Ethiopian Airlines	0/0+?	–	Asmara	Destroyed by shelling at airport. Several loaders killed.
31/8/91	CP-1365	-323C	18692/358	Lloyd Aéreo Boliviano–LAB	0/0	–	La Paz.	Destroyed in hangar fire.
29/10/91	A20-103	-368C	21103/905	Royal Australian Air Force – RAAF	5/5	Richmond-	150 miles (240 km) E Melbourne.	Stalled and crashed on training flight.
26/11/91	7O-ACS	-369C	20547/861	Yemenia Airways	?/0	–Amman	Amman, Jordan	Undercarriage collapsed on landing.
7/12/91	5A-DJT	-351C	18888/425	Libyan Arab Airlines	199/0	Tripoli-	Tripoli, Libya	Wrecked in take-off accident.
20/2/92	D2-TOJ	-349C	19355/553	TAAG Angola Airlines	4/0	?	Luanda Airport	Nosegear collapsed.
24/3/92	ST-ALX	-321C	18715/364	Golden Star Air Cargo	7/7	Amsterdam–Athens	3 miles (5 km) SE Athens Airport	Hit mountain on late missed approach.
31/3/92	5N-MAS	-321C	18718/368	Trans-Air Service	4/0	Luxembourg–Kano	Istres, France	No.4 engine came off, taking no.3 with it. Successful emergency landing made.
29/4/92	9G-RBO	-351C	18746/367	GAS Air Nigeria	?/0	Test flight	Ilorin, Nigeria	Made gear-up landing.
25/11/92	5X-DAR	-321C	18825/386	DAS Air Cargo	4/0	Gatwick–Port Harcourt	3 miles (5 km) from Kano, Nigeria	Undershot in sandstorm, hit barracks.
26/11/92	PT-TCP	-365C	19416/556	Aerobrasil	5/0	Manaus-	Manaus, Brazil	Struck tower on take-off. Right gear collapsed on landing. Not repaired.
15/1/93	YR-ABM	-3F9C	19272/578	Air Afrique	5/3	Jeddah–Kano	Near Hadeija, Nigeria	Smoke in cabin, crashlanded in swamp.
31/1/93	LV-ISA	-387B	19238/528	LADE	168/0	Maceio–Fortaleza	Recife-Guarapes Airport, Brazil	Gear extended manually after hydraulics failure. Collapsed.
26/7/93	OD-AFY	-327C	19108/511	TMA	3/0	Amsterdam–Beirut	Amsterdam-Schiphol Airport	Structural failure of right maingear while taxiing.
?/6/94	N6232G	-131	17661/22	'World Air Freight'	0/0	–	Mojave Airport, California	Blown up in making of film 'Speed'.
9/10/94	HK-3355X	-324C	18886/430	TAMPA Colombia	5/0	Sao Paulo–Santa Cruz	Sao Paulo-Guarulhos Airport	Hydraulic leak. Gear collapsed on landing.
19/12/94	5N-ABK	-3F9C	20669/864	Nigeria Airways	5/3	Kano-	Near Hadejia, Nigeria	Smoke in cockpit, crashed in marsh.
17/8/95	YR-ABN	-321C	19379/677	Air Afrique	6/0	Paris–N'Djamena	N'Djamena, Chad	Thrust reverse failure in wet, ran off runway and left gear collapsed.
22/9/95	77-0354	E-3A	21554/933	USAF 962 ACS	20/20	Elmendorf AFB-	Elmendorf AFB, AK	Struck flock of geese on take-off, struck hill while trying to return.
30/11/95	4K-401	-323C	19584/663	Baku Air / Azerbaijan Airlines	6/2	Urumqi–Baku	Baku, Azerbaijan.	Struck bridge during flyby to check landing gear.
30/6/96	5X-JON	-369C	20546/860	DAS Air Cargo	4/0	Niamey–Bamako-Senou	Bamako-Senou Airport, Mali	Windshear on landing, wing hit ground, aircraft left runway and hit obstacle.
14/7/96	LX-N90457	E-3A	22852/969	NATO	16/0	Aktion-	Preveza AFB, Aktion, Greece	Birdstrike, ran off runway, hit sea wall and broke in two.

Date	Reg	Model	c/n + l/n	Operator	Aboard/killed (+ on ground)	Route	Location	Details
21/8/96	SU-AVX	-366C	20760/865	Egypt Air	128/0	Cairo–Istanbul	Istanbul-Atatürk Airport	Overran runway in rain, hit taxi and burned.
22/10/96	N751MA	-323C	19582/639	Millon Air	4/4+23	Manta–Miami	Manta, Equador	Crashed in suburb after engine fire spread after take-off.
23/10/96	LV-LGP	-327C	20077/728	Fuerza Aerea Argentina	8/2	Santiago–Buenos Aires	Buenos Aires-Ezeiza Airport	Banked and hit ground on approach. Incorrect use of spoilers.
16/1/97	P4-000	-331C	19435/629	First International Airways	5/0	Kinshasa–Kananga	Kananga, Zaire.	Right gear collapsed on landing. Caught fire.
1/11/97	9Q-CKK	-323C	19577/722	Congo Airlines	?/0	–Kinshasa	Kinshasa, Zaire	Landed nosegear up. Later broken up for spares.
10/3/98	SU-PBA	-336C	19843/735	Air Memphis	6/6	Mombassa–Cairo	Mombasa-Moi Airport	Struck approach lights on take-off, then a hill. Crashed and burned.
5/9/98	N138SR	-138B	17697/39	Jaffe Group	0/0	–	Port Harcourt, Nigeria	Badly damaged in hangar fire.
14/11/98	5N-VRG	-355C	19664/643	International Air Tour – IAT	5/0	Ostend–Lagos	Ostend, Belgian	No.3 engine separated in turbulence. Made belly landing on return.
7/2/99	9G-ROX	-328C	19521/584	Avistar	0/0	Bratislava–N'Djamena	Bratislava-Ivanka, Slovakia	No.2 and 3 engines failed on take-off. Aircraft overran runway.
14/8/99	ST-ANP	-351C	19632/649	TAAT	?/0	–Juba	Juba, Sudan	Landed with tailwind, overran.
3/2/00	ST-APY	-351C	19412/563	TAAT	5/0	Kharthoum–Mwanza	Mwanza, Tanzania	Struck lake on second night approach with defective instruments and landing aids.
14/4/00	9Q-CGC	-327C	19531/646	Government of Congo	0/0+100?	–	Kinshasa, Zaire	Destroyed in fire and explosion of ammunition at airport.
21/9/00	5V-TAG	-321B	19739/765	Togo Government	10/0	Paris–Lomé	Niamey, Niger	Onboard fire and engine problems. Crash landed and burnt out at airport.
7/3/01	PT-MST	-331C	18711/370	Skymaster Airlines	3/0	Belem–Sao Paulo	Sao Paulo, Brazil	Main undercarriage failed after heavy landing.
23/3/01	SU-BMV	-3B4C	20260/823	Luxor Air Egypt	182/0	–Monrovia	Monrovia, Liberia	Damaged beyond repair on landing.
7/9/01	TN-AGO	-323C	19519/619	Equaflight Services	240/0	–Lubumbashi	Lubumbashi, Congo	Undercarriage collapsed on landing.

ABOVE: 707s continue to fall victim to accidents, particularly in Africa, where many of those still in use serve as freighters. 5X-JON was an ex-Kuwait Airways 707-369C belonging to DAS Air Cargo but leased to Air Afrique when it encountered windshear on landing at Bamako, Mali, on 30 June 1996. A wingtip struck the ground and the aircraft left the runway. Seriously damaged, it never flew again. It is seen here performing a flyby at the 1994 Biggin Hill Air Fair. *Author*

9 CHRONOLOGY

27 July 1949	De Havilland Comet first flight
10 August 1949	Avro C-102 jetliner first flight
1952	367-80 configuration established
2 May 1952	Comet enters service
20 May 1952	Go-ahead for prototype given
14 May 1954	Roll-out of 367-80 prototype
15 July 1954	First flight of 367-80
3 August 1954	First USAF order, for 29 KC-135As
27 May 1955	First flight Sud-Est Caravelle
13 October 1955	First 707 orders, 20 from Pan Am (plus 25 DC-8s)
16 October 1955	Record-breaking demonstration flight; Seattle–Andrews AFB at average speed of 612 mph
Late 1955	707 orders from Air France, American, Braniff, Continental, Sabena. Total of seventy ordered by end of year
31 August 1956	First flight of KC-135A
15 September 1956	Tu-104 enters service
27 January 1957	First flight Convair 880
11 March 1957	Record-breaking demonstration flight; Seattle–Baltimore in three hours, forty-eight minutes
28 June 1957	KC-135 deliveries begin at Castle AFB, California
28 October 1957	Roll-out of first production 707 (N708PA)
20 December 1957	First flight 707 (N708PA)
30 May 1958	DC-8 maiden flight
18 September 1958	Full certification awarded for 707-120
September 1958	First commercial transatlantic jet service with BOAC Comet 4s
26 October 1958	First commercial 707 service, N711PA Pan Am New York–Paris
11 January 1959	First flight 707-320 series (-321)
25 January 1959	American Airlines first US domestic service 707 Los Angeles–New York
6 May 1959	Air France introduces Caravelle service
May 1959	First VC-137A delivered
11 May 1959	First flight 707-220
19 May 1959	First flight Conway turbofan-powered 707-420
15 July 1959	707-320 ATC awarded
18 September 1959	DC-8 enters revenue service
5 November 1959	ATC awarded for 707-220
23 November 1959	First flight 720
12 February 1960	ATC awarded for 707-420
15 May 1960	Convair 990 enters service
	First flight 720B
22 June 1960	First flight 707-120B
30 June 1960	Type approval for 720 granted
5 July 1960	720 enters service
31 March 1961	ATC awarded for 720B
31 January 1962	First flight 707-320B (l/n 268 N60PA)
1965	Peak year for orders (135)
1966	Peak year for deliveries (118)
14 March 1966	DC-8-61 first flight
February 1972	AWACS testbeds flown
31 October 1975	First E-3A flown
1975	Peak of 684 707s in service
1979	707 tested with CFM-56 engines
1982	Last 707 airliner delivered (l/n 941 for Moroccan Government)
January 1982	First NATO E-3 delivered
September 1985	FSD contract awarded to Grumman for J-STARS
1985	464 707s still in service
1986	Royal Air Force orders six E-3Ds
1987	France orders four E-3Fs
19 February 1987	First E-6A flown
22 December 1988	First YE-8 flown (86-0416)
1990	Last orders
March 1991	RAF E-3 deliveries begin
1991	Last deliveries
15 July 1991	Dash-80 prototype flown Davis-Monthan to Seattle for restoration
21 December 1991	Last E-6 delivered
15 Feb 92	Last E-3F delivered
12 May 1992	Last 707 airframe (E-3D ZH107) delivered to Royal Air Force
1997	First E-6B delivered
1998	707 tested with winglets

BIBLIOGRAPHY

BOOKS

Balch, Adrian M., *Airline Nostalgia: Classic Aircraft in Colour*. Airlife, Shrewsbury, 1999

Bowers, Peter M., *Boeing Aircraft Since 1916*. Third edition. Putnam Aeronautical Books, London, 1989

Cook, William H., *The Road to the 707: The Inside Story of Designing the 707*. TYC Publishing Company, Bellevue, Washington, 1991

Francillion, René J., *Boeing 707: Pioneer Jetliner*. MBI Publishing, Osceola, Wisconsin, 1999

Gero, David, *Flights of Terror: Aerial Hijack and Sabotage Since 1930*. Patrick Stephens, Sparkford, 1997

– *Aviation Disasters: The World's Major Civil Airliner Crashes Since 1950*. Patrick Stephens, Sparkford, 2001

Hersh, Seymour M., *The Target is Destroyed*. Random House, New York, 1986

Heppenheimer, T.A., *Turbulent Skies: The History of Commercial Aviation*. John Wiley and Sons, New York, 1995

Hewson, Robert (editor), *The Vital Guide to Commercial Aircraft and Airliners*. Airlife, Shrewsbury, 2000

– *The Vital Guide to Military Aircraft*. Airlife, Shrewsbury, 2001

Hopkins, Robert S. III, *Boeing KC-135 Stratotanker: More Than Just a Tanker*. Midland Publishing, Leicester, 1997

Hurturk, Kivnac N., *Individual Aircraft History of the Boeing 707*. BUCHair (USA) Inc., Forest Hills, New York, 1998

Irving, Clive, *Wide-Body: The Making of the 747*. Hodder and Stoughton, Sevenoaks, 1993

Job, Macarthur, *Air Disaster: Volume 1*. Aerospace Publications, Weston Creek, ACT, Australia, 1994

Johnston, A.M. with Barton, Charles, *Tex Johnston: Jet-Age Test Pilot*. Smithsonian Institution Press, Washington DC, 1992

Mondey, David and Taylor, Michael J.H., *The Guinness Book of Aircraft Records Facts and Feats*. Sixth edition. Guinness Publishing, Enfield, 1992

Nicholls, Mark (Editor), *Boeing Jetliners*. Airliner World Special. Key Publishing, Stamford, 2001

Pither, Tony, *The Boeing 707, 720 and KC-135*. Air-Britain (Historians) Limited, Tunbridge Wells, 1998

Proctor, Jon, *Boeing 720*. Great Airliners Series volume 7. World Transport Press, Miami, 2001.

Smith, P. R., *Boeing 707*. Airline Markings series. Airlife, Shrewsbury 1991

Willis, David (Editor), *The Aerospace Encyclopaedia of World Air Forces*. Aerospace Publishing, London, 1999

Wright, Alan J., *Boeing 707*. Classic Civil Aircraft 2. Ian Allan, Shepperton, Surrey, 1990

Wilson, Stewart, *Boeing 707 Douglas DC-8 and Vickers VC10*. Legends of the Air 6. Aerospace Publications, Fishwyck, ACT, Australia, 1988.

PERIODICALS

The Aeroplane and Astronautics
Air Forces Monthly
American Aviation
Aviation Week
Boeing Magazine
Flight International
Interavia

WEBSITES

The Boeing Company	www.boeing.com
The Aviation Safety Network	http://aviation-safety.net
Air Disaster	www.airdisaster.com
Plane Crash Info	www.planecrashinfo.com
Wassim's Cedarjet Pages	http://wassch71.tripod.com /cedarjet
The Braniff Site	http://www.braniffinternational.org
The Airline History Site	http://airlines.afriqonline.com
Air-India	http://www.airindia.com
Federation of American Scientists	http://www.fas.org
SC's Airliner lists	http://members.ams.chello.nl/ s.c.verbrugge/707.html
Bill Harm's Airliner Census	http://www.bird.ch /bharms/asr_boei.htm

Special thanks to: The San Diego Aerospace Museum, The Royal Aeronautical Society Library, Michael Oakey at *Aeroplane* magazine, Robert Hewson, Robert F. Dorr, Austin J. Brown, Mike Hooks, Graham Robson, David Willis and Ian Bott.

INDEX

Page numbers in *italics* refer to illustrations.

AWACS programme 54-56, 58
Aer Lingus *46*
Air China *115*
Air France *49*, *64*, *84*
Air-India International 50
Air Malta *108*
Air Manila International 70
Allen, William M. 'Bill' 6, 7, 9, 11, 12, 13, 14
Allied Signal Aerospace *102*
American Airlines 11, 25-26, *25*, 29, *40*, *42*
Argentina, Fuerza Aerea 60
Australian Air Force, Royal 60-61
Avianca *50*, *67*
Azerbaijan Airlines *104*

BOAC (British Overseas Airways Corporation)
    18-19, *37*, 51-52, *51*, *111*, *112*
Binegar, L.A. 'Bert' 10
Boeing, William and Bertha 9
Boeing Aircraft Company 6
    B-47 Stratojet 8; B-50 Superfortress 6, 7; C-
    18: *62*; C-97: 7; CC-137: *54*
    E-3 Sentry (AWACS) 54-56, *55*, 58; E-3A
    Sentry *55*; E-6 Mercury *57*, 58; E-8 Joint
    STARS (J-Stars) *57*, 58; EC-18B (ARIA)
    55, 62-63; EC-137D *56*
    KC-135: 10, 13, 53, *79*, 104; KC-137E/KC-
    707: *61*
    Model 367 Stratofreighter 7, 8
    Model 367-80 (Dash 80) 8-10, *8*, *9*, 12-16, *12*,
    17, 19-20, *20*; cockpit *11*; mock-up *7*; nose
    experiments *14*, *18*, *22*; undercarriage *12*,
    13, *17*, *19*
    Model 377 Stratocruiser 7
    Model 450 (XB-47) Stratojet 6-7, *12*; Model
    473: *6*, *8*; Model 473-47: *8*
    Model 707: name given 13, 15; projects 4
    707-3B4C *116*; 707-3D3C *114*;
    707-3H7C *48*; 707-3J6B/C *47*; 707-3J8C
    47; 707-3J9C *61*; 707-3P1C *59*
    707-020 (720) 18; 707-023B *68*; 707-030B
    71; 707-048: *46*
    707-100: *16*, *39*, 40, *40*; 707-121: *19*; 707-
    123/B *41*, *42*; 707-131: *90*; 707-138: *43*;
    707-138B *17*, *65*; 707-220: *24*, *43*; 707-
    227: *113*
    707-300: *16*, *18*, *45*, *63*; 707-300C *49*; 707-
    307C *62*; 707-309C *115*; 707-312B *48*;
    707-320B *33*, *34*; 707-320C *77*; 707-321:
    73; 707-321B *103*, *109*, 117-118, *118*; 707-
    321C *24*, 74, *79*; 707-323C *107*; 707-
    324C *68*; 707-326: *111*, *112*; 707-327C *69*;
    707-328: *49*; 707-328C *22*, *64*; 707-329: *2-
    3*, *35*; 707-330B *106*, *108*; 707-331: *70*,
    120; 707-331B *109*; 707-331C *104*; 707-
    338C *66*; 707-344: *46*; 707-348C *46*
    707-358C *73*; 707-359C *48*; 707-366C *117*;
    707-368C *59*; 707-369C *119*
    707-430: *71*; 707-436: 18-19, *51*, *107*; 707-437:
    113; 707-441: *78*; 707-458: *105*; 707-465:
    76; 707-700: 4
    707AR *31*, 106, *108*; 707RE 106
    Model 717: 18, 53, *79 see also* Boeing KC-135
    Model 720: 14, 18-19, 44, 59, *102*, 116, 119-
    120; 720-023B *51*; 720-047B *48*, 108;
    720-059B *50*; 720-061: *76*; 720B *22*, *32*,
    40, 41-43, *41*, 45, *67*, *74*

Phalcon (Condor) *56*, 60
    RC-707: 59-60
    VC-137 Stratoliner *62*; VC-137A *23*, *27*, *53*;
    VC-137C *58*, *62*; VC-707: *54*
    XB-47 (Model 450) Stratojet 6-7, 12
    YB-52 Stratofortress 12; YE-8B J-Stars *57*
Braniff International 43, 46, *69*, *113*
British Airways *107*

CAAC (Civil Aviation Administration of China)
    47
cabin 10, 11, *25*, *26*, *27*, *66*, *71*, *73 see also* fuselage,
    lavatories
cabin service staff 11, *65*, *66*, *69*, *71*, *72*, *73*
Cameroon Airlines *48*
Canadian Armed Forces *54*
Chile, Fuerza Aérea de *56*, 60, *63*
Civil Air Reserve Fleet *74*, *75*
cockpit *21*, 22-24, *22*, *23*, *24*, *72*
commercial service, first 40
Continental Airlines *74*
control surfaces 32, *32*, *33*, 34-35, *34*, 37-38
control system 32
Cunard Eagle Airways *34*, *76*

DAS Air Cargo *119*
Davis-Monthan AFB, Arizona *109*
design 8-10
designation system 21-22
Douglas 7, 10; DC-8: 10-11, 16

Ecuatoriana *51*
El Al *73*
electrical system 31
engines 27-30; noise-reducer nozzles *27*, *29*; Pratt
    & Whitney JT3: 9-10, 28, *28*, *29*, 30, *31*, *33*,
    48; pylon-mounted 10; pylons 31, *31*; Rolls-
    Royce Conway 28-29, 52; water injection 30

FAA (Federal Aviation Administration) 18-19, 76
fares 77
film props *104*
fire extinguishers 32
flight crew *72*
Flying Tiger Line 51, *69*
fuel 31
fuselage 24-27, *25*, *80*, *81*, *82 see also* cabin

German Air Force (*Luftwaffe*) *62*

HeavyLift Cargo Airlines *68*
Hong Kong, Kai Tak Airport *78*
hydraulics 31

Iran Air Force, Islamic Republic of 60, *61*
Iraqi Airways *77*
Israel Aircraft Industries (IAI) 60
Israeli Air Force *54*, 60

Johnston, Alvin 'Tex' 10, *11*, 12, 14, 15, 16
Jordanian Airlines, Alia Royal *114*

Korean Airlines 117-118, *118*

Lan Chile *108*
lavatories *27*
Lloyd Aereo Boliviano *107*
Lockheed 7; L-193 design 13
Loesch, Richards L. 'Dix' 10, 14

Lowa Inc. *106*
Lufthansa *71*, *105*

maiden flight 14
Malaysia-Singapore Airlines *48*
Middle East Airlines (MEA) 46-48, *116*
Monarch Airlines *68*

NATO 54-55, *55*, 56-57
New York International Airport *75*
Nigeria Airways *48*
noise *27*, 29, 67, 105-106
Northwest Orient *37*
nose 22, *80*

Omega Air *34*, *57*, *103*, 106, 108, 110

Pakistan International (PIA) 32, 48, 50-51, *73*
Pan American 10-11, *13*, *19*, *24*, 39-41, *39*, *40*, *74*,
    79
passengers, service to *66*, *71*, *72*, *73*, *75*
preservation 105
production roll-out, first 16
prototype construction 11 *see also* Boeing Model
    367-80 (Dash 80)

Qantas *43*, *65*, *66*, *78*, *84*
Qatar government 59

RAF *55*
roll, Dutch 38, 40, 43, 65
roll performed 14

Sabena *46*
Seattle 7, 14, *19*, *79*, *80*, *81*, *82*, *84*, *87*
South African Airways *70*
Spanish Air Force *59*, *61*
static rig tests 7
Sudan Airways *47*

TWA *45*, *90*, *113*, *120*
tailplane 37-38, *37*
tanker conversions 60-62, *61*
terrorism 116-117
test programme 14-16, *14*, *19*
Trans Mediterranean Airways (TMA) 48, 50
Trippe, Juan 10-11

undercarriage *35*, *35*, *36*, *37*
United *44*
United Arab Airlines *117*
US Air Force 13, 53-54, *53*, 55-57, *56*, *57*, 62-63,
    79
US Navy 58

VIP role 58-59, *58*, *59*, *62*
Varig *78*

war 56-57, 116-117
wing 7, 8-9, 16, 18, *82*
World Airways *45*
Wright, Captain Waldo *37*

Zambia Airways *49*